The Young Russians

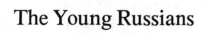

Previous Publications:
    The New Latins
    The New 100 Years War

THE YOUNG RUSSIANS

By

Georgie Anne Geyer

An ETC Publication

1975

C I P

Library of Congress Cataloging in Publication Data

Geyer, Georgie Anne, 1935 -
   The young Russians.

   1. Young adults — Russia. I. Title.

HQ799.8R9G48   301.43'15'0947   74-23874

ISBN 0-88280-021-3

Copyright © 1975 by ETC PUBLICATIONS
18512 Pierce Terrace
Homewood, Illinois 60430

Printed in the United States of America

❧ Table of Contents

For Pamela and Mandelot,
who shared this curious odyssey
and so many others . . .
and to Herve, who bore it all
with his innate savoir faire.

✿ Introduction

"There's no need to tell the truth about Russia to a foreigner; the sores of the fatherland should be hidden."

Pyotr Dolgorukov,
Russian writer and colleague of Alexander Herzen's in the 1850s.

*J*UST PAST the mid-20th century, the young people of most of the world exploded in a rebellion of the youth that historically could be compared only to the European student revolts of 1848. But in that year, ancient monarchical states were falling before the imperatives of the new industrialism, the new ideologies and the passionate new experimental concepts — Capitalism, Socialism, Nationalism, for the Proletariat. The 1960s were something quite different, for by then the catchwords had become the established concepts to rebel against anew.

What was curious about the turbulence was that in each area of the world — developed, underdeveloped, Capitalist, Socialist, rich, poor — the revolt arose out of different causes yet expressed itself in uncannily similar ways.

The United States and the Western Europe of the '60s saw young people in ferment — demonstrating, rioting, mocking their elders' most sacred beliefs with pedantic vulgarity, challenging their societies' often inane and callow values of affluence and perversely poisoning themselves with drugs, as they went about corrupting the language and block by block building their own new youth culture of challenge and mockery.

In the Third World of Africa, Asia and Latin America, where affluence was not something to purge yourself of but something to rise to at virtually any cost, the situation was quite different. There young men and women embraced guerrilla movements and died massively in a, first, joyous and, then, squalid and futile abandon, their hungers feeding ravenously upon a most exotic and inconsistent mixture of ideologies which they dreamed could develop their backward nations.

In Communist China, on the other hand, the youth presented the curious picture of children walking backwards. There youth flowed as one vast, angry, collective Red Guard out to the streets, trying to carry a relaxing society back to its first revolutionary purity. And in eastern Europe, Czech, Polish and Hungarian young people pitted themselves hopelessly against a Russian imperialism that held them in its great bear-like embrace.

Of all the youths in the world during this tortured, searching and violent period, only one remained silent. Only Soviet youth. Oh, there were minor youth "disturbances" in the early '60s as a consequence of the shock of Nikita Khrushchev's stunning revelations at the 20th party Congress in 1956 about the crimes of Joseph Stalin, but a "disturbance" in the Soviet Union looks more like a common high school debate elsewhere.

All this "youth revolution" really amounted to were some university meetings where Central Committee officials were disrespectfully questioned and a few lyrical poetry readings in Mayokovsky Square — the Russian "molodyosh" were amateurs compared to the perfervid youth of the rest of the erupting world.

So it was that, as parents elsewhere in the world wrung their hands and damned themselves for being either too permissive or too authoritarian, the Russians sat with smug self-satisfaction, knowing that at least *they* had no "generation gap" and no "youth rebellion" like the Capitalist countries of the West.

The reasons, of course, seemed quite obvious to them: The victory of Marxist Socialism historically outmoded the very concept of the generation gap because the social and economic inequities that caused such a generational chasm were wiped out. The energies of youth were formed, forged and channeled from birth by the Socialist state and, on the way to the "New Socialist Man," there was too much work to be done to play at revolution.

Meanwhile, many Western parents - tormented by their own children's apparent ingratitude for their sacrifices, deeply disturbed by the violence and the nihilism, catapaulted into a new world where all of the old values were called to judgment - looked from time to time to Russia, wondering if, indeed, the Russians might not be partially right.

So it was that, when I first visited the Soviet Union in 1967, on the 50th anniversary of the Bolshevik revolution that "shook the world," I immediately was caught up in the idea of investigating the Russian young people of this era. What kind of a "New Man" had the Soviets really created after 50 years of revolutionary passion, upheaval, beauty, brutality and suffering? Was he really different from the querulous, quarrelsome youth of the rest of the world? Had the Soviet experiment indeed found a way to insulate its siblings and sprouts from the contagion of world-wide youth fevers?

It seemed to me an ideal time to probe these questions, not only because of the youth "scene" outside but because of the "objective conditions" inside. For the first time since the revolution, there was a really "new" Marxist generation — a generation that represented the ultimate outcome of the great Leninist experiment. It was the first generation born and bred since the Stalinist time of troubles and the days of war. It was a generation free of the fear that has permeated Russian life and it was a generation which, if one watched and listened very carefully, might just be able to give us a shadowy preview of what the future Russian man and world might be like.

Would he speak in riddles, like his fathers? Was he ideologically convinced of the single truth of Communism? How much of the searching individual was there in him? How much of a seeking after meaning in modern, industrialized society? Did he, as the Russians always have, see the rest of the outside world as fraught with unspeakable dangers and filled with threatening strangers?

I knew all the questions — but I had no idea how fascinating and untouched many of the answers would be.

On my first trip to what that inveterate French traveler, the Marquis de Custine, described in 1839 as "that inpenetrable nation," I began by traveling from Japan to Nahotka, the port of Vladivostok, by boat. From there, partly by train and partly by plane, I made my way to Khabarovsk, Irkutsk, Bratsk, Novosibirsk, Tashkent, Samarkand, Bokhara, Moscow, Leningrad, Riga, Tallinn, Vilnius, Sochi, Tbilisi, Kiev, Baku and Volgograd. In short, the trip included most of the open cities that a foreigner could visit and a good representation of all areas of the country.

Insofar as possible in the Soviet Union, I tried to work systematically. At this time, the Soviet government press agency, Novosti, was working with foreign journalists for a fee, arranging official interviews (which were almost impossible to get any other way) and providing guidance and help. My paper, the Chicago Daily News, which sent me for three months, paid them for this service.

In my approach to research, I went down the line: high school and university officials, Komsomol (Young Communist League) officers, sociologists and psychologists who work with youth, writers who write about youth, parents who give birth to youth and . . . youth. I wanted as good a cross-section of ideas as possible.

In general, I decided, I would be covering that group of Russians who were between 15 and 35 at the end of the '60s and the beginning of the '70s — the post-war, post-Stalin generation, which could barely remember what war and hunger were like, if at all. I decided to use "Russian" and "Soviet" interchangeably, which is generally considered proper usage, because it is the Russian people, the Russian landmass and the Russian spiritual and political experience that still dominate and give form to the Soviet experience. It is the Russians' fear of outside and the Russians' compulsive submission to authority — not the Ukrainians', not the Estonians', not the Buryats' nor the Yakuts' nor the other Russified nationalities — that hang like a shroud over the other peoples of the Soviet Union, who often have quite other ideas of freedom, collectivism, authority, life and death.

My main concern, in my official conversations and particularly in my private conversations, which took place in parks, university vestibules, youth clubs and beaches, was to get beneath the facade of dull standardization that the Russians so love to present to the world and to permeate the human life I knew must be there. For my official interviews, I used an interpreter, because there were always other people present anyway. For my private conversations, I used my imperfect but highly employable Russian and on numerous occasions spoke English or either German or Spanish, both of which I speak fluently.

I was trying to describe the Russians, youth and old, not, as many Western observers do, simply on whether they "liked" or "disliked" their government or had read "Dr. Zhivago." I was trying to describe them in their own terms: on what they were and what they thought in their own terms: on what they were and what they thought themselves to be. I soon learned how to deal with the programmed nastiness of Soviet officials, or to sidestep it, which was to ignore it, but it took me much longer to learn to deal with the inate difficulties of interviewing in the Soviet Union.

The direct question, I soon discovered, was disastrous, simply because it further frightened a people already, even today, deathly frightened of foreigners. I found myself asking questions in their favorite form — the allegorical — and then weaving myself out of the answers (Russia is a magician, the master of the finely-woven, whispered web of riddle). You have to let Russians tell you things in their own time and in their own way and, as likely as not, having told you, they will scurry away like timid does.

Sometimes, I found, it is simply best not to ask anything; often it is then that they suddenly overflow, sharing with you their ideas and feelings. Sometimes it is best to discuss subjects rhetorically — "If you were living in the 19th century . . .?" And many times, no matter how hard you tried, the answers were in the vein of one of Dostoevsky's characters, who exclaimed, "But if there is no God, what kind of Captain can I be?"

Another problem was the apparent facelessness of the people and the immense and wearing standardization of the urban landscape. Although you have been warned of this, you don't fully realize until you enter deeply enough into the maze that everyone seems to be saying the same words to you. Everybody seems to *look* the same; each Soviet human seems, at first, to be in his person a one-dimensional, humanly-undefined, socialist realism character straight out of the pages of the flat, monotonous Soviet period. It is not only, coming from society where paens are sung to the power of the individual, that the collective quality of everything Russian is so tiring to the mind and Spirit, it is that, as a journalist, you find so little new to describe. Before I went there, I had wondered why all the writing about Russia was so flat, so without flavor, character or dimensional form. Once there, it was obvious — the whole country *appeared* so. From Siberia to Central Asia to Moscow, the people marched in lines, eyes straight ahead, like the blank windows in the new buildings.

Nevertheless, by the time I left after my first trip, I knew that I had gotten through to some fascinating insights. In the state based solely upon materialism, the young people were impassioned with the "spiritual life of man." In a community built around a fervent collectivism, more and more youngsters were trying to be their individual selves. In a system that inserted ideology into every corner of life, the new generation was heartily tired of its constant imperatives.

By the time I returned to Russia in 1971, after several years covering Vietnam, Latin America, the Middle East and Europe, several things had changed. Novosti, now under the directorship of one of the hard-liners who had put down the Czechoslovakian liberalization in 1968, was not working with foreign correspondents any more. I was on my own — an easy way to defeat you in Russia.

So I used every means I could muster to get to people. I enlisted everyone I knew. My excellent Intourist guide, Nellie Genina, helped a great deal. I telephoned many people directly — something that is not done in Russia, if only because there is no phone book — and many responded. Other interviews were arranged through friends or simply by accosting people where I knew they'd be.

This second trip — in which I visited Moscow, Leningrad, Novgorod, Petrozabots, Kiev, Odessa and Tbilisi — enabled me not only to check out my previous observations but to discover that some wholly new elements, such as an intense Russian nationalism and a thriving dissident movement, had come to the fore. I found many of the best young people "dropping out" of Soviet society, and I found a much greater ease of conversation with people in general, perhaps because my Russian was better but more probably because the country *is* slowly and painfully but constantly opening up.

Much more than on the first trip, I had the feeling that people were telling me what they really thought. The "moments of truth" came closer together, as with a young woman friend who told me frankly one day, "You've got a terrible job. You know by now that we all change when we talk with foreigners and don't tell them what we're really thinking. We don't know it ourselves sometimes, but we change."

Or the day when, after talking for a long time with a highly proficient and able academic, he asked me, "Now, tell me please, what do you not like about the Soviet Union?"

"Let me tell you first what I like," I said. And I outlined several areas — the egalitarianism, the respect for work, the quest for cultural values. "But there is one thing I could not abide, living here. That is the fact that your entire society is built upon dishonesty. You all live it every minute, you speak it, and sometimes even you yourselves don't know where honesty ends and dishonesty begins."

On my first trip, observations like this (which I used sparingly) always evoked the most acid, even vicious retorts. This time it was greeted by the din of total silence. The man looked down at the table. The two other women present looked away from me. No one would meet my eye.

Finally the silence became so deafening that *I* broke it. "And now, let me ask you something else," I said. In our moment of silence, we had all agreed, and they were willing even to recognize — in their very wordlessness — this agreement.

By the time I left, I had had lengthy personal and individual interviews with several hundred young people representing all areas, professions and idea groups of the country. In groups, I spoke with several thousand. I had interviewed several dozen leading poets and writers. I had had lengthy interviews with a dozen Western Sovietologists and about forty diplomats, and by now I have read very nearly everything published (not very much) on every aspect of "Russki Molodyosh" — Russian youth. I have purposefully quoted key sections from other journalists, writers, scholars and diplomats to show where there is agreement or disagreement with others on conclusions I reached.

I want to stress that I clearly recognize the limitations imposed both by the country and the subject matter. I did not reach nearly enough village youth or soldiers — the hardest groups to get to. It is easy to gravitate toward the students — the budding intelligentsia. But on the other hand, in this country more than perhaps any other, it is this intelligentsia that will dictate the world of the future.

I do not consider, however, that only visiting Russia — and not living there — was in any way a limitation. On the contrary, it is an advantage, so long as you have ample time. The visiting correspondent has innumerable advantages that the hard-pressed and unwanted resident correspondent or diplomat does not have, not the least of which is the fact that Russians are far more afraid of seeing or confiding in foreigners who are going to be there the next week (reminding them of their indiscretion) than they are of itinerant gypsy Westerners like me. Here today, gone tomorrow. Forget the fact that you talked too much with a little more vodka. The secret is not to have too little time . . . or too much.

At the end, of course, one has to admit that it is impossible at this time to do any definitive analyis of Russian youth such as you might do of non-Communist youths. Maybe in twenty years. But what one can do — and what I have attempted to do — is to present informed and carefully thought-out *observations* on Russian youth.

I left eventually, therefore, with feelings of confidence about my material, with a sense of excitement about the many unexpected charateristics of Russian young people that I had uncovered and, even, with a perverse admiration and affection for Russia's remarkable people and places.

The darkness of a winter noon in Tallinn, as the November snows flickered with the reflection of the still-burning neon lights . . . the sun shining at midnight in July in Karelia, as if a gauzy film were stretched out between you and the world before your eyes . . . the vast stillness of Siberia, with its open-faced people, so similar to our early settlers of the Old West . . . . the shining golden domes of Suzdal, the black rock beaches of the Black Sea, the dusty blue minarets of Central Asia lying between the deserts of the Black Sands and the Red Sands.

Perhaps the moment I felt I had finally escaped Russia's omnipresent modern standardization and begun to penetrate the world of old and real Russia that still exists was one day when I walked into the Tsarina Katherine's beautiful blue and white palace outside Leningrad in Pushkintown. It was a glorious October morning, with yellow leaves falling like flat golden raindrops on sidewalks still wet and black from the night's rain. I, reacting to the cold weather we had been having, was wearing my heavy Russian fur coat on a day much too warm for it.

Behind the coatcheck counter stood a typical old babushka (grandma) looking like a flat little gnome in her black coat with scarf tied tight around her temples. When she saw me, she started, then clapped her fat hands together as if to ward off a bad omen. "Oh," she said, her eyes wide and disturbed as she looked at my coat, "Oh my, you're frightening summer."

Georgie Anne Geyer   Chicago, Illinois

❧ Part I
Fathers and Sons

❧ Chapter One
The Children of Victory

The boy asks: Why?
The boy asks: Why?
Two hundred and three hundred times, "Why?"
But papa is cutting his ham,
Papa is cutting his ham,
He chomps and cuts his ham
And does not answer.

From an underground song by Alexander Galich

𝒥HE fragrant city of Sochi stretches in a beautiful green half moon along a stretch of the Black Sea coastline, sitting magisterially atop a crown of cliffs facing the water where in ancient times Jason sought the Golden Fleece. Jason never found his gilded fate, but much later the Turks found quick death there at the hands of the Russians. It was they who named it the "Black" sea.

But aside from this single threatening typically Russian strain of "darkness," Sochi is a most un-Russian city. Although described in the guide books as "the jewel of the Russian federation," Sochi is a perversely individualistic jewel. The city is filled with rustling trees, blooming bushes and even an occasional romantic outdoor coffee bar. There is a delicacy and variety about it, with its fine old hotels and spas, that is so rare among all those other Soviet cities so grimly celebrating conformity and mediocrity.

Even the Russians seem less feral in Sochi. Perhaps the breeze calms them. Even they seem less standardized and more individualized. Perhaps it is because Sochi itself is an old, pre-Soviet city

3

that still whispers, when the wind blows off of Jason's sea, of other times and other worlds.

But there is something else unusual about Sochi. There is an unusual monument — a shrine, really — that is probably the most illuminating spot in Russia concerning the officially approved hopes and ideals of youth in the Soviet age. It is the house of Nikolai Ostrovsky, the famous writer of the years of the revolution and a man whose life and work became the arch symbol of an age.

His two-volume classic, "How the Steel was Tempered," consistently has been cited by Soviet youth as its favorite and most inspirational book. But the symbolism and importance of Ostrovsky reaches much further than simply his work — his importance lies in the example of his courageous life.

It was quite by accident that I strolled up one warm afternoon about 3 o'clock to see Ostrovsky's house. The immediate purpose was to escape from my guide, a particularly cantankerous Russian named Nikolai. That particular afternoon he was baiting me with the endless and tiresome argument of Capitalism versus Communism, when I asked him quietly, "Do you think I am not educated at all?" When he answered, vehemently, "That is just your problem — you are too educated," I decided it was time to take a walk.

A pathway filled with flowering trees and buzzing flies led me to Ostrovsky's house.

The main part of the shrine is a dark, cool room with a bed in the center of it, and I immediately had the feeling that the bed was an altar. Tiles lined the walls and fresh flowers bloomed on the old-fashioned dark wood tables.

"This is where he lay for ten years while he wrote 'How the Steel was Tempered'," the guide, one of those pleasant, stolid, no-nonsense women who seem to thrive in Russia, told us in a whispered voice. Of the twenty or so visitors, no one spoke. Then she led us upstairs to the museum itself, where the accumulated papers and pictures of Ostrovsky, inspired of Russian youth, were on display.

One does not have to be a Communist to admire the life of a man like Ostrovsky. From the blurred and strangely stylistic old pictures — placed under dusty glass in that peculiarly unkempt Russian way — stared out a scarecrow of a boy with eyes too big for his head.

Something of the tormented eyes of Dachau was in them, though he was no Nazi victim but only a simple boy from the Ukraine who had become a Communist at an early age. As you passed by the pictures, you saw him grow up — poor country boy, partisan, always a Communist, always a fighter. And as he grew and his spiritual life became more full, in a terrible inversion his body became more wilted and more tormented. Several crippling illnesses hit him all at once until, still only in his early 20's, he lay totally paralyzed and very nearly blind.

The pictures of him lying in bed left a vivid impression: a long gaunt man dressed in uniform and covered with a throw blanket, smiling objectlessly as he stared sightlessly out at you.

But Ostrovsky was not famous because he suffered; Marxism is not Orthodoxy or Catholicism, where suffering is purifying. While bed-ridden and while blind, he lay writing his book with one hand on specially ruled paper; and he wrote the most popular book of his time.

Why were his two small volumes so important for their era? When I sat down to read them, I began to understand. They were written with childlike simplicity. Bursting with faith and good will, they resembled nothing so much as an exhortative American children's book of times now past. Ostrovsky's hero — who was himself — was a Marxist Horatio Alger of a time of innocence and purity.

Absolute belief. Absolute courage. Absolute conviction. The desire to work without question for the revolution and to rise above the past, above history, above self. This is what Ostrovsky thought of as he lay on his bed of nails.

Here there were no kulaks destroyed, here there were no purges, here there were no concentration camps. This was the age when man would perfect himself.

Hear, for instance, the voice of Ostrovsky's wiry young hero Pavel Korchagin, whose life nearly exactly follows Ostrovsky's:

"I'm not smoking any more . . . A man who can't break himself of a bad habit isn't worth anything. That leaves only the swearing to be taken care of. I know I haven't quite overcome that shameful habit, but even Dimka admits that he doesn't hear me curse very often. It's harder to stop a foul word from slipping out than to stop smoking, so I can't say at the moment that I've finished with that too. But I will."

Or, talking to his mother:

"No, Mother, I've given my word to keep away from girls until we've finished with all the bourgeois in the world. Bit long to wait, you say? No, Mother, the bourgeoisie can't hold out very long now. Soon there will be one big republic for all men, and you old folk, who've worked all your lives, will go to Italy, a beautiful warm country by the sea. We'll install you in the rich men's palaces, and you'll lie about in the sun warming your old bones while we'll go and finish off the bourgeois in America."

Or, perhaps the key paragraph, as Pavel stands at the cemetery where his fallen friends lie buried:

"Man's dearest possession is life. It is given to him but once, and he must live it so as to feel no torturing regrets for wasted years, never knowing the burning shame of a mean and petty past; so live that, dying, he might say: all my life, all my strength were given to the finest cause in all the world — the fight for the liberation of Mankind."

Simplistic? Innocent? Naive? Heroic? Ingenuous? Great?

Of course. It was all of these things — that is why it was the Bible for a Marxist beginning. And that is why Ostrovsky has remained, until recently, *the* hero of Russian youth. It was simple stuff, and it held conviction. When the young, with those open fresh faces, were asked who their favorite was, they almost always said Ostrovsky — or some other officially-blessed hero very like him. It gave their Bolshevik elders the assurance that all was right with the world and that everything they had struggled for was being fulfilled in these young people.

But now it has been more than 50 years since the revolution and more than 50 years since Ostrovsky's ordeal. In place of the children of the revolution, in place of the "children of strife," has arisen a new generation that has known neither war nor revolution nor Stalinism nor hunger nor Ostrovsky's partisan battles in the Ukraine. The "children of victory" the Russians sometimes call them — for they are what the revolution was fought for and what 50 years of agony were endured for.

And who are the heroes of *this* generation?

It was a beautiful July day in Leningrad, that most beautiful and Western of Russian cities, and several of us were having lunch in the New Frigate Restaurant, a spot of unusual charm that was decorated with maps of the Baltic and picturesque folk scenes. As we sipped a curious Russian "koktail" of vodka, champagne and syrup, I put this question to Dr. Vladimir Lisovsky, the man who is considered the top sociologist on youth in the Soviet Union. He answered with extraordinary candor.

"Until recently, they were Aksyonov and Rozov, Dr. Lisovsky, a young brown-haired man with a warm and open personality, began. He was speaking of Vasily Aksyonov and Victor Rozov, the two writers whose literary heroes, more than any others in modern Russian literature, were uncertain, tentative, unconvinced men. "Now it's much more complicated," he went on.

"When you ask them who their heroes are, somehow they do not want to tell you. They can't express them. It's not that they don't like the old heroes. They still like Ostrovsky, for instance. But they don't like them unconditionally. They feel they're a little overdone. And . . . they don't know who their new heroes are."

A short while later we were strolling past the old pastel-shaded Petrine palaces along the Neva, as a soft breeze rippled the water. Now I asked Lisovsky about ideals among the young today. "Again, it's difficult for them to express their ideals," he said, as we paused before an old aristocratic palace turned into a modern, state-run wedding palace. "It's not that they don't have them, but that they're somehow not formed. They have many choices now. When you ask them their ideals, they're somehow hesitant about talking about it."

Was it because they wanted privacy? I asked. Or was it because of uncertainty? He paused thoughtfully. "They have ideals, but they're not all the same," he summed up.

A government official who was with us — a woman who generally took a moderately hard line — to my surprise, agreed. "I think one cycle is ending," she said, "and that one is beginning. You can't see what the new cycle will be."

Nor were these unusual expressions.

Fathers and Sons

When Colette Shulman, the Soviet specialist at Columbia University, chatted with three 16-year-old Russian girls one afternoon in a park in Moscow in 1969, she asked them if young people were becoming more independent in their thinking.

One, Lena, answered, "Perhaps it is true, because now there are no heroes whom we can personally admire, and we have to combine all the heroes and take what we need from each one of them. And the characteristic features of this combination are what will suit us and not any one single person. In this way, youth is independent — taking only some features and not the whole person."

The young people agreed that what their generation prized most was courage and honesty, and when Mrs. Shulman went on to talk to "a famous writer" who had written about young people for many years, he agreed with this. "I would say that the outstanding quality of these thinking young people is their tremendous passion for truth," he told her. As to heroes, he said, "The young people do not like authority of any kind, and that is one reason why there are no heroes at the moment, neither in literature nor in life. At one time, they admired the cosmonauts, and the death of Yuri Gagarin was deeply felt by many people. Pavel Korchagin, Ostrovsky's hero, is still something of a hero for the 15-year-olds, but our writers are afraid to create a new hero, because no one will believe in him — to the young he will seem too crystal-like and monumental for the complexities of our time. This is why no new literary hero has appeared."

When I first came to Russia and looked around, I immediately saw and felt this uncertainty among the young; but, being American, I saw it as a perfectly normal and healthy development. I looked around and I thought that this was a generation of which the old Bolsheviks must be proud. There they were — industrious, ambitious, fun-loving, individualistic, addicted to science, patriotic in an unobtrusive way, unchauvinistic, questioning, well-dressed, normally respectful to their parents and searching for truth and for the spirit. No drugs to speak of. No counter-culture. No pessimism. No pornography.

And, indeed, almost always officially the Soviets insisted that they had a splendid flowering of youth — no "youth problem," no "generation gap," no "alienation." Ideologically, the very idea was impossible; publicly, the very concept was denied. Social scientists were even under ideological orders to deny that there was any longer what is still popularly called in Russia a "fathers and sons" problem — the type of generational break written about so brilliantly by Ivan Turgenev in his famous and prophetic novel of that theme in the 1860's. Today's Soviet world, with all its answers, has no room for "heroes" like Turgenev's Bazarov, the archsymbol of youth of his age, the "nihilist" — or, as Turgenev himself described him, "the person who does not look up to any authorities, does not accept a single principle on faith, no matter how highly that principle may be esteemed."

No, nobody was going to get away with very much of that sort of talk today. In 1965, for instance, Victor Nekrasov, the beloved and highly independent liberal writer who lives in Kiev, wrote in an essay of a young man who tells a group of older people; "We do not believe you. We do not believe a word. We 20-year-olds do not believe anyone who is over 30." When the elders try to convince him, he answers angrily, "I have seen my own father. He believes himself to be an honest man . . . but all his life he has lied. Lied to me, to my friends, to mama, to himself. He lied when he eulogized Stalin . . . He lies now . . ." Even though Nekrasov carefully qualified this outburst, stating that there were many other kinds of youngster besides this, this passage was cut by the censors.

So the doubts begin to set in; And so it turns out that with youth, as with so many things in the Soviet Union, what you hear is most definitely *not* what you see. Soon, underneath the solid official assurances and the rosy-cheeked youngsters, you discover that just about everybody considers the country to be in the grip of a "terrible youth problem."

"If anyone here tells you there isn't a youth problem, he's lying," Igor Danilan, a well-placed Moscow journalist told me one night over dinner in Moscow. "This is a generation that has not gone through a war. It doesn't know how hard we suffered for socialism. They want everything right away — a car, clothes, apartments, travel — and they don't understand you have to work to get it." He shook his head, as we sat at a caviar-laden table in the Hotel National. Yet this man, himself only in his early 40's, was also critical of *his* father's generation. "*My* generation is different," he said. "We are socialists, yes, but with open eyes. They were only building, building, building socialism. It is very tiresome. Now, I . . ."

His eyes, so dull until then, suddenly danced. "I would like to be a guerrilla. Why, I'd be a guerrilla for Capitalism if that were the only way."

It was the same way in Odessa. A 50ish journalist with the maritime newspaper, "The Sailor," asked how this new generation was different, answered, with an air of total disgust in his voice, "It has no profound understanding of anything."

And in Moscow, a leading and highly perceptive Western ambassador told me, as we sipped tea in his genteel drawing room, that "the biggest concern Soviet officials voice is that their children will not be responsible when they take over."

Perhaps the man I met who best characterized the changes in the generations over the Soviet period was the liberal playwright Victor Rozov. I met Rozov in the Writer's Union, that nest of literary lions and snakes which was once the town house of the aristocratic "War and Peace" Rostov family, and found him a simple, engaging, honest man. We sat in a corner of the snack room, where authors had scrawled irreverent bits on the walls, and talked about the mysteries of the generations.

It turned out that he was writing a new play with a modern "Fathers and Sons" theme. "I write about three young people of the last three generations," he said, his voice excited. "The boy is of the civil war — dirty and unkempt. The man is on the eve of the Second World War — already a quarter of a gentleman with a part in his hair. Then there is a man of the present — with big grey, thoughtful eyes, working a cybernetic machine. All three parts will be played by one actor." Of course. They were the three archtypes of the three generations since the Bolshevik revolution.

"Of course, the conflict of 'Fathers and Sons' exists!" he averred then, with some vehemence. "If you did not have it, society would perish. It existed always, as long as the world existed. It existed in the cave, when the baby started crawling out and the father said, 'Don't crawl out,' " Rozov, a homey, down-to-earth man with sad, sensitive eyes, paused. A bitter-sweet smile passed over his lips and he sighed. "In my age," he summed up, "many of us stayed in the cave."

But what really frightens and threatens the blinking cave-dwellers of the older generation is not the Rozovs but the extra-ordinary sunshine-seeking of the younger generation. Far, far to the

Left even of Rozov, a man who is always at least three quarters "out" of establishment favor, lie the real outspoken critics: the all-out dissidents who speak their mind with suicidal fervor, as they demonstrate openly their disgust and repugnance for the paranoia that has poisoned very nearly every generation of Russians. Interviewed in his Moscow apartment before he was exiled to the remote Siberian region of Chita on the Chinese border, the young dissenter Pavel Litvinov told Western correspondents, "In our country, those of more than 40 years of age are scared of everything. Theirs is the fear described by the English writer, George Orwell, in '1984.' It is a psychological, not a rational condition, and those who feel this fear deep inside themselves can do nothing against it. It is up to my generation to bring about a change."

Neither is Litvinov any ordinary complainer. As the grandson of the famous Maxim M. Litvinov, long-time Foreign Minister of the early Bolshevik era, he is typical of the free-thinking, outspoken sons of many of the top Communists. It is they who are dissatisfied, just as it was the tormented sons of priests and aristocrats who led the youth rebellion in Russia in the last century. And, despite everything, he is convinced that change will come. "On the whole, I am an optimist," he said further. "I believe my country will become a just country. But I don't know when."

Then, as you begin prying about the Soviet Union in the search for just where in the devil youth really stands in terms of the other generations, you find something even more astonishing than these private exclamations: you find, despite all the official muffling, that there are even Communist officials who admit to their concern over generational conflict under the ideology that was to banish it from the earth.

To cite only a couple of dates:

In November, 1969, I. G. Kebin, 1st secretary of the Estonian Komsomol, said in a public address, "Of course, the problem of 'fathers and sons' exists. It is the problem of generations. We should not shut them up but convince them:"

And in the plenum of the Writer's Union in 1967, Union Secretary Victor Pankov said, more benignly, "The problem of 'fathers and sons' is one of the eternal themes of literature. The entire matter is what kind of accent is given to it — whether the continuity or the conflict is stressed."

Even, occasionally, the forbidden theme slips out — modulated, of course — in the Central Committee. It was none other than Party Leader Leonid Brezhnev himself who warned at the 1967 Communist Congress that "The present generation does not have the severe schooling of revolutionary struggle and is not hardened as the older generation has been."

While nothing definitive has been written inside or outside of Russia on the new "fathers and sons" tale within that secretive land, some of the best foreign observers have, at one time or another, commented briefly on the changes now in full bloom.

Writing in the London Observer in 1968, Edward Crankshaw, one of the West's most respected Sovietologists, observed that: "This generation is separated from its fathers by a gulf which we, even with our own familiar alienation problem, can measure only with difficulty. Their fathers grew up under the terror, and their responses were conditioned by fear long after the terror was diminished. The young grew up under a regime which, though still harsh and arbitrary and conducted by men who had been Stalin's henchmen, was relatively permissive. Unlike their fathers, they have no reason to be thankful for small mercies. They see only the continuing crassness and heavy handedness of high authority, the corruption and brutality of its instruments. They are no more conscious of the improved circumstances of their existence under a modified police regime than our own children are conscious of the difference between the welfare state and the doom-laden era of the '30s. So they protest!"

And Laurens van der Post, one of the most evocative and intuitive writers on Russia, has written: "Yet I felt that the young were most fortunate in that their Revolution was truly over and they were free not only to be bored by it but to begin their own reformation. This, perhaps, is one of the reasons the old writers and artists feel so bitter about the new trends among the 'ungrateful' young, and why the aging Party stalwarts stand at bay, like old bulls in danger of being driven from the herd they have protected from so many dangers."

Still other careful observers analyze the changes, not only in terms of a reaction to Stalinism, but in terms of the enormous social changes that have taken place in the last 20 years. To Mrs. Shulman, for instance, there are three related themes which are changing the attitudes of Soviet youth and thus many aspects of Soviet life:

1.) the migration of young people from the countryside to the cities
2.) the rise in the standard of living in recent years and
3.) the long period of peace.

"In the period before 1945," she told me, as we discussed Russian youth in her New York city apartment, "Soviet life was a succession of world war, civil war, social upheaval and political purges. The main effect of this is that, in times of great stress, the authority of the Communist party is accepted. Under stress, it was easier to get people to give of themselves unquestioningly, especially in Russia, where obedience to authority is ingrained. But now the Russians have had many years of relative tranquility, and one can see that the young people are concentrating more on their own lives and careers. This has introduced an attitude of questioning authority, and the young are less willing to put their lives uncritically at the service of the state."

Lisovsky generally agreed with this prognosis. The young, he said, accept nothing without investigation, and the difference has produced an "authority clash." "The fathers are used to getting the word," he says. "The sons don't have the same attitude toward authority. Parents try to force their children to accept their views without any criticism. The kids disagree. They want to lead their own lives."

Some of the parents realize this and, at times, rarely but always unforgettably, it comes out on the stage. One of the most popular films of the mid-'60s was a film called, "I am 20." Krushchev disliked it so intensely he had the ending changed, but he didn't really alter the message. The father, who had been turned into a silent statue for so long during the Stalin years, tells his 24-year-old son that he can give him no advice because, "You are 24, but I am only 20."

Despite the concern over youth and its foibles in the Soviet Union, it is curious that if you are to look purely at numbers, youth represents proportionally fewer there than in almost any other country on earth. Here there has been no mammoth infusion of "war babies" such as hit the U.S. in the '60s and played a special role in the development and flowering of the radical movement. On the contrary, because of the low birth rate of approximately one child per family, the under-16 bloc in the U.S.S.R. is actually declining. It represented 30 percent in 1970 and, if present trends continue, it will comprise 20 percent by 1980. To illustrate the trend with other figures, 24 was the country's median age in 1950, 26 was the median age in 1960, and 30 was the median age in 1970. Predictions are it will be 34 by 1990.

Still, despite the fact that the Soviet Union is not being overrun, as in many developed and underdeveloped countries, with disproportionate masses of youngsters it cannot handle, it *is* more threatened by the very concept of the "youth problem" than many other countries simply because of Marxism's claim to do away with generational hostilities. Under Marxism, a youth eruption is not simply something you greet with a stoical "This, too, shall pass" — it is an insufferable threat to the entire underpinnings of the state.

The Russians, too, are more aware of the power that youth can bring to sway in society because of the extraordinary formative and apocalyptic role youth has played in Russian history since the beginnings of the 19th century.

Until the 1800's, Russia was, culturally, a silent country. While the West was going through the Renaissance and the Enlightenment, Russia was isolated from the Western world, turned in upon itself by the repeated invasions from the East of Tatars, Mongols, and so many other barbaric hordes. In the process, she became herself a world half-West and half-East, mutely yearning for Europe but never able to speak with her, as, for instance, Kievan Russia did — a fact which to this day accounts for the greater openness and the more European qualities of the Ukrainians.

Then, in the 19th century, following the Westernization of Peter the Great, Russia suddenly strode, only half prepared for the fatal examination, onto the European stage. And, as in no other country, it was her youth who both led her and distorted her march.

It was the young officers of the nobility who caused the famous "Decembrist uprising" in 1825; the intense young sons and daughters of priests and aristocrats who, out of guilt and self-effacement, became "narodniks", trying to carry the revolution "back to the people" by marching out to live in the miserable peasant villages; the nihilists like Bazarov who negated everything extant so that something new should bud and bloom; and those ultimate revolutionaries, the Bolsheviks, who lived to become the adumbrants of the 20th century.

In terms of its sense in the modern world, generational conflict *began* in Russia. It was in Russia in the 19th century that a man was dated by his generation — one was a "man of the '40s" or the " '60s" or the " '80s.", with all that represented in terms of his philosophical outlook about the revolutionary fate of Russia. It was in Russia of the 19th century that modern philosophers first point to the concept of the "de-authorization" of the older generation — the same feeling of an older generation that has failed that one finds in the United States today and that one also finds, to a lesser degree, among young Russians today.

Always the young led, either galloping too far ahead of their countrymen (the masses of whom were mired in ignorance and misery) or taking some desperate apocalyptic step — like the assassination of the Czar Alexander II in 1881, just as he was about to institute liberal reforms — which turned the clock back irrevocably and made total revolution in the Marxist fashion inevitable. When the "narod" or the people rejected them, the young turned to the most extreme forms of terrorism, making evolutionary change impossible.

There were literary heroes who illustrated the types of young Russians of that fated century — roles that, interestingly enough, one can find repeated even today in this positivistic era. In addition to the rebel, plotting in his basement apartment lair in St. Petersburg or Odessa or Minsk, there were the superfluous man, and the nihilists. The superfluous men floundered and suffered their way through 19th century history, exemplified by Lermontov's hopeless anti-hero in "A Hero of Our Time." Their lives pointless, their souls without succour, their intellects withered by the hopelessness of changing their societies or their lives. The superfluous men were the Hamletian intellectuals of their time. Only, in Russia, their torpor was unnaturally exaggerated by the fact that the intelligentsia was totally divorced from the peasant masses and from the aristocracy by its spiritual and intellectual addiction to the ideas and social solutions of the West — of Europe.

The nihilist was equally a negation of life, but an active negation, a man who believed that everything must be destroyed before anything could be built anew.

The only positive characters in this brooding and romantic assembly of young people were the revolutionaries and the young women — the girls like Natasha in "War and Peace" and Turgenev's heroine in "On the Eve" who was off to fight the Balkan wars.

And behind and beneath them — a vast pillow that absorbed and cancelled all their noble hopes — were the "dark masses," the peasants still revering the isolated Czarist "little father" in the Winter Palace in St. Petersburg.

If this age was typified by "beautiful sufferers and superfluous men," as one writer has put it, it was to give way to an age of glinty-eyed revolutionaries and self-righteous men shouting Maxim Gorky's cry that, "One must say firmly 'yes' or 'no!' " By 1917, as the Russian tsarist state collapsed from war and internal dissolution, the archtype of the young man and woman became the Marxist revolutionary who came to power bearing the religious passion of the ancient Christian martyrs, a vision of omnipotence, and a sense of inhabiting the center of the world that can only be compared to that of the Chinese emperors — or the Muscovite Orthodox Church of the Middle Ages.

The Bolsheviks never took youth for granted. They never allowed it to grow freely, like a weed, taking sustenance promiscuously from the wind and the rain. To them, youth was a precious flower, but a flower that must be mechanistically trained and trimmed and systematically cultivated to grow arrow-straight toward the sun — the Marxist sun, which would shine down upon a new generation of "New Men" the likes of which had never before been seen on this earth.

The first post-revolution generation grew straight. This was the passionate generation — Rozov's "unkempt boy" of the Civil War and Ostrovsky's Pavel. The next generation, the one that was born since the revolution and that came to manhood and womanhood in the late '30s and '40s, was already a little polished, a little more removed from the revolution, a little less impassioned — Rozov's man, "already a quarter a gentleman with a part in his hair." This was the son of the revolution who went on to fight the Great Patriotic War," as the Russians call World War II, with a fierce bravery, but who fought first for the "Rodina" — the "motherland" — and only secondarily for Communism.

The third post-revolution generation — the generation born and raised since World War II — is something totally new again. This generation — which was between 15 and 35 by the end of the 1960s — remembers as the most "unforgettable" moment of its collective life, not the day the Siege of Leningrad was lifted nor the day the Nazis surrendered at Stalingrad, but that memorable day at the 20th party congress in 1956 when Nikita Khrushchev told them that the man who had ruled their country for nearly 30 years and the man their fathers had worshipped was a paranoid megalomaniac and killer who had slaughtered millions of their innocent countrymen. And, remember, they were only children at the time — impressionable children!

The staggering disillusionment that swept Russia in the wake of Khrushchev's announcements stunned the young people, particularly those with impulses, normal to that age, of extreme idealism. It shocked them so much so that, in the early '60s, the universities were filled with stormy meetings at which students accosted party officials with their accusations of guilt, massively attended poetry readings that became the symbol of the resistance of that generation, and insolently published such underground journals as "Phoenix" and held "discussion groups" at which anything was open to discussion.

It was the time that caused the young American William Taubman, who was a student at Moscow University in those days, to write: "It is too late to recapture lost innocence. The inescapable truth is that young Russians are largely disenchanted with the Party's official answers . . . The simple truth is that Soviet indoctrination has backfired. It has ended in doubt and dissent."

But today, already a new half-generation has come to the fore. The university students of the early '60s — the most uproarious time for Soviet youth — are now in their early 30's. They are now either deep in careers or family. What came ten years behind them?

This generation of teen-agers and 20-year-olds, the poet Andrei Voznesensky, one of the heroes of the early '60s, told me, is "more quiet" than his generation was. And that is true. The excitement at the universities is largely over, and many of the young seem either very indifferent or very loyal.

Fathers and Sons

Vladimir Voronof, a pleasant, soft-spoken and non-pedantic editor at Yunost, one of the most popular and liberal youth magazines, insisted to me one summer day in 1971 that this new generation *is* really quite different from that of the Voznesensky era. "Their faith in the principles of the revolution is as pure as that of the first generation of the revolution," he said, as we sat in a pleasant little room that opened off the court of one of the old Moscow palaces. "Fifteen years ago, the young generation had no positive program. Something was broken by the 20th congress, but new principles were not created. For that generation, the main thing was a negative attitude to the old, to the past. But for the present generation, the difficult facts of the 20th congress are history for them."

Others do not see the "new quietism" in such an optimistic light. Writing in "Literaturnaya Gazyeta" or the "Literary Gazette," in 1969 about this "completely new generation coming in to take the place of those who were young just . . . six or seven years ago," Victor Rozov observed that: "There is one feature inherent in some of these 16- and 17-year-olds that troubles me. It is their peculiar kind of alienation. We adults coexist with them in the same space and time, but we don't get through to each other. You say things to your son or daughter. The boys and girls of six to seven years ago . . . would shout back passionately, 'You're wrong, your ideas are rigid, you are ancient.' Today's youngsters don't shout and argue. They listen to what you say, then go ahead and do what they themselves think should be done, even when they are on good terms with their parents.

"How do I explain this alienation? Evidently there is something extremely important that we have not given our children and there are areas where we don't understand one another. As a result, they have developed a kind of self-defense around their own world of feelings."

Who is right — is this generation terribly patriotic or terribly alienated? — or, somehow, both?

Who is telling the truth — or is there none?

What really *is* this new generation?

✢ Chapter Two
The Resurgence of the Spirit

"Lenin did not believe in man. He recognized in him no sort of inward principle; he did not believe in spirit and the freedom of the spirit, but he had a boundless faith in the social regimentation of man. He believed that a compulsory social organization could create any sort of new man you like — for instance, a completely social man who would no longer need the use of force. Marx believed the same thing, that the new man could be manufactured in factories."

The Russian Orthodox philosopher Nikolai Berdyaev

*A*T FIRST, I could barely believe what I was hearing.

When I began asking young Russians necessarily generalized questions, such as "What is your greatest passion in life?" or "What interests your generation most?" given the resounding, interminable indoctrination of the last 50 years, I assumed that at least some young people, if only for the sake of form, would say things like: "Creating the new Communist man" or "Destroying the bourgeoisie throughout the world and establishing Communism for all men."

I soon discovered how naive I was.

In my entire five months in the Soviet Union, not one young person offered anything even approximating these answers. When I finally, gingerly, suggested them as possibilities, the young people looked at me blankly. This blankness was often accompanied with quizzical, bemused smiles that indicated they found my questioning curiously outdated or found me someone ripe for membership in the Central Committee.

19

But if none of these textbook answers were given, there *was* one answer that came through loud and strong and constant: "the spiritual life of man."

This generation of young Russians — bred in the world's first materialist state supposedly weaned away from the dark old mysticism of the Russian past, raised to enjoy the material fruits of labor — is obsessed with the spiritual side of life.

One of the most interesting men I met in my whole time in the Soviet Union — and the young man who elaborated most fully on this phenomenon — was a 28-year-old physicist-turned-psychologist at Kiev State University. His name was Valerie Melko, and he seemed to incorporate in himself the conflicts between the searchings of objective science and the seekings toward a subjective inner world of man.

In looks, Valerie could have been an American post-graduate student. He had medium long brown hair, unhurried eyes, a sharp mind and an unfettered, honest way about him. By everyone's account, he was a brilliant physicist, but — and this is typical of his age group — he soon tired of pure, lonely, dehumanized science and took on psychology as an antidote to it.

"Even if you know how to do things, the problems of *what for* still remain," he told me, as we sat in a small drab study room of the university that cool October day, talking for well into four hours. "For what do we use modern technical things? What do they give to man? What do they give on a spiritual level?

"The world of things is known well. But what concerns man we know least because it is the most complex system. This tendency can be compared with the tendency of the Renaissance — to put man in the main spot, to make man the most precious thing in the world."

Valerie smiled — the kind of open, genuine smile one finds in this type of Russian young person.

"There was a revolution in physics at the beginning of the century which first influenced biology and now influences all the sciences which deal with man," he went on, "But the process which is going on in science also influences the desire of youth for independent thinking in all spheres — to find our own views and opinions. Youth does not share the opinion that technical progress will solve all social problems automatically. Fascism showed that. If there is one thing typical of this generation, it is its tendency to analyze everything and understand everything independently."

He shifted on his chair, then continued in the same intense tones; "The formation of the inner consciousness of man is not decided scientifically. The formation of the consciousness of man is going haphazardly, without order. We don't know on what it depends. We suppose it depends on social and economic conditions. But what? We don't know. We can only surmise. We hope that many features can be improved in man. But the first thing is to awaken a will in man to improve. To do this, we must know on what the will depends."

I must have started. Here was a young Marxist, a man quite within the system and indeed a jewel of its intellectual world, saying that his generation did not trust social and economic advances to solve psychological problems . . . in a society which consistently has claimed that man's psychological and personal problems were simply an outgrowth of the social imbalances that Communism would solve.

Son of a former pilot, Valerie had been doing work on the theory of relativity, when he decided that the study of man was more interesting than pure science. "In science, I felt I could only work on theoretical developments," he related. "You couldn't check the results with reality. Gravitational waves — no one knows if they really exist or not.

"I came to feel that knowing people was much more difficult — that and studying psychological behavior."

But Valerie was only one of hundreds of young people who spoke — passionately — along these lines. Sometimes they called it the "spiritual needs" of man. Often they used the term "inner man." "Creative" was popular and occasionally "individual" was used, particularly in referring to changes in education.

In Volgograd one afternoon, for instance, I wandered into the House of Culture, entered into a conversation with a young art teacher, and asked him if there were many new trends in painting among his students. "Yes," he said thoughtfully, "they are all trying to depict man in a different way — not just to show what he looks like. They want to show his inner life." And, of course, I thought, as I perused the paintings carefully, this no longer was socialist realism, the one approved art form of the Marxist state in which the humanity of every human figure was stylized out into some symbolic figure representative of all humanity. Now the figures had eyes of their own, thoughts of their own. They were real human beings: individuals.

But what surprised me most was not that this passion for the "spiritual life of man" was omnipresent among artists — nor only found among psychologists — but that, perhaps out of duress, it had been taken up by the toughest, least sentimental, most hardened organization of them all — the Komsomol or the Communist Youth League.

Certainly no one could accuse the Komosol of sentimentality. It was the Komsomol, founded in 1918 immediately after the Bolshevik revolution, that inspired Communist youth to fanatic deeds. When the state felt it must destroy the kulaks, the wealthy farmers whose annihilation was the first step to collectivization, it was the Komsomolers, sometimes sobbing but all the same knowing full well what they must do if Communism were to win, who dragged them from their homes and sent them to death in Siberian exile. When lakes were needed, it was the Komosomol who dug them with shovels, cracking through the frozen ground with their bare hands and bare will. When cities were built in the wilderness, these youths built them. They controlled taste, too, punishing deviations into jazz and other Western attractions with ostracism, in their own courts, and there was a time when they employed such brutish punishments as shaving a girl's hair off if she wore Western style clothes.

The Mafia is not an equal opportunity employer and the Komsomol is not a ladies' bridge club.

Even more reason why I had reason to be initially surprised at the new route the Komsomol was taking. Like so many ruling, formative bodies within the Soviet system, it was in the midst of a profound transformation from the old reliance on sheer force and terror to a new, unsure, unsteady, but constantly proceeding reliance on persuasion in order to mold and mark the more than 20 million Soviet youths between the ages of 14 and 28 who came under its sway.

Once again, and in this most unlikely place, the "spiritual man" came up. Komsomol magazines and units themselves were calling for a new "humanized" type of leader. In Volgograd one day, for instance, in the office of the youth newspaper "Young Leninist," the editor, Galina Rezhabek, put it this way:

"If earlier we elected Komsomol leaders taking into consideration whether he was a good worker and how many bricks he laid, now we considered how he knows a person, how he understands things and how clever he is."

She seemed very excited and pleased to be able to tell me they had just published an article on the subject and that the author, a tall, serious and bespectacled young man named Vladimir Ryashun was there. He added modestly that, "Now we like a Komsomol leader who shows initiative. There is a distinct tendency to have leaders who pay attention to the spiritual demands of members." What did he mean by "initiative?" "They are no longer strictly fulfillers," he went on, referring to the time when the drab, faceless, brutalized leaders existed only to force people to fulfill production quotas. "Now they are thinking, making analyses, finding new forms of work with young people. They are educated and very clever. They try to find the key to the heart of every member. It means a thoughtful approach to the person."

"Komsomol wants to know about the wishes and demands of every member," another Volgograd Komsomol leader broke in. "When we know the needs of each person, we are able to increase interest in each activity."

Moreover, this new passion for a more humanized and efficient leader and a more humanized life style was not proceeding only on the level of the "intellectual" Komsomol — that is, the university and school cells of the organization. It was proceeding, although at a slower rate, in the factories and farms. Just outside Volgograd, the next day, I visited the Volski chemical factory and put the same question about the new type of leadership to Oleg Besedin, secretary of the Volski city Komsomol.

"Life prompts us to work with people more individually now," he said. "Yes, our role has changed. If before we worked with Komsomol in general, now we divide our people into categories. This factory, for instance, has mostly girls working in it. We try to organize it so we can satisfy their interests and needs.

"All our organizations have this task of working with the person's inner life. It brings us into close contact with members and non-members. We are interested in the mood and spirit of youth.

We are interested in their interests, hobbies and abilities. When we take the whole complex into account, we have excellent results."

Even in architecture, young architects talk about the spirit, and they are beginning to create works tremendously different from the old standardized architecture that marched stolidly through the bolshevik period. In the beautiful old Ukrainian capital of Kiev, for instance, I stopped in at the city planning office one day and chatted with a young architect, Avram Miletzkubi, who had just designed a strikingly beautiful crematorium for the city to deal with the shortage of space for burials within close distances of Kiev. The crematorium had a flowing, blooming quality about it that arrested the eye and soothed the mourner. Its gates were two tall soaring wings just barely passing each other, and the central building itself was formed with receding circles, like a flower blooming — or closing its petals for the night.

"There is a symbolic meaning of the form," Miletzkubi said, pointing to the model of his marker. "There are two symbolic events in life — birth and death. But birth is not the beginning of life. The birth of each person begins with the birth of his parents, and there is something left after each person. So I designed the gates to look as though they were moving — as if one person was being exchanged for another. The form of the building is the form of a shell opening, but also the form of the setting sun. I wanted the idea of moving time." He paused and smiled what struck me as a sad smile. "I didn't want a mechanical thing," he said. "I wanted it to have a spiritual feeling."

But even if one agrees that there is this spiritual search proceeding in the Soviet Union, the question of what it signifies is harder to answer. Does it denote a religious search — a return to past forms of spirituality? Does it mean simply cultural things — beauty of form, beauty of expression, beauty of the creative spirit? Or does it mean human decency — a minimal level of courtesy toward one another and an ethical approach to man?

Communist theorists have certainly recognized this trend, — they have had to because it is so demandingly present — and they have their own explanations. When I asked Dr. Vladimir Kolobkov, head of the Chair of Scientific Communism at Kiev State University, about this, he immediately fit the fascination with "the spirit" scientifically into the development of Communism.

"Until the mid-'50s." he said, "our main objective was to recreate the national economy to cope with defense and living standards. These tasks were mainly solved in the mid- or end- '50s, and we began to build Communism itself. Our world outlook is that when the material needs are satisfied, spiritual and social problems come to the fore and must be solved according to social demands."

But despite the obvious sincerity and conviction of men like this, most objective observers are convinced that the reaction of the Soviet hierarchy is just that — a *reaction* to what the young people are demanding and not something that Communist ideologues always foresaw and predicted. It is being written into "scientific" Communism now; it was not there in the beginning.

The truth, rather, lies elsewhere.

A good part of what these young people — so much better educated, so much more cultured and so far better-mannered than their crude and often brutish elders — called "spiritual" was simply what would be called human decency in much of the West. As one Sovietologist in the United States, in a skeptical mood, put it: "Yevtushenko can work up tears about not beating women. Yet this is not going to keep him from it. The whole search is not on a very ethereal level. It's rather that they have had so many hacks that what we in the West think of as a normal decent person they think of as a saint. To have normal human instincts and affirm them makes you abnormal."

There is no question that the Soviet young are deeply ashamed, embarrassed and disgusted with the boorishness and cruelty — the traditional "khamstvo" — that has characterized their fathers for so many generations. Even Soviet leaders like Krushchev were known for their peasant curses, usually having to do with human excrement and someone else's mother.

One sees it, too, in public life. One foreign woman friend of mine who had lived for several years in Moscow was pushed off an overcrowded bus one day as it started up and landed on her back in a snowdrift. A Russian man approached her, glanced at her lying there and, before she could get up, walked not over her but on her — he stepped right on her stomach as he went on his way. This is typical.

It was typical, too, when, one night in Moscow, Henry Gill and I were ushered to a table in the enormous new Hotel Rossiya and, though the rest of the restaurant was empty, we had to sit with two very, very drunken Russian working men. The one next to me was slavering from both sides of his mouth as he sat there; he was also dead asleep. As we watched, fascinated, the other (awake) man took his napkin (this is the fanciest hotel in Russia, remember!) and gathered into it everything left on the table but the dinnerware. A few pieces of chicken, bread, butter, the salt shaker, some dripping salad and a bottle of beer — all went into the hastily-rigged knapsack. Grasping this tightly in his hand, he started out the door. Then, suddenly remembering his friend, he returned, elbowed the sleeping, slavering man in the ribs and led him, staggering, out.

But it is not only these crude manners — the result of centuries of war and hardship — that "turn off" the critical and relatively pampered young, it is also the long-accepted brutality that one finds everywhere in the country.

This came through to me most forcibly and poignantly one afternoon in 1971, when I was sitting in the studio of my friend the renowned Armenian sculptor, Nikolai Bogranovich Nikoroyan, in Moscow. He was sketching me. In between furious bouts of work, he would dig into his little "cellar" under the floor, bring out excellent bottles of Armenian wine and several of us would sit down to eat and drink. This day, as we ate, he reminisced about his father who, on the brink of dying from a fatal disease, had committed suicide by throwing himself under a train after he bade farewell to his family at a warm family dinner.

Nikolai himself was a wild creature of the wind, always doing curious little dances, throwing his arms around the nearest woman, shouting, singing and jumping up in the air. A free spirit. But when you looked at him closely, you saw beneath the shaggy head of curls two sad, supplicating eyes that belonged to a vulnerable soul.

"I remember one day," he reminisced this day. "I was just a small child — five or six. My father was making shishkabob outside our house and my mother called him a fool. He took a knife off the fire and threw it in her back. Then he took it out and wiped it off and went on cooking. At the time, I thought he was quite right. She had insulted him. He was a man who had his own rules.

"Later, when I was a bit older, I decided to make myself a different pair of shoes from the kind that all the villagers wore. I was very proud of them, and, when my father was critical of them, I said that they were very modern and that everybody was wearing them. My father made me a wager: 'We'll walk through the village and if we see anybody else wearing them, you can beat me. If we don't, I can beat you.' He beat me so badly I lay unconscious for four hours. Finally he came and poured water on me. Many years later, I asked him if he remembered this. 'Yes.' he said. 'I had to do it. I had to show you to respect other people.' "

In effect the "spiritual search" *is* in great part a search for simple human kindness, for simple human decency. And much of this expresses itself, on the part of the young, in a tremendous interest in good manners.

Etiquette books are snapped up as soon as they come on the bookstands. There are constant youth panel discussions on radio and television about creating a "new code of Communist etiquette," and the young obviously do not believe, as did the original Bolsheviks, that "crude manners often conceal wonderful hearts." Hand-kissing is widely approved among the young and the whole phenomenon even takes on political contours.

Manners matter in politics. Nine out of ten of the young persons I met had no regard for the late Nikita Khrushchev, despite his de-Stalinization. Why? "Because he's a boor," was the common reply. "When he went to the U.N. and took his shoe off, we all nearly died with embarrassment and rage. We want our country to be respected, not laughed at." And Andrei Voznesensky wrote a poignant poem picturing those who "take their shoes off wondering only which foot they have washed the night before."

The new courtesy, if it can be called that, is a bonus to foreigners. Except for professional young Communist officials, neither I nor any other American I met in Russia (and this includes many who had studied and lived there) was ever deliberately embarrased by a *young* person. "They seem to go out of their way to avoid sensitive or provocative subjects altogether," was the way one American girl studying there put it. "They don't want to insult you. If they know you're against the Vietnam war, nothing more is ever said."

All of this, of course, causes part of the "Fathers and Sons" problem between children and parents. In one popular recent story the son tells his father bruskly, "Oh, you old fool, you're not up to date." Answers the father, sadly, "I had to work so hard I couldn't do anything else. If I had your education, I'd be better-mannered, too."

An ever-present theme here is that the younger generation thinks the older are "boors" because of their social manners; but the older thinks the same of them . . . because of their free-swinging sexual morality.

Still, the "spiritual search" is not only a search for basic human decency and courtesy, it is also a search for many other things. It certainly signifies a turning away from industrialization, not as a means to material well-being but as a means to discovering the answers to life. It does mean a need for something beyond material goods. It does signify an overwhelming boredom with Marxism. And it does show a demand for answers to the question that never again was supposed to be asked under Communism: "What for?"

That question, in turn, leads to the religious aspects of the search. If it is not, at this point in time, a religious search, at least not in any traditional organized religion sense, it is on many levels a mystical search. And if there is not any real flocking back to the Orthodox church, it must be remembered that it is holding its own (in some cities, like Gorki, the Russian press reports that 60 percent of the children are baptized in church and 55 percent of young couples are married in church), that the Baptists are thriving, that there is a Jewish revival, and that, if there were true religious freedom, they would certainly be undergoing much of the kind of religious experimentation going on among youth in the United States.

What was naive on the part of Westerners, of course, was to believe, because the Marxists tried so hard to make us believe it, that the historic and often fanatical spirituality of the Russians had somehow been bred out of them by Marxism. All Marxism showed was that they are such a deeply spiritual people that they can make a spiritual truth even out of materialism.

I have watched with fascination how a slightly mad look comes over them even when they talk about electricity, as if this new technological light had somehow taken the place of the old light of salvation. I have felt it in the Orthodox churches in Russia today, when the women begin to sob and one feels the fever and frenzy of passionate belief rising. And I have felt it with Marxist officials who, in their fanatic aversion to everything mystical and in their fear of freedom — which they relate to anarchic mysticism and dissolution — illustrate the power these concepts still hold over them.

Many of the spiritual and religious motifs of the past have been transmogrified into new forms for the present. The peasants, for instance, can easily see in Lenin lying in his tomb the descendant of the petrified saints of the Old Orthodox faith. I remember standing in Red Square just before the 50th anniversary of the revolution in 1967 talking to a young artist named Misha from Lvov. "I was in the tomb two years ago," he told me in a hushed voice. "Lenin is our god."

Really, God? I asked him. Really? "Why not?" he asked, unruffled. "We walk in his footsteps. Jesus was a man first, so why can't Lenin be God. That is why we keep the square quiet. That is why we keep traffic out. So there will be no noise and no confusion where Lenin lies."

The old mysticism is still there, it has only been resting, waiting for better days.

On a religious-intellectual level, the "search" takes still other forms. Already, because of so much renewed interest in religion, the Soviet state has had to make certain old Orthodox philosophers available for young readers. In 1967, the Political Literature Publishing House issued in a Russian translation the Polish author Zenon Kasidowski's "Tales from the Bible." Since the Bible is not generally available in the Soviet Union, this was the closest thing to it that the Russian people had had in two generations.

"The first break in the exorcism of silence surrounding the Bible in Communist countries," the liberal magazine "Novi Mir" or "New World" commented, as the book sold out and was reissued. The magazine also noted that "School children know the Greek legends. Have the Old Testament stories really failed to leave a noticeable imprint on the history of world culture?"

It must be remembered, too, that in Eastern and Western Europe, many of the most provocative scholars are attempting a "dialogue" between Marxists and Christians — a trend that has only begun to reach Muscovy, the seat of Marxism as it was of Orthodox orthodoxy. As the Czech Marxist philosopher, Milan Machovec, a professor of philosophy at Charles University, has said, "Both Christians and Marxists ask the ultimate questions. Christians call it the problem of salvation, we call it the problem of alienation." It is the basic convergent humanism present in such a statement that is probably the closest thing to what the young Russians desire in their "spiritual" quest.

Russia never had the Protestant work ethnic of the Calvinist countries of the North, and, outside of officialdom, she does not have it today. Salvation, to them, came not through the expending of energies in productive industry but through an intangible, mystical "goodness" that is precisely what the young people, albeit without any hanging of it onto religious practice, are talking about today.

But when they talk about "the spirit", they are talking about other things besides decency and a mystical goodness. They are talking about the ethical content of life, as embodied in the individual — about personal honesty and integrity, something that the young Russians speak about constantly while at the same time not quite coming to the point of knowing how to apply it to real life. They are talking about living with verve in a country that reeks of boredom, and just living as they want to live, without constant reproval by the state.

"We Russians like to daydream," Giselle Amalrik, the beautiful almond eyed Tartar girl who is married to dissident writer Andrei Amalrik, told me. "I think a lot. I like to sit in the countryside staring at the sky. Many young people are now interested in religion. It's just not enough to live in this society with no spirit. Material values are just not enough."

They want beauty in their lives. They want to reach out from the geographical, historical and human isolation of the Soviet period — beyond the feeling of suffocation that was common to tsarist and to Communist Russia — and they want to have some fun as they take their place on the spinning human stage. They want to reorient their spiritual lives in a way that is far more Western than Eastern.

✿ Chapter Three
The New Quest for the Old Russia

*"One cannot understand Russia by reason
And measure her by a common yardstick.
She has a peculiar nature.
One must simply believe in Russia."*

Poem by the noted Slavophile Fedor Tyuchev in the 1860s

𝒯HE major direction that the young are carrying the spiritual quest in Russia today is backwards. I soon had to turn around and join this curious march to the past when I returned to the Soviet Union in 1971, for, after four years the evidences of it were everywhere.

At the Smolny Institute in Leningrad, which was headquarters for Lenin's forces during the revolution, my guide, Sonja, pointed to the beautiful adjoining blue and white church and said smartly, as if it were the most normal thing in the world, "We just put the crosses back on the church this year." The golden crosses gleamed in the sun — the same sun which, since 1917, has seen churches burned and looted and used as poolhalls, storage warehouses and museums of atheism.

In Novgorod, when I walked into the old Cathedral of St. Sophia in that ancient city's Kremlin, recorded Orthodox church music was playing, as Russian tourists sat and stood, listening intently to it. Church music has rarely been heard in the Soviet Union since the revolution.

In Moscow, I visited the Society for the Preservation of Ancient Landmarks and found that no fewer than 6 million Soviet citizens of all ages are now deeply engaged in the work of this *voluntary* organization to restore and save the symbols of the old Russia. "Voluntary" organizations are practically unknown in Russia — particularly to preserve old churches.

And at Yunost magazine, one of the most popular magazines for youth, editor Vladimir Voronof told me, "One of the differences in the young people today is they are reading the reactionary Orthodox philosophers from before the revolution. The idea is they should know what they are against in these works." It has most definitely *not* been the idea of the state over the last fifty years to take this sort of a chance.

What is happening is one of the most fascinating and broad-reaching currents of spiritual and intellectual development in Russia today — a return to Russian nationalism and even to 19th century Slavophilsm (that ingrown tendency that Leon Trotsky, always the internationalist, ungenerously called "the messianism of backwardness").

"It is Russian nationalism," says Dr. Edward Keenan, leading Sovietologist at the Russian Research Institute at Harvard University. "It tends to be a conservative and anti-industrial movement that has enormous affinity for the old days: for peasants and for things unspoiled by politics. And one of the wonderful things about the old Russia, of course, is that it's not Marxist."

Arising out of what many young Russians and even officials acknowledge as a "spiritual emptiness" in Soviet society and a lack of charismatic qualities on the part of the leadership, this chauvinistic nationalism is Russian rather than Christian, although the saints are, for the first time since the revolution, marching in again.

Cut off from the tentative and largely unsatisfying modern answers to alienation being put forward by the rest of the world, the young Russians are searching in the only place open to them — their own mystic, semi-forbidden, 1,000-year-old, pre-revolutionary past. And, here, the only voluptuous spiritual ideas they come upon that they are free to use are the God-seeking ones of the 19th century Slavophiles, those apocalyptic Russians who believed in the spiritual superiority of the Slav, the moral bankruptcy of the West and the mission of Muscovy, the "third Rome."

Perhaps the most remarkable thing about the "movement," if, in its amorphousness, it can be called that, is that it was in no way formed or forced by the state. On the contrary, between 1965 and 1972, it arose on many levels and in many places at once and always in an individual and voluntary manner. Obviously reflecting some great need felt — across age and cultural and professional groups — it was joined by masses of Russians. At first the Komsomol and the organs of the government held back. But once its popularity became too obvious to ignore, they jumped in and tried to coop it.

If there is one watershed date that marks the public beginnings of this new phenomenon, it is probably 1965, when a group of the cultural and scientific intelligentsia, having become concerned with preserving the Russian cultural heritage from the growing voraciousness of the Soviet Marxist bulldozer, started the remarkable Society for the Preservation of National Monuments. With its 6 million members (almost all from the European Russian peoples) paying 30 kopecks or cents a year, it works with the government on projects but actually operates mostly on a private basis. It raises millions of rubles a year for restoration work, mostly for old churches and monasteries, inspires children to seek out old ruins and legends among the populace, and sends students and specialists all over the country to work.

The home of the society in Moscow is itself a lovely old monastery. Like so much of Old Russia, it is somehow unfinished and neglected, but also wild and free. The courts behind the facade facing a Moscow street are lined with mellowed old buildings and high-growing grass and wildflowers. One gets a feeling of beauty and freedom — so different from the clipped, utilitarian standardization so prevalent in New Russia.

Inside the building, Vladimir Ivanov, a charming elderly art historian who is a member of the society's presidium, spoke of "Why, the society?"

"Members of the society can be school children," the genteel, white-haired man said, leaning back in his old chair. "Their duties are to look for new monuments not yet uncovered. They take pictures and describe the places and find out the legends among the local population. Then we have a council of scientists here which studies objects and decides what to include in a special list for restoration. This then goes to the government for approval. The government, of course, does most of the restoration, because it is very expensive, but the society helps. During the last year, the society gave 5 million rubles (roughly 5 million dollars) for restoration. Then we organize teams of students who go during vacations to work. This year we had 16 teams of 40 to 50 each from Moscow alone. The students have a great enthusiasm for the romantic, and sometimes we open a competition to find which team can go the farthest. They've worked in Tamerlane's ruins, in the Solovetsky Monastery on the White Sea island . . . Bilizerski Monastery . . . in Irkutsk, where we're reconstructing three very old fortresses of the Old Believers in a kind of Disney Park . . ."

Why? He had very definite ideas on "Why." "People living in the big cities want to learn the sort of life of other times . . . " he went on, speaking gently, in a tone very like the ruins themselves. "The new construction, too, is somehow a contradiction of nature, whereas the old monasteries are allied with nature and the old churches do not deprive you of a feeling of the trees. They have found that physics is not enough to satisfy man — they need something to excite the mind and the soul."

Something to excite the mind and the soul might be the description of one society-aided project in Novgorod. For the last six years, an art historian, Alexander Petrovich Grekoff, aided by 35 students sent out by the society, has been piecing together 440 cases of tiny pieces of frescoes of the 14th century Monastery of the Savior, destroyed by the Nazis in World War II. The pieces were deep in the ground and have been dug up, matched and newly placed together; soon a new church will be built to house them.

The mysticism surrounding this work is typical of the latent mysticism behind all of this work. "There is a mystic communication between the artist and this work," Grekoff said, sitting in his Novgorod studio amidst these living ruins. "Sometimes I think I am getting a bit crazy. I will take two pieces of the frescoes and they seem to unite, to go together by themselves. The students tell me they have the same experience."

When Grekoff and his handsome wife, Valentina, also a restorer, were drawn to the spot in 1963, they were not, originally, sanguine about the possibilities. "In the beginning, I agreed that it was hopeless," Grekoff said. "But it was such a beautiful spot — the wild roses were blooming. Why not spend two weeks here?"

He smiled. "Now I am a prisoner to the work. It is absolutely impossible not to finish it. I feel a kind of moral obligation. In times when so many things are being ruined, I want to create things. And you can't create things as beautiful as these old ones. I am happy so many young people take part — part of the soul of art comes to them."

Much the same thing is happening in the field of music. Here, the stellar figure is the famous pianist Andrei Volkonsky — a romantic figure to many young Russians partly because he is the grandson and namesake of the immortal "Prince Andrei" of "War and Peace."

When he reminisces about his family, one does, indeed, feel for just a moment transported back to the Old Russia. "I am a great grandson of the Volkonsky of the Decembrist uprising," he said, unassumingly, as we sat one day in the elegant National Hotel restaurant overlooking the Kremlin, its gold onion domes gleaming in the sun. "We are related to all the czars of the Romanoff family. And also to Prince Vladimir of Kiev and to Alexander Nevsky."

Then he said, with just a touch of an ironic smile. "They're just relatives. The family had its own czars and saints. But I have nothing to do with saints any more." A pregnant pause. "Besides," he went on, smiling now more broadly. "I'm not a saint myself."

Volkonsky doubtless is no saint, but, to many young Russians he is a modern Soviet version of one. A commanding and memorable figure, tall and gaunt with burning eyes and long black hair he throws about at will, Volkonsky began in 1965 what six years later had become a wildly popular renaissance of early pre-Peter the Great (and thus pre-European influence) Orthodox church music.

"At the time of Peter, there were reforms in the church services," he explained, "and part of the reform was a kind of Europeanization of the service. The old type of music was forgotten. A new singing during the services was introduced that had nothing to do with the old music. I believe everyone must feel very sorry because the music today is poorer. It lost its Russian features."

Volkonsky formed a performing group called the "Madrigals," which by 1971 was giving 100 totally sold-out concerts a year all over the Soviet Union — but not before he personally had done the mammothly intricate job of personally searching out and decoding the music, which lay untouched in old libraries and monasteries.

"For thousands of people, particularly students, this ancient classical music replaces pop music," he summed up, "In a way, it's a kind of social experiment.

Perhaps nowhere is the "social experiment" so interesting as on the literary level, however. In the underground "samizdat" (literally "self-published") press, which consists of hand-typed carbon copies passed from hand to hand, there are now underground Slavophille "magazines" such as "Veche" (the word the early Slavophiles used for their town meetings) and "The Word of the Nation," one whose contents typify the blood nationalism of the most fanatic Slavophiles.

On an incalculably important level is the debate in the official press. From 1968 on, the youth journals have been so filled with references to white stone churches, golden domes and Christian saints — many portrayed for the first time since the revolution as national heroes — that the more sedate magazine, "Soviet Russia" warned: "This undue emphasis on gilded cupolas detracts from the display of what Russia has achieved during 50 years of Soviet rule. We must treat (patriotism and pride) only from clear Marxist positions."

The major current of the debate has proceeded in a most unlikely vehicle, however: the Komosomol's popular magazine "Molodaya Gvardia" or "Young Guard." Here two popular young writers, Vladimir Soloukhin and Victor Chalmayov, have sparked the debate.

In 1968, Chalmayov, the more controversial, printed an article entitled "Inevitabilities," averring that the great, crude industrialized society was getting into trouble because it lacked spiritual values. For a man whose idols are Ivan the Terrible, Peter the Great and Joseph Stalin and for a man who believes that Peter's merit was not that he opened a window to Europe for closed and secretive Russia but that he gave Europe a window to "virtuous Russia," it was obvious where his ideas were leading.

Not surprisingly, trouble followed.

"His theme was that if it was old, then it was good," Igor Zaharoskho, an editor of Young Guard, explained to me in the journal's offices. "He wanted to take everything old and use it today. He forgot that first you have to have a class position."

Others soon reminded him and, in the summer of 1969, a spirited discussion developed within the entire Moscow press among the Russian nationalists, the proletarian Stalinists and the more Western-minded liberals. At one point, it reached such a heated level nationally that Brezhnev himself found it necessary to warn that patriotism was good but that extremes of patriotism represented the dangers of a departure from class consciousness; he particularly warned against Russian nationalistic exclusivism.

But the real attack has been waged by the state's atheistic journal, "Nauka i Religii" or "Science and Religion," which attacked the implicit religiosity of Chalmayov and much of the new Slavophilism; by the Western-oriented liberals of the magazine "Novi Mir" or "New World," who were against its backwardness and closed qualities; and by Party Ideologist Mikhail Suslov himself, who has talked about it as being inimical to party creed.

And, of course, there is an inevitable core of controversy in their ideas and approach. The U.S.S.R. is established in its official ideology as a Marxist internationalist state, embracing all peoples and negating the need for any further search for meaning in life, while the new Slavophiles, implicitly and often explicitly, would carry the state back to the ingrown, purely Russian nationalism of the past.

What's more, the Russian nationalist position brings together some of the most unlikely bedfellows: Nobel prize-winner and dissident writer Alexander Solzhenitsyn (though a critic of Stalinism, a believer in God and in the Russian mission), dissident writer Andrei Sinyavsky (an avid icon-collector, who, described by his prosecutor in his trial as a "cosmopolitan", retorted that he was actually a "Pan-Slav"), and, to a lesser degree, the top conservative Nobel prize-winning author Mikhail Sholokov.

Not surprisingly, this fascination with the old — and thus, to many, the beautiful — has seeped over into art and into what is, in effect, interior decorating. The apartments of the intelligentsia today are filled with icons, now being collected from farmers who hid them under floors and barns during the war, and other antiquities. Some of the effects are breathtaking. One evening in Kiev, I was taken by friends to the apartment of Sergi Parazhonov, the famous Armenian movie director. When I stepped inside the front door I had to catch my breath.

Here was an ordinary modern apartment, as box-like and sterile as any other in the Soviet Union. But Parazhonov, a short stocky man with quizzical eyes, a bemused curl of the lip, tremendous personal assurance and a devilish beard, had made it into a lair of ancient Russia. One almost expected Rasputin to step out at any minute, rolling his eyes and licking his lips over some ripe peasant girl. In one room was a long, heavy, wood-carved banquet table, on which was spread every sort of fish, caviar, cold meat and delicacy. Wine was served in huge wooden mugs. All over the apartment hung animal skins, icons, hand-woven cloths and scabrous old crosses, while the young men and women who lolled insouciantly against the tables with their curious feline smiles seemed escapees into some strange netherworld. One young woman artist immediately showed me her sketches of Dante's "Inferno" and they seemed somehow appropriate.

This artistic strain has also led to many young artists painting old religious themes. Ilia Glazunov, officially recognized by the Union of Artists, paints a kind of contemporary iconography, and in one corner of his Moscow studio he has a replica of a peasant hut. Many others are painting crucifixes. Soloukhin has ever written in the monthly "Moskva" or "Moscow" an article classifying people according to their attitude toward icons — religious devotees, collectors and iconoclasts, to name just a few.

This combination of artistic creation coupled with a religious theme is also beginning to be seen in an occasional new film. One of these, "Andrei Rublyov," a remarkable film about the great 15th century icon painter, was completed in 1966, but it was not shown in Russia until 1972, although in the meantime it won a prize at the Cannes Festival for its dark and brutal portrayal of Rublyov against the background of the wanton destruction of Russia by the Tatar hords.

The other great icon painter of the time, Feofan Grek, says at one time during the film, "Everything is on a treadmill. And it turns and turns. If Jesus descended again, he would be crucified anew." Rublyov says to him in another scene. "Rus, Rus, it endures everything, it will bear everything. How long will this continue?"

"Probably always," Grek answers.

But, in the end, is all of it really important? Will it really influence the development of the future of the Soviet Union, or will this trend eventually simply be absorbed into the massive authoritarian pillow that is the Soviet state?

The numbers of Soviets, particularly young people, influenced by this Russian nationalist "discussion" or "movement" are enormous. Aside from the members of the Soviety, millions read the magazines involved in the debate and 50 million Soviet tourists (a number which had doubled since 1964) in 1971 and '72 scoured the U.S.S.R.'s historic spots in their dogged, unsmiling Russian way.

On the level of restoration and preservation, the preservationists have been extraordinarily successful. The Society, through its persistent efforts, was able to save such valuable things as the six old churches surrounding the new Hotel Rossiya in Moscow, the Romanov palace, the English court built by Ivan the Terrible, and Kolomenskoye, the 13th century village housing the summer residents of the czars near Moscow. "We got out backs up and fought to preserve these areas," Prof. Pyotr A. Volodin, the ministry of Culture official in charge of preservation and a leading member of the society, says.

On the literary level, the fact that young Russians are now permitted to read formerly forbidden pre-revolution philosophers indicates a general reaching out beyond the intellectual prison walls of the Soviet period. Since they cannot reach out around them today, they are reaching out to the past, and the Soviet state, taking the relatively enlightened new position in ideological warfare — that this generation is too well-educated not to know its enemy — is allowing them to do this.

But it must be remembered how unusual — how tremendously new within the Soviet period — this phenomenon is, as well as what it means historically.

In their time, the Slavophiles advocated the emancipation of the peasants, but they totally rejected the idea of a formal, Western-style constitution. They celebrated Russia's mysticism, her closed qualities, her dark peasant masses, her familial clans and her "sobornost" or "togetherness" in the church. In everything they were wholly opposed to the other major current of 19th century Russian intellectual thought, that of the Westernizers — the pro-Western liberals who wanted reform on the European principles of democratic and republican change.

In many ways, the Slavophiles, in their typically anti-Capitalism Russian attitude that the land belonged to everyone and in their sense of the Russian mission were certainly closer to the Bolsheviks than were the Westernizers. Still, when the revolution came, they were all but destroyed. Their lineal descendancy did not go so far as to develop into Marxist internationalism and their God-seeking nature hardly found a place in a regime that was destroying the Orthodox church.

Still, the mysticism underlying them lived on, covertly, like so many things in Soviet Russia, and it lived on with a continuity never remotely expected in the West, which naively assumed that a "total" revolution like Russia's could wipe out 2,000 years with one great 50-year sweep. Leningraders, for instance, tell the story of the nearby village church which the authorities converted into a school; they covered the frescoes with a coat of green paint. But soon the paint began to streak. The unbelieving and the believing villagers alike soon came by the hundreds to see the "miracle." "Really it was because of the bad quality of Russian paint," one Leningrader commented, "but you will never get the people to believe this."

In those years, there was no such tolerance as today about fixing up the churches because they were "beautiful" or "becoming acquainted with" the old philosophers.

Indeed, I observed a typical phenomenon of this epoch in Vilnius, where the former St. Casimir's Roman Catholic Church had been turned into a "Museum of Atheism" directed by the former priest, Stasis Marconis. "The priests had made lists of people to be executed by the Germans," Marconis' deputy Joses Matusabuchus told me, somewhat breathlessly, the day I visited. Then he showed me a picture of Hitler with a messenger of the Pope. When I suggested that there were a good many Protestant "priests" in Estonia exterminated by the Nazis, he answered quickly. "That shows how the church adapts to modern conditions."

So the changes today are dramatic ones. And they indicate, first, the intellectual and spiritual, if not the economic, vacuity of Marxism after 50 years. Materially, the country has progressed dramatically, and it has progressed to such a point where now new needs come into play — needs for which the system has no immediate answers.

Interestingly enough, the two movements that have developed spontaneously — this one and the political dissident movement — almost exactly parallel the two major movements of the last century, the Slavophiles and the Westernizers; this one looking inward to everything Russian, the dissident movement looking outward to everything Western. In terms of food for real spiritual thought, it becomes clear that there has been little since then.

But this movement probably occurred now, not only because the material level is high enough to permit such intellectual meanderings, but also because there is a resurgence of the primeval Russian fear of threat from outside. "Czechoslovakia had a lot to do with it," one Sovietologist said, referring to the threat and fear many Russians felt at the 1968 liberalization there, "and China does, too. They know that in comparison they're not reproducing."

Russian nationalism is important, of course, because of the tremendous hegemony which the Great Russians (the Russians) and secondarily the Little Russians (the Ukrainians) and the White Russians (the Belorussians) play in terms of the cultural and political dominance of the U.S.S.R. The Great Russians themselves comprise over half of the Soviet people, and, with the Ukrainians and the White Russians, they comprise three fourths of the Soviet peoples. The Great Russians dominate the politburo, the culture, and the language and Russians have spread throughout the non-Russian areas, often dominating them internally.

But. . . .the purely Great Russian birthrate is so low today and the Asiatic and non-Russian Soviet birthrates are so high that some Soviet demographers estimate that in between 30 and 50 years "Russia" will be a predominately Asiatic country. When you take this fact, plus the growingly obstreperous claims of various nationalities (Ukrainians, Moldavians, Jews, Armenians, Georgians, Crimean Tatars, Turks), it is clear that the Russian people, who have totally controlled the levers of power since 1917, are increasingly fearful that their time may be drawing to a close. Almost instinctively, they are reaching back into their own past for nourishment and sustenance to face a hard winter period.

And so, ironically, today the archaic philosophy of Slavophilism or Russian Nationalism, by the quirk of a great leap backwards in history, is serving to open the Soviet age - to break the taboos of reading books of the non-Soviet era and to initiate a search. While the search is, at this moment in the past, one has to remember that there were many things in the Russian past quite outside of Slavophilism that would be looked at as quite daring today — these include not only Western ideas, but the pure, relatively tolerant and humanistic ideas of Marx and other Socialist philosophers.

But as important as these intellectual ideas are, in its essence the search through the Old Russia is a metaphysical, poetical search, with an undoubted magic about it. It takes one into deep, dark woods that have always had a quiet sense of doom about them. It takes you to the White Sea, where the summer sun paints a white film between you and the world. It takes you into the Dostoevskian, Tolstoyan passions of the past — and away from the fleshless, tiresome, utilitarian passions of the present.

It restores beauty and mystery in a country whose system thought it could squeeze the need for them out of people.

A Russian sculptor friend of mine, asked why so many of his friends and colleagues were hanging icons in their apartments, said simply, "Because they're beautiful. We want things made by man, not by a machine, something that someone put love into, something human. We're tired of machines." A pause. "We've become machines ourselves."

❧ Chapter Four
An End to Ideology?

"We are one of those nations which do not seem to be an integral part of the human race, but which exist only to give some great lesson to the world. The instruction which we are destined to give will certainly not be lost; but who knows the day when we will find ourselves a part of humanity, and how much misery we shall experience before the fulfillment of our destiny?"

The famous 19th century Russian thinker Peter Chaadayev, pronounced by the czar in 1836 a lunatic.

*9*T WAS a cool September night in Irkutsk, the funny, surprisingly picturesque old city that sits right in the middle of Siberia. Already you could feel the threat of winter moving toward you through the night. Siberians, who tend to take on an air of deliriousness during the brief, hurried magic of the summer months, were beginning to bundle down for the long season of darkness.

Irkutsk is one of the few Siberian cities with real charm and character. Its streets are lined with the colorful palaces of the merchants of the last century; its people, like all Siberians, are far more open than other "Russians"; and their faces often betray the blood and the free-roving spirits of the original tribes who lived here — the Irkuts, who worshiped the bear paw as their icon, and the Buryats, who lived in yerts and drank the intoxicating mare's milk, Kumas, favored by their southern neighbors in Mongolia.

There is a feeling, too, in Irkutsk, of the time when Russian, Ukrainian and Polish political prisoners, as well as Old Believers, made Irkutsk their home — because they had to. With the Decembrists, the anti-czarist rebels who were exiled here in 1825, all these intelligent, life-asserting rebels created in Irkutsk a thriving political life of the intellect and a Siberian citadel of free thought. By the time I got there they were restoring the old Polish Catholic Church, which had been used in Soviet Times as a warehouse, and creating a museum village of the rustic wooden houses and fortresses of the Old Believers.

Besides, Irkutsk is the main plane stop in the Soviet Union on the way to the Russian Far East, where they catch tigers with their bare hands. It is also, quite literally, the dropping off place for Mongolia, Outer.

This night I was sitting in the Komsomol office of the university with several officers who should be the most convinced and fanatic of the young Russians, talking about everything from freedom to revolution. Appropriately prepared for a Soviet-American confrontation, the little room was hung with posters of Patrice Lumumba, Lenin and others emitting strident anti-American cries. All the accoutrements of revolutionary outrage!

Lubimov Leonid Stepanovich, a young journalism teacher, kept saying over and over, with apparent sincerity, that he simply could not understand how Americans could put up with so much pornography. "Before the revolution," he said earnestly, leaning forward across the desk where he was sitting, "Lenin said there must be no cruelty or anything justifying cruelty."

"Now, if we are going to talk about cruelty," I said, referring to the millions killed under Stalin, "we think you must have a balance of power to prevent real cruelty. If you put too much power in one person, then you have real cruelty. Then you have Stalin and concentration camps. We think it is better to have a few pornographic books."

There was a great silence. Later one of the students would whisper to me, as we went out, "I agree with you. All the students feel the same way."

But now the conversation changed and the students began urging me to be "objective" in everything I wrote. I assured them I would be. Then I pointed to one poster that read, "Resist the struggles of the gorillas and Yankees in Latin America," and said, "But I don't think *that* is very objective."

Had this been Cuba, whose present generation is engulfed in the passions of early revolution, they would have eaten me alive. But what was fascinating to me was that these students did not even defend the poster.

"Well, you know, that isn't ours," one said, a little defensively. "That came from Cuba."

Then the young woman official walked over to it with a distinctly worried look on her face and stared at it for a moment. She took it off the wall, picked up a poster that was hanging under it and hung it on top. She turned and smiled at me with perceptible relief.

The new one read: "Free Greek Political Prisoners."

"We can all agree on that," she said briskly, smiling now even more broadly. We proceeded with our conversation in an atmosphere of solidarity.

What this — and an overwhelming number of other similar incidents and discussions — proved to me was that, for Russian youth today, the revolution is over. The old symbols of revolution do not fit this generation, the posters and slogans do not accurately reflect its interests. They resemble people who, from habit or impoverishment, wear clothes they have outgrown.

This Russian generation is not out to change the world; it is out to serve it and to enjoy it. It has *its* revolution, but it is an internal one — a revolution turned inward to the soul and the mind. The old idea that dominated Bolshevik passions — that the whole world *must* become Communist and that every true Communist must spread the faith, even to those who resisted — finds little response in this sophisticated generation of Soviets. This would mean little if it were occurring only among the relatively small percentage of active dissidents, misfits and malcontents; but it is also occurring on the part of the young people who consider themselves genuine, but intelligent, young Marxists.

Galina Mamayeva, a 23-year-old teacher in Khabarovsk and one of the most perfect specimens of what young official Soviet womanhood should be, put it this way: "Now the main problem of young people is not to think about Communism or Capitalism but peace. They see people as all very much alike."

Sonia Zubareva, a beautiful guide of 30 from Leningrad, almost exactly echoed this relativistic approach when she said, "You think you are moral and we think we are moral. But that's not important. It's only important to live in peace."

In discussion with a group of journalists in Kiev, I volunteered to them the fact that I did not approve of either Vietnam nor Santo Domingo, and they listened attentively. Then I added quickly, "But don't forget that you have your Hungary and Czechoslovakia." No one said a word in rebuke. They all sat quietly for a moment and nodded in agreement. "A man is a man," one finally volunteered.

When Leonard Gross, then Look magazine's foreign correspondent, looked into the story of Soviet youth on the eve of the 50th anniversary, an "old professor" in Moscow told him: "When I was a child, it was downright indecent for me to say I wanted a decent flat or car or good clothes. My preoccupation was the world revolution, the overthrow of Capitalism. To think of anything else was inconceivable, unethical. I don't say the young man today doesn't care about revolution. But the modern view is that the human being has the right to be happy as a human being, as an individual. In my day, we could be happy only when we were sacrificing our lives."

Perhaps the most sophisticated youthful response came from Valerie Melko, the brilliant young physicist-psychologist at Kiev State University. "What are your generation's ideas about your systems?" I asked him. Were other systems considered, per se, antithetical to Communism? Could there really be coexistence? He thought carefully for a moment, then answered.

"It depends upon what you mean by different systems," he answered, in his pleasant, unassuming way. "If there are two groups of people and they are both happy, they can coexist. But if there are two systems and one group considers the other system better, it is another thing. The question is whether the system meets the needs of its people. The question can be put only by the people who live in the system."

Gone are the Comintern passions of the early years, when the Russians used to say, as the Cubans now say, "The duty of every revolutionary is to make the revolution." Gone is the fervid belief that, if a man is not a Communist today, he must become one tomorrow. Going is the early rigidity that said the only moral man was the Marxist man. Indeed, the young tend to use a new Russian word, "sozialnost," which means responsibility not to the Party but to the broader community — a concept remarkably similar to the traditional concept of community responsibility in the West.

This does not mean that the majority of Soviet youth is against the system or that they are going to, or want to, overthrow Marxism.

Not even the dissidents want this. This generation, despite its parents' ill-founded fears, is patriotic and loyal. . . but in its own way.

They are tremendously proud of what their people, under Communism, have accomplished in 50 years — "from the most backward country in Europe to the leader of the world." They feel the system is economically rational and that, despite everything, society *is* gradually being perfected. But at the same time they feel no need to celebrate Marxism as endlessly (and tiresomely) as their fathers do. To them the system is given; it simply *is*. The study of Marxism bores them to death ("We can get into a better discussion of Marxism at Harvard than in Moscow," one American who studied there remarked) and so does ideology. They simply want to live.

What has happened is that ideology has been transformed from a struggling, assertive force, trying to impose its own order from without, to the central, integrated, invisible force in society. This is a perfectly natural progression, of course, but it seems thoroughly threatening to the parents, who lived through the passions of the first era and innocently thought it would never end.

Something that hits the visitor, if he is honest, is the manner in which the omnipresent pictures of Lenin, the tools of ideology, and the symbols of revolution have simply become part of the scene. They remind one of nothing so much as our own pictures of George Washington and Abraham Lincoln and the red, white and blue. Now that ideology is accepted as an integral and natural part of things, instead of something mammoth and glorious and all-powerful, young people feel the room to move around as individuals, to act out of conscience instead of mass fealty and to stand alone.

Perhaps Stanislaus, a young Muscovite I got to know well, put it most exactly. "The young Russian of today," he told me one evening, as we sat in a youth cafe sipping champagne and eating ice cream, "is much like the American of ten years ago. He wants a good job, a flat, a car, love, the human things in life. That, psychologically, is the way I would characterize the typical young Russian."

Among many of the most intelligent young people, the most important thing is their friends and how they are accepted by them

— what kind of a"man among men" they are. Valerie, a factory manager in Bokhara, voiced this to me when I asked him what he wanted out of life. "I want good friends," he said, with a kind of muted passion. "I want them to hold me in high regard and when I die I want them to remember I was a good man. Maybe it's not much, but it's what I want."

Some Russian young people see this generation as a total break with the apocalyptic, maximalist, deeply-involved generations of the past, who were always searching for an absolute answer to life. In an interview with the British correspondent John Morgan in Encounter in 1968, one young man said, "For the last 100 years of the history of young people in Russia, every new generation has interested itself in something outside of itself — either revolution, or religion, or some special purity in relationships, or something else. But now, for the first time, the new generation — the generation born about 1945, the 'children of victory', as they are called — are interested above all in themselves . . . And that is a lot more interesting than the sort of young people who can be led here and there."

Some keen observers see the high degree of privatistic withdrawal as based wholly upon material desires. "At this point in history, youth is more concerned with material things," Pyotr Yakir, a historian who was one of the leaders of the dissidents, told me in Moscow before his arrest. "It wants to do as little as possible and obtain as much as possible — to be somebody with status, like a diplomat. Historically, it's been true in any country that, if there is a moderate standard of living, like here, the main goal in life is to make life better. If there is no starvation and people are clothed, they don't worry about social problems — you try to make your corner a better place to live. If there is affluence and free time as in the United States, then people become concenred about these things."

But I felt, personally, that it was a little more complicated than any of them had made it. There may, at first, appear to be contradictions in these analyses. On the one hand, youth is seeking out spiritual values, and on the other hand it is tremendously materialistic. But actually there is no contradiction here. What brings them together is the inward-seeking qualities of so many young Russians today — that and the missing element of ideological passion.

The Soviet state knows this quite well; for it is not only foreign writers who discover it and tell them, it is also found in their own surveys. At the University of Leningrad, for instance, surveys were done in 1966 of a representative sampling of Russian youth on what they wanted out of life. Not a word was mentioned about revolutionary or ideological values. Dr. Vladimir Lisovsky, the U.S.S.R.'s preeminent youth sociologist, found that youth wanted, in this order: to get an interesting job, to receive a higher education, to visit foreign countries, to be well off, to have good housing conditions, to improve one's qualification (for work), to find loyal friends, to bring up children to be worthy people, to find one's true love, to build a family, to buy a car, to receive secondary education and to go to a project under construction.

At Kiev State University, sociologists point out a comparison of surveys done of youth in 1910, in 1930 and recently. "In 1910," said Dr. Vladimir Kolobkov, head of the Chair of Scientific Communism, "youth showed a preference for parties, balls and material things. They strove for officers' ranks and beautiful women. By the 1930s, their major interest was to acquire qualifications for jobs. But if youth then wanted to acquire qualifications for work, youth today wants to acquire *interesting* qualifications. They want good clothes and houses. Our material base has created a great sphere of new interests."

Other events showing the lack of interest in ideology include the growing lack of interest in the Komsomol, the growth of juvenile delinquency and laws to deal with it, the obvious boredom of youth with the spare "entertainments" of Soviet life.

For the young— active, life-loving, healthy, curious, life's blood pulsing — the worst thing about their society is its very tiresomeness. Where can young people go? What can they do? In the big cities there are "youth cafes," but it is difficult to imagine less sensuous or blood-stirring places. Bright lights knocking your eyeballs out. Scruffy, nasty waitresses who make you wait an hour to get a glass of champagne or an ice cream. Other people seated routinely at your table who listen to every word you say.

When a young American wife, who had studied several years earlier in Leningrad, returned in the summer of 1971 to see her Russian friends there, the major thing she found among them was a stifling sense of boredom. She was at first apologetic about the chaos and violence in her own country, only to find that her friends did not criticize this.

"We don't know whether it's better to live in all this calm or in a little turmoil," one friend told her.

"The point was unmistakable," the American girl noted.

Beyond this tiresome public life, there are home parties with your own trusted "krushki" or circle of friends (these parties are unquestionably considered the best form of entertainment) and there is alcoholism, which most analysts are convinced is so overwhelming a problem in the Soviet Union simply because it is the only escape from the boredom and the psychic pressures.

When Maria Vovchok, a pretty, blond-haired, thoughtful 22-year-old Russian student defected to England in 1970, one of the things she mentioned was that "I think that young people drink to fill a vacuum. All students in Russia, whatever their faculty, must study the history of the Communist Party, Marxist philosophy, Marxist economics and so on, but few are so stupid or so naive as to take it all seriously. And, because they must pretend, they become cynical. In fact, I think cynicism is the most remarkable feature of the younger generation in Russia."

Harvard University Professor Paul Hollander also reported to the American Sociological Association meeting in 1966 that delinquency had become a problem for the Soviets largely because they were boring their children to death." An institution that does more than its share in injecting boredom into the life of the young is the Komsomol," he said, because "lifelong membership in one huge bureaucratic organization that concerns itself with every detail of life leaves little room for chance, luck, imagination or excitement."

The older Soviets do not like to face this, of course. As the Minister for Safeguarding Public Order has said: "What is the matter? Why is it that in our wonderful time, when the material well-being and culture of the people is rising steadily this evil is so tenacious? Why is it that the hooligan continues to commit outrages . . . ?"

Another gauge of the withdrawal from ideological fervor into personalism, skepticism, and finally, black cynicism, lies in the joke and the song.

When I returned in 1971, I found that the most popular new series of jokes was the one about Vassili Ivanovich Chapayev, the great general of the revolution. It seems that the Soviets had made a movie of Chapayhev's life and, as is their wont, they overdramatized it and overheroized it. The new generation hates maudlin emotions.

The Chapayev joke I liked best had the schoolchildren being taken to the Chapayev museum. At the entrance hung two skeletons, one big one and one small one. "Now, children," the guide instructs them as they enter, "this was Vassili Ivanovich when he was big, and this was Vassili Ivanovich when he was little."

But the most poignant satire most closely approaching tragedy is best known in the plaintive, bitter, angry underground songs that the young people sing. Of these, perhaps the most moving is "My Friend Has Gone to Magadan."

In this song, a"friend" has left for Magadan — a notorious prison colony in far eastern Siberia which has become a symbol for political dissidents — not because he *has* to but because he *wants* to.

"Take off your hats, wish him the best!" wrote Vladimir Vysotsky, the well-known film actor who has written many of these songs. "He went himself — Without police, without arrest. Not because he wasn't doing well. Or 'cause he's an oddball, as some tell.

"He simply went."

Why should a young Soviet, for whom life is supposed to be filled with promise and with meaning "drop out" (Vysotsky's term) and go voluntarily where convicts and the exiled are driven?

That is the question.

"What's out there but labor camps galore, full of murderers, full of murderers?" the song goes on. "He answers them, 'the rumors are untrue. Moscow has as many murderers, too.'

"Then he packed a suitcase — only one — and left for Magadan, for Magadan."

Why has this happened? Why should the new generation become so bored and so often disillusioned with the ideology at the precise point when that ideology, in power, is providing them with the best material life any Russian generation has ever enjoyed?

Lisovsky thinks it began after the 20th party congress in 1956, when Stalin was denounced and an era in Soviet life ended. It was then that the new generation's needs and desires came into their own. "Social life became more free," he explained to me. "It gave more range to the inclinations of the masses."

Certainly this is true. But that is the positive side. It also made true-believing very nearly impossible any more for any but the most rigid party hacks and the totally unthinking — and, of course, formed in their own authoritarian history and mentally manicured by constant fear, there are many questioning people in Russia. "We know that if something like this could rise, there must be something wrong with the system," one girl ruminated, thoughtfully. "I think it taught us not to praise someone too much," another boy said. And for incalculably many others, who had believed in passionate submission to the "vozhd" or great leader, Krushchev's truths were almost more agonizing to bear then were Stalin's heinous crimes.

The most poignant and disturbing story I heard — and there were many — of what happened inside the young Russians upon Krushchev's denunciation came from a pretty, blond teacher I met one night on the stairs of my hotel in Kiev. Actually, I had grown so inured by that time to the lack of spontaneity and the distrustfulness on the part of most Russians that I was stunned when Natasha Orlova, with her wispy smile, began to pour out her heart to me.

But Natasha had been drinking a lot of wine, and so for just a little while the curtains parted and I was able to see what a Russian was really thinking behind them. A precious moment, and a rare one.

It started with a chauvinistic remark on her part — a typical, often-heard and absurd one — that Russians could not create anywhere except Russia. "They say that the composer of the 'Volga Boatman', couldn't compose anything ever again when he went to America." She shook her head and tears came to her eyes, it was so sad. "When a Russian is out of touch with Russia, he can't create." she went on. "I think those who have gone, they went because they couldn't believe that working men could create a society."

"Now, no, Natasha," I said, going down the line of all the early poets of the revolution. "You must know that many of them went because they were persecuted here. Take Yesenin — he committed suicide. Even Mayakovsky killed himself. Akhmatova can't be published."

She raised her head defensively. "Mayakovsky got in with the wrong crowd. He was very melancholy. He worried a lot."

"He was persecuted," I repeated. "He couldn't write what he wanted."

She hesitated. "Maybe that happened to some," she acknowledged.

"Why, look under Stalin — look at all the people killed. The top members of the party, the politburo . . . "

"You know more than we." She said it now not defensively, but with a sadness in her voice. How many times I was to hear that phrase from young people in Russia!

"And they were the top members of the party. It's the Communists who should hate him, not us." I went on.

"Maybe this is why the ordinary people do not hate him," she suggested, tentatively. "He did things for them. He just persecuted the Communists. You ask people today if they hate Stalin and you'll be surprised . . ." Then her mood suddenly changed. She became very upset. Tears rolled down her cheeks.

"After the death of Stalin," she went on, "I was terribly upset." We sat down on the steps in the slightly darkened hall. "It was a great disillusionment for me to hear about his crimes — I can't tell you know deep it was. I couldn't even go to the institute to study for two years. I lost all interest in everything. It wasn't until my marriage and my husband began to explain things to me that I began to feel again." She was crying very gently.

"Now . . . " Her voice suddenly became fierce. "Now I don't want to know things."

When I suggested to her that to be fully human you had to "know" things, she shook her head with a fierce insistence.

"Why?" she demanded. "I don't think it's at all necessary. So what if Stalin killed a million people, as you say? There are still 200 million of us left."

There it all was, caught on one single square on the film: first disbelief, then disillusionment, then cynicism and wanting to escape from truth and reality rather than deal with it.

As suddenly as she had revealed herself, just as suddenly Natasha closed herself up like a tight bud, as if for the night, and left. Although I saw her again, she always averted her eyes and never spoke to me again.

Fathers and Sons

This is a common type of story. Writing in Realite's for instance, about a "typical" Russian today, the perceptive French journalist Georges Bortoli attempted to tell the story of a typical Soviet man of today — loyal, hard-working, sober. But "Vassili" had never joined the party, he points out. Why? Because of the 20th party congress! When Vassili was 25 and in the sudden freedom of talk that followed the congress, he suddenly started hearing "strange tales about Uncle Victor, who had last been heard of somewhere in Siberia, from where he had never returned."

"In his confusion," Bortoli wrote, "Vassili had felt as if the earth was giving way beneath his feet. As one who had been a boy during the war, brought up to the sound of patriotic marches and announcements of victories, he did not want to be deprived of the reasons for living which had been planted in his mind. Without really admitting it to himself, he decided to ignore these later developments, and to become, in effect, a nonpolitical animal. Along with 227 million other Soviet citizens, he decided to remain outside the Party as a 'Bespartiiny' , or, as the approved abbreviation has it, a BP."

But for some it is not enough to simply learn to accept Stalin's crimes or to ignore them or to live one's own life "bespartiiny" or "without party" or to absorb the post-mortem explanations now being offered, often so cynically, for them. For these young people, the most important element of life is "truth" — it is abstract and amorphous, it is on a painfully low level, compared to the rest of the world, and they have not the slightest idea in the world how to reach it, but what matter? At the moment, it is enough to stand for honor by avoiding politics and seeking personal nobility.

They hate hypocrisy and they hate cant. As one Soviet journalist told me with disgust, "What I hate most are those who pretend. Some Russians go abroad to live, and they change. Then they come back and they change again." And occasionally, a Solzhenitsyn or a Yevtushenko or another writer will speak out *in public*, as Konstantin Paustovsky did in May, 1959, in his letter to the Third Congress of the Writer's Union, when he proclaimed that "We shout so much and so loudly about truth, precisely because we lack it."

When Colette Shulman interviewed "a Soviet writer who has written for and about young people for many years", he told her that the "outstanding quality of these thinking young people is their tremendous passion for truth. If you evade the hard and sensitive questions when you talk with them, if you try to smooth over the rough edges and use cliches, they right away stop believing in you and even listening to you. In comparison with our generation of the late 1920's, these youngsters today are politically unsteady and less sure of themselves. They hesitate, they waver."

The obvious last question, if the present ideology evokes so little passion, is what kind of ideology *would* evoke interest. It seems clear that, except for that relatively small percentage of apparatchiki who embrace Communism either out of belief or ambition, what the masses of the young people want is "good Communism." They know now that Stalin was a maniac; they think Krushchev was a late-repenting killer; many think, as one boy put it to me, with amused eyes, that Brezhnev is a "klutz — neither dreaded nor respected"; and they tended to think that Kosygin was the only educated, cultured man among the later leadership, if only because he mingled with the intelligentsia.

"But youth has no alternate program, no alternate leaders, no alternate solution," one foreign diplomat in Moscow commented. "The present regime is not popular with youth. They feel it doesn't have imagination. What it comes down to — the overwhelming theme — is that they want 'good communism,' and that is Leninism. Their cultural heritage is in the '20s."

In effect, what they want is a humanized and liberalized Marxism. They want to get beyond the society of basics, which was all right for the beginnings of Marxism, and move on to a new, more sophisticated and more exciting state. "If only," one young Russian day-dreamed to me one day, "if only someone would think out some great Marxist-humanist idea. We have such a great need for that." And that, of course, would mean the general economic distribution and organization of Communism without the political and social horrors of Stalinism and with the personal liberties and the collective democratic organization of society that Lenin, at least theoretically, wanted.

So this is the key to why the elders feel there is a "youth problem." This, as normal and natural as it seems, poses a real threat to the older generation, steeled in obedience and the true faith. To its members, the sins of this generation are sins not of commission but of omission. They are not *enthusiastic* enough, and passive acquiescence, if you are a Marxist, is never an acceptable substitute for revolutionary passion. This is a society where *not* to constantly pronounce your *loyalty* is quite as suspect as to pronounce your *disloyalty.*

Even after 50 years, the typical old Bolshevik wants a Marxist monk, a revolutionary aesthete, a choir of Communist angels singing the praises of his generation's sacrifices and carrying on the point-counterpoint, synthesis-antithesis of Communist internationalism.

This is *not* the way it was supposed to turn out.

✌ Chapter Five
The Edge of The Earth:
The Outside World

"Of course, we know about the rest of the world. But, tell me, do you have restaurants like this in New York?"

A Russian working woman at a simple restaurant in Moscow.

9 F the majority of young Russians are bored with the ideology of their own state, how do they look upon countries outside their homeland? What is their reaction to the United States? Does the rabid, and often morbid, anti-Americanism eventually permeate their consciousness, despite their innate, youthful good will? How do they regard the "third world", which Communism has determined theoretically to "save", and its other races? Are they outward-looking — or do they look only toward themselves?

Here, the differences between the older generation and the younger are stunning. The older people hate the Western styles which they look upon as "infecting" their own pristine children, of the revolution ("music from the jungles, hairdos from monkeys," cried Vsevolod Sysoev, the museum director in Khabarovsk). They are touchy to the point of absurdity about the shortcomings of their country, when compared to others, and so they become unbearably arrogant and give themselves to ridiculous pretensions ("Dr. Zhivago is a very bad book," snapped a Moscow journalist. "You don't publish books in the West that are critical of you, either.").

They are convinced that Americans are terribly selfish people ("They think only of themselves and then of other people," said Josip Khan Shakir, an official of the central mosque in Tashkent). From the world, they want to take. They want to give only to impose their own ideological form. ("They want our information, but they don't want to give out any," said two English welding firm contractors in Kiev, in anger and astonishment, "and they don't even want to recognize our achievements.").

Russians, with their own pervasive insecurity, have traditionally had a compulsion to judge themselves through foreigners' eyes, and part of this was due to their dual attitude toward foreigners. On the other hand, the original word for "foreigner" was "German" in Russian. It meant "dumb," because many of the earliest foreigners were Germans and they could not understand their language. On the other hand, the Russians soon learned that "foreigners" were often far more advanced than they were. At any rate, largely because of Mongol and Tatar invasions, Muscovite Russia found itself, from the 13th century on, isolated from the rest of the Christian world. This physically separated the Russians from Europe and caused them to turn in upon themselves in an orgy of egoism, pride and fear.

But what about today? Does this same fear of outside — this same deep sense, common to Columbus' time, that if you leave your own horizon you will fall off the edge of the earth — inform *this* generation?

One of the first things you discover about the young Russians today is that they may ask curiously convoluted or distorted questions, but they are not at all afraid to ask. Go to a place like the Ananeya Society (the Knowledge Society) next door to the KGB on Derzhinsky Square (the same building where public discussions were held in tsarist times) and you'll find no holds barred. The question period following a speaker may last two hours. Why don't we have more consumer goods? Why is it that a two-party system is so bad? Why is the convergence theory so harmful? Why are the Egyptians purging all the pro-Soviets? What was the attitudes of the Czechs toward us after the invasion?

In one of my more interesting discussions, this one with about 45 students at the Novosibirsk Institute of Electrical Engineering, every possible question — and answer — was voiced. The eager-eyed teen-agers sat in a large classroom with all eyes fixed on me and their first questions were repeated as by rote: "How could you respect Steinbeck any more when he came out in favor of the Vietnam War?" "What can Egypt do when attacked?" "Why did we go into Hungary? — Hungary fought against us in the great war."...

Then, gradually, the conversation shifted — shifted to the things that really interested them.

This day, one boy suddenly stood up, saying wearily, "That's enough of politics." Then he began asking, with a totally fresh eagerness, what was obviously on his mind: "What do American students do at night? Where do they go? Do they worry about their futures? How do they get jobs?"

The first thing you discover in conversations with young people is the extent to which the things they want to know about other countries are the *human* things — the same personal, private, individual things they are so concerned about in themselves and their own lives. The pattern was repeated everywhere — first the wearied, half-disinterested repetition of official questions; then the excitement of asking what they really wanted to know.

Interestingly, many Soviets in official positions acknowledge this. At Literaturnaya Gazyeta or the Literary Gazette, for instance, I chatted one afternoon in 1971 with the editor who handled American news, Anna Ivanova Martinova. When I asked her what her young readers wanted to know about the U.S., she was quite candid. "Not political things," the slim, dark-haired young woman said, with a wave of her hand. "They want to know how young people live, what they do in the evenings . . . things like that."

But despite the fact that the younger generation looks at the West with more openness and curiosity and with less fear than its parents, they still know painfully little in real terms and their observations are often a most curious combination of insight and absurdity that bear no resemblance to any American conception of right, left and center. Angela Davis . . . the Kennedy assassination . . . the fact that there are "no workers in the American Congress" — these kinds of things crop up in conversations constantly because these are the only things they have been told.

The young people I met, however, were convinced they were beginning to get a more reasonable picture of the U.S. and the rest of the world. After all, between 1965 and 1970, the traditional isolation was broken when some 300,000 Soviet young men and women visited 60 other countries, and some 350,000 of their counterparts visited the Soviet Union. They cited magazines such as "Za Rubeshom" or "Abroad", a Soviet magazine which reprinted verbatim items from the American press, the fact that some

American newspapers are available to a limited number of people in the libraries, and the radio broadcasts of Voice of America and B.B.C. There are even some wildly-popular books like "Delovaya America" or "Business America," written by a Soviet engineer, which accurately and even complimentarily describe American business, know-how and energy. "We read about America," one student said, "and today, if anything is really unobjective, any educated man would notice it." This is not true, but it shows how deeply ashamed they are to be thought of as men who do not know about the world.

Ironically, it is the United States, and almost primarily the United States, which interests both young and old Russians. Europe is a second, but a poor second. The reason is simple and clear — "Because the U.S. is the only other important and powerful country in the world," they told me unanimously, almost as if a ventriloquist were manipulating their tongues.

However, when Novosti did a Gallop-style poll in 1966 of what the Russian young knew and felt about America — and then followed it up with a similar poll of Americans on Russia — it turned out that both were well disposed toward each other but less than well-informed about each other. It showed that 91 percent of the Russians were definitely interested in America, that Abraham Lincoln and John Kennedy were their heroes, and that for the majority, "America" represented technological progress and a high standard of living.

Sometimes one wonders where the Russian youngster gets even the amount of information he has. One day on a beach in Odessa, I was chatting with a young engineer named Ivan, who happened to notice my book, "The Mind of Modern Russia," which has selections from all the great Russian thinkers of the last two centuries — from Chaadayev to Lenin. When I asked him if he and his friends ever read anything like that about American thinkers, he said, "No." Then he said, "But it should be. Why shouldn't we read about your leaders? We want to know everything about the U.S."

The views of the Marxist hierarchy about the United States are of course, clear and fixed. They are sure it is going just the way the Communists always thought it was going — and that, most definitely, does not mean that the going is good. I dropped in one day to see one of Moscow's prime "interpreters" of the American scene, V. P. Filatov, an "Americanologist" at the U.S.A. Institute in Moscow, which studies the U.S. for the Academy of Sciences. He said, at first calmly: "We see things occurring just as we always thought. Capitalism is living through increasing economic crises. There was 1930 and 1950 and 1960. We don't know how close together these crises are apt to come, but the cycles are certainly growing shorter. Politically, the country is going from a democracy to an oligarchy. It is run by an oligarchy of military and political and business leaders who bypass Congress with executive agreements. Why, even in the last century, people still admired your democracy. Even Marx admired it. Now, no one admires it."

The nondescript man — mousy brown hair, light frame, pinched face — smiled sleekly. Wearing a soft, well-tailored sport shirt that was certainly from the West with stylish pants and sitting in a carpeted office with light modern furniture and the soothing presence of an expensive modern Hi-Fi, he looked much like an up-and-coming young Western businessman. And, of course, he is an apparatchik — the Soviet equivalent.

Then he went on to say that the American system was the "most primitive one known to man." When I suggested, in a soft voice, that the totalitarian system was the most primitive system known to man, Filatov, an excitable type, erupted like a Russian samovar at boiling point. Getting up out of his chair in order to stand, he shouted, "You will have socialism, you will have a one-party state, and you will *enjoy* it!"

The younger Russians do not only not *enjoy* this kind of super-chauvinism, they do not believe this kind of analysis (though it does worry some of them, who fear some of it may be true). And even when they criticize our government, most of the young people I knew thought that Americans as individuals were very kind and good people.

One night I had brought a Russian student and former guide named Volodie up to the foreign currency bar at the Hotel National and suddenly a Texas couple at the next table began chatting with us good-humoredly about the awful food in most of Russia. "I wanted to say in one restaurant, when they brought me that scrawny chicken, 'Did you put it out of its misery?' "

When the American man went to the bar for a moment to get cigarettes, Volodie whispered to me in urgent tones, "Don't tell them I'm Russian. I've never heard Americans complain about anything — they're always so polite — and I want to hear what they really think."

Whenever you are with the average person, indeed, you are struck by the curiosity that Russia is probably the only country in the world where, among the people, there is the least anti-Americanism.

One is also beginning to find a type of Russian that one did not find even five or six years ago — a Russian who has traveled abroad and is able to look at things realistically. In 1971, at the height of problems with the Jewish Defense League, for instance, when the Soviet government was accusing the American government of aiding the JDL in its attacks on Soviet diplomats, I spoke with Victor Lipsky, one of the top Intourist officials in Moscow. He saw things in quite a true light. "We know that Mr. Nixon does not like this," he told me, "and most of the travel agents in New York are Jewish and they don't like it either. They tell me this is a bit of fascism that will die down."

On the other hand, the very nearly bottomless well of an inferiority complex on the part of officialdom toward the U.S. still comes out at many a turn. They spit and rail against America because, like so many countries, they want so much either to be like it or to catch up to it. Sitting in Leningrad one evening with the sociologist, Dr. Lisovsky, and my two guides, Nellie and Sonia, the conversation suddenly took such a turn. Suddenly, Lisovsky, such an otherwise rational man, was sputtering at me, "You Americans are always criticizing us. No hot water. No amenities. No . . . " All three glared at me. Eyes which had been friendly a moment ago now blazed.

"Now, wait," I interjected, as calmly but firmly as I could. "Think a minute. I've never criticized anything here. Nothing at all." They looked at me in astonishment. To their minds, my very *being* there was a kind of implicit criticism.

The young people were fascinated with American hippies (though many of their guides, who have worked with them, most definitely are *not*), with the free press and with the extraordinary amount of personal freedom in the U.S. — something, however, that often troubles them as much as it attracts them. Moreover, they, like their parents, are apparently across-the-board convinced that Americans are "so much like Russians."

This conviction that the two peoples are so much alike has various roots. My guide, Nellie put it this way; "I think it's the open spaces. It creates a bigness about both peoples, and a generosity and frankness. If they don't like something, they say so. I had a group of American and European tourists for the theater and I went to get the tickets. When I came back, the Americans were all waiting with rubles in hand. The Frenchman searched around in a big bag, took out a notebook, made a lot of figures, and then said, 'No.' Americans would never do that. We still like Americans from the time when Ilf and Petrov (two beloved Russian writers) traveled to America in the '30s and wrote 'One-Storied America', about the America of the little houses. It created a legend about America because everyone was so kind and gracious to them." Closely allied with this idea of similarity between the two peoples is the idea of world power, the idea of personal equality and the idea of missionary energy and zeal.

Of course, many of the worst types of Russians identify with America, too, seeing only its lust for money, its clamour for power and its rampant lack of concern for beauty and culture.

Second to the United States, the Russians tend to be interested in Europe. The idea of a two-front war, with their two ancient enemies, the Chinese on one side and the Germans on the other, is something that has not been yet bred out of the generations. And while many young people, mostly in the intelligentsia, were traumatized by the brutal invasion of Czechoslovakia in 1968, I had a number tell me, as one boy in his late 20s said, "Sure, ideally all peoples should be free, but with Czechoslovakia, people think it's better they're with us than against us. After all, we fought to free Czechoslovakia in the Great Patriotic War and we couldn't let the German revanchists take it over again. Our security comes first."

But at the same time that there is this outlook politically, there is also a cultural outlook toward eastern Europe that is fraught with jealousy — for their greater freedom and for their blue jeans and rock bands and for their access to the Western Goodlife. How many times did I hear young Russians say, "We can get that in Poland" or "They've got that already in Prague," and always the voice was tinged with yearning and desire.

What perhaps surprised me most was the young Russians' total and unequivocal disinterest in the "Third World" — in Africa, Asia and Latin America — despite the fact that some 16,000 Third Worlders were studying in the U.S.S.R. and some 12,000 of them were in on-the-job training there. "Little peoples" arising and developing seem to evoke on the part of the young as well as the old an aversion bordering on disdain and disgust. I found little equivalent on a personal level to our Peace Corps mentality, out to help and change the world, and I found little academic or intellectual interest in these countries, whose cultures the Soviets look down upon and disdain. Did their backwardness remind the Russians too poignantly of that from which they had so recently come?

Fidel Castro? "When he came here to visit, I was fascinated with him," a Bratsk teacher told me, "but now no one cares about him." "A prostitute," was the way a journalist in Leningrad characterized him. "We were only 20 minutes from war with the U.S. because of him, and he doesn't even want to work — it's just carnival, carnival, all the time." And from three workingmen on the street in Volgograd the most common plaint of all: "Why are we behind? If we weren't helping them, we'd be equal with you."

The Middle East? Here the attitude has changed. Before the 1967 war, there seemed to be a good deal of criticism of the Arabs and of Russian involvement there. But by 1971, most of the young people I talked to looked at Israel as a "racist state" and at the Arabs as the victims; they were happy to see Russian expansion proceeding in that part of the world at so little personal cost to the Russian State by the 1973 war.

As to what happens when Russians go abroad, I have seen them all over the world and they are always the same. Whether in Cuba or Egypt, they live in their own private compounds, buy the best food at their own stores, mix with each other and shake their heads about how "savage" the "natives" are. Not the most arrogant British colonialist or the most impatient American would act as they do. And the "third worlders" in general return the compliments with a savage dislike of everything Russian.

"Mechanical people," an Egyptian student said. "They invited me to Russia for three weeks," a hotel manager in Cairo said, "I said one week would be quite enough." And an Egyptian editor recalled his first trip to Russia. "We got to Kiev," he said, and one of our party made an emotional speech about how Russia had been behind a curtain for so long, like a woman with a veil, that it was wonderful now to see how beautiful she was. He meant it as a compliment, but the Russians were furious. One got up and said angrily, 'First, Russia is not a woman, and second there is no veil. You are talking the same kind of Iron Curtain nonsense of the West.' " He shrugged. There was no understanding such people.

Because of misunderstanding and simply a lack of compatibility in both directions, and because of inborn prejudices against anyone outside, the racial feelings among Russians — and this goes for the young as well as the old — are intense. They can, without exaggeration, be said to be far more racially-prejudiced, particularly against blacks (with the exception of their regard for certain "political" cultural figures as Paul Robeson), than are even white Americans.

Orientals are admired, but feared. A fear of the East — from whence came the Mongols, the Tatars, the Khazaks and all those folks who gave them such things as the Mongol devastation — is deeply ingrained in them even today. It accounts partially for the continuous attempts to people the Eastern borders with China with Soviets of European Russian blood (a nine-to-one Russian-Oriental ratio is that desired on these borders). These fears are so real, even today, that in modish circles of the intelligentsia, it was fashionable to replace the traditional Russian word for stranger ("eenorodyets") with "chitshmesh", a newly-coined word meaning only European Russians and illustrating clearly the new Russian exclusivism.

As for the Africans studying or working in the U.S.S.R., it is hard to imagine a sadder lot. Everywhere I went, young Africans sought me out, usually to pour out their troubles to me, a sympathetic Westerner who might understand . . .

A typical case, a Nigerian student in Leningrad: "I've been here two years, and I'm so homesick I think if I have to stay any longer I really might die. These people are not alive. They don't know how to live. Why, *our* cities are livelier than *theirs*. They start their parties at 8:30 and end at 10:30. I tell them that's when we're just starting. I don't even go out anymore. You know, they are very primitive people. Why? Because they're ignorant. They don't know anything. They're afraid of each other. They tell me there's a color bar in the 'States, but I was there two months and I made a lot of friends. The color bar is here. Nobody likes us. A Russian friend? Is there such a thing?"

In Volgograd, I had an experience which sheds some light on racial feelings. A group of Cuban baseball players was staying at the same hotel as I was and one evening I went to a youth cafe with one of them, an attractive, lively young man named Alfredo Street. His father had been an Episcopal minister from Jamaica and, though he considered himself a good Marxist, Alfredo admitted that "Sometimes I wake up on Sunday morning and hear in my mind the choir singing, 'Savior, savior, lift me,' and I want to sing." His brother, also a star baseball player, was not quite so religious. "On Sunday mornings when we were kids, I would tell him we had to go to church and he'd ask, 'Are you a man or a cucaracha?' and we'd go to play baseball."

At any rate, I got along splendidly with Alfredo Street, for I was accustomed both to Cubans and to people of dark skins — if the Russians were not.

When we returned to the hotel that night about 10 p.m., several of the Cubans were singing and playing guitars in the lobby while a group of Russians and Poles were grouped around them, swaying and listening.

Everything was fine until one of the Cubans, speaking to me in Spanish, asked me to tell one of the Russian guides, a cute readhead, that he liked her. When I passed on this relatively innocent remark to her in Russian, a look of disgust came over her face. She turned on her heel and sat down with a group of the Poles. When I approached them to apologize for anything *I* might have done, one of the Poles said, soothingly, "But we *understand* your racial problems. We don't like them either."

"You misunderstand us," I said, "Our racial problems are very bad but most of us of my generation approach every man as a man."

He ignored this. "No, no," he insisted, "we understand it. You'll see if you come to Poland." Then he grew very confidential and leaned over close to my ear. "But you mustn't dance with those black men, even if they speak English to you."

Upstairs, later, I ran into the redheaded guide and she was still angry at the poor Cuban. "Black men have no courtesy at all. They're just crude. And they can't even dance. They just shuffle."

A few last points need to be made on the question of how the young Russians look at the outside world.

One important point is that in the '60s and '70s there has been a growing disillusionment being superimposed upon the basic liking for the United States. It has arisen over the assassination of their hero, President Kennedy, the brutality of the war in Vietnam, such "incidents" as Santo Domingo, the support of Pakistan in the East Bengal oppression, Watergate, and the inability to solve racial problems at home. It has made the U.S. less of a respectable alternative to Russian youth — it has bitterly frustrated the hopes of many in Western democracy — and it has turned many critics of the Soviet regime into people who say, "But what else is there?" Or, as an East European Communist remarked when Dr. Boris Dotsenko, a Ukrainian nuclear physicist defected to Canada in 1967, "were it not for your war in Vietnam, which horrifies our people, there might have been many more such cases."

Concomitantly, as Soviet foreign policy has passed from the early adventurist period of the early '60s — when the Soviets attempted directly to support revolution in the Congo and failed — to a policy of more traditional diplomatic and cultural penetration in the Middle East, Latin America and the Indian subcontinent, the young Russians have begun to see their own country more often than not being involved on the right side of the moral question. Czechoslovakia was an exception, but they see that more than out-balanced by Vietnam. Attitudes on the Arabs have changed dramatically, as Israel's line came to seem harder and more intransigent and exclusivist. They began to see their own country as less reckless than the U.S. and to see it even more on the side of international legality in the U.N. (the Middle East) and of common justice (East Pakistan or Cyprus), than the U.S. Besides, theirs has been a highly successful foreign policy, spreading Soviet influence at minimal cost and risk throughout the world. It has begun to give the impression of a great, respectable and dignified world power — and this is precisely what the young Russians want.

In the last analysis, of course, even the young Russians have very confused and limited views of the United States. They are just beginning to understand that ideally in the U.S. individualism was based, not on libertinism, but on an internalized responsibility and law. Little more than their rigidly Marxist fathers can they understand why we tolerate such disorder in the name of freedom. They try to but they still find it difficult to grasp a society made up of such diversity and of so many individual rights, just as we find it hard to understand a society where order is not self-imposed, by inner beliefs and inner voices, but imposed from outside, by the collective.

Beyond this, there is, I think, one enormous and major generational change occurring.

The older generation's attitudes toward the outside world were manic. They feared it, as Russians have for centuries, and thus they sought both to close themselves off from it and, when that did not work, to subdue it. Communism internationalism was not so much a reaching out to help other people as it was an attempt to impose Russian messianism on the world — in much the same way that Russian Orthodoxy centuries earlier dreamed of bringing all Christendom under the holy hegemony of Muscovy, the third, and last, Rome.

The younger generation, while it is equally determined that its own nation remain inviolate, has little of that passion to impose itself and its ideas on the world. It is just beginning to want, instead, to know the world, to *understand* its people.

One could hardly imagine a greater change.

❧ Chapter Six
Freedom, Collectivism and Individualism

He who is conceived in a cage yearns for the cage.
With horror I understand that I love
That cage where they hide me behind a fence,
And that animal farm, my native land.

Yevgeny Yevtushenko

𝓘T WAS a clear, shining June day in Leningrad. I was walking down one of the mellow old streets near the river, chatting casually with a good friend of mine — an extremely pretty, delicate-faced Russian girl who at that time was a student of philosophy in the university — when suddenly her whole expression changed. Her usually pleasant face took on an angry look. Her lips pursed. She tossed her head back angrily and pointed with a throw of her arm to a line of women waiting patiently in front of a grocery store.

I looked and saw nothing I had not seen hundreds of times in the Soviet Union. Mostly old, babushkaed, dark-coated "grandmas", the women were standing patiently, with those outwardly vacant, non-telling eyes, shopping bags held dutifully in hand, in front of a shop not yet opened. I glanced at Galya, for I couldn't understand what was wrong.

"Do you know," she said, disgust edging her voice, "that there are no shortages in that store? They don't even have to wait in line. But they're so used to waiting for everything all their lives, they do it automatically. That is what I really hate about our people. They accept everything."

Galya was right, of course. Habits of subservience and obedience are deeply ingrained in the Russian peasant character, and such habits persist today in the older people long after much of the need for them has died. These habits — formed by hundreds of years of turning in upon oneself and upon one's own people under attack from without — lay the grim base for one of the most important character traits of the Russian people even today: the extent to which they are afraid of freedom.

Americans have found it comforting to think that Russians were a people imprisoned by the totalitarianism of their system, whereas in reality Russians are a people imprisoned by themselves. They created the system before the system created them. It was, after all, only Russians who would, as thousands of them did. in the '30s, march off to prison camps and even to execution, condemning themselves by publicly admitting guilt to crimes they never committed. Probably even today, a majority of Russians do not really *want* to know the truth about life. They think such exorbitant freedom is dangerous, that it will somehow lead to anarchy and dissolution. Traditionally they have been a people who conform easily, who cannot stand the slightest straying from the norm; and this is not political in origin, but deeply psychological. They are a people who found it easier to sacrifice freedom and truth than order and progress.

"They are utopians here," one Western ambassador in Moscow put it. "They are thinking in terms of the perfect society, and their fear of freedom is a fear of anarchy and the loss of impetus in creating a new society. They think of *giving* people more, not of *liberating* them."

Or, as dissident writer Andrei Amalrik has written: "To the majority of the people, the very word 'freedom' is synonymous with 'disorder' or the opportunity to indulge with impunity in some kind of antisocial or dangerous activity. As for respecting the rights of an individual as such, the idea simply arouses bewilderment. One can respect strength, authority, even intellect or education, but it is preposterous to the popular mind that the human personality should represent any kind of value."

Even the Russian word for "freedom" — "volya" — has a basically unpleasant ring. It means ignoring the needs of others, stepping upon them in order to escape into the immensity of the steppes and into one's own desires. The tyrant has "volya" in its purest form. As the brilliant Orthodox philosopher Georgii Fedotov has written, "Since 'volya,' like anarchy, is impossible in a civilized community, the Russian ideal of 'volya' finds its expression in the worship of the desert, of wild nature, of nomadic life, of gypsy songs, wine, revelry, passionate self-oblivion, brigandry, tyranny and revolt."

There is also the situation that, even while the Russian hates authority, at the same time he is craving it. "There is this attitude of not even being conscious of resisting the regime," Dr. Edward Wasiolek, an engaging young Soviet specialist at the University of Chicago, told me one afternoon in his small office on the campus. "When I was a student in Moscow and I told them about Americans suing the government . . . well, it was absolutely inconceivable to them that the government could lose. They didn't even like the idea — it made them uneasy."

Or, as one young Russian engineer told me, We're afraid too much freedom might interfere with building socialism. We must give the right ideas to our people. We think it's better to follow one line."

But while this conscious belief that it is better at this point in history for Russians not to have too much freedom is prevalent, so, too, is the idea that it is the Russians — and not the Americans or the Europeans — who are genuinely free.

One night at dinner in the Hotel National in Moscow, Igor Danilen, a prominent Moscow journalist with "Moscow News," told me flatly, "I could not live in the West, you have no freedom." And he was not being provocative. Nor was the woman in her 40s who said, "It's better to have a secure job and a pension than all the 'freedom' you talk about."

For Karl Marx, freedom was "realized necessity" — and this fit in beautifully with traditional Russian feelings. To Soviet Communists, freedom, therefore, is having the necessities of life and having, at least theoretically, a Communist society in which all are equal.

But there was nothing really new or even really "Communist" in this. "This was a collective society long before Lenin," Wasiolek went on. "They always had a different idea of freedom. Here in the United States, freedom meant doing what you wanted — we idolized the free individual, the man at 'High Noon.' To the Russians, this kind of freedom was coercion. You could be free only by coercing others, by cutting a wide swath through others.

"To them, freedom is fulfillment rather than independence of action. Napoleon could sign directives that thousands of men go to Russia, but Natasha, that wisp of a girl in 'War and Peace,' is free and he is not because she stopped coercing life and started receiving it. Napoleon's way cut people out of life. Her way brought them in."

In their attitudes toward freedom, the two societies stand at polar limits to each other. Americans find it hard to understand the complexity within sameness that is Russia and the Russians most certainly do not understand the unity within diversity that is America. They enjoy a forced communalism, whereas in the United States neighborliness is bred into people individually and largely accepted voluntarily. Yet within their hushed collectivity, the Russians often seemed to me more apart from one another than do the super-individualistic Americans.

When American and European "individuals" come into contact with the communal sense of the Russians, some curious things happen. I was in Leningrad in 1967 and I had gone down with some Russian friends to the foreign currency bar of the Astoria Hotel. In their feverish quest for foreign currency, the Soviets allow these bars, where you can buy foreign drinks such as scotch and bourbon with foreign monies, in all the Intourist hotels.

The contrast between the tiresome order and understatement of Soviet society and this bar was stunning. The bar had the mood of a city besieged, where anything goes. It was the last night of the world, a kind of Leningrad Babylon. People were falling out of chairs and sprawling across tables. Braless girls shook like jelly on the dance floor, and at the bar men pawed at the women like tethered wild animals. Otherwise sedate and proper Europeans I had earlier seen in the hallways of the hotel were behaving as though Berlin were falling.

This bizarre and desperate scene, I felt certain, would only convince most Russians anew of the awful dangers of too much freedom. But it was really, I felt, simply an overreaction on the part of the Westerners to the imposed order of Soviet society — to the walking-in-step and lack of liveliness everywhere. That little room, like a foreign embassy in Latin America, was the place where people desperate to live took assylum from the grey uniformity.

But the salient fact among the new generation — people like Galya — is that, relatively quickly, this "fear of freedom" is disappearing. This is the first generation to have confidence in itself and thus not fear the "outside." Western concepts of law and individual rights do not frighten them and, in fact, fascinate them.

The older generation acted and often thought as one man. The new generation is composed of many men with many ideas.

The older generation really often believes it when they say, "But those guards at the buildings are there to *protect* you, not to keep people from you." The younger generation scoffs at such errant "nonsense."

The older generation often welcomed restrictions. The younger generation, almost to a man and woman, is both irate and impatient with the restrictions.

A student in Kiev, who only wanted to buy some Western records, suddenly grew angry, as did my friend Galya, just talking about it. "I'm not doing anything wrong," he said. "All I want to do is listen to some music. Why should I have to everything underhandedly?"

An artist's wife in Tallinn said impatiently, "We have more in common with intellectuals in other countries than we do with workers here. Yet we're not supposed to talk with these intellectuals. Can you imagine this? — in an age when man is going to the moon?"

And it's not surprising that when the magazine "I am 19" took a survey and asked 3,500 young people what shortcoming most disturbed them, the overwhelming answer was "Servility!"

These are only limited changes, of course. The Soviet Union, with its enormous state apparatus, is not about to become any kind of Western-style democracy. Even the most liberal young Russians (like many Americans) feel that freedom in the West is often excessive and that it is accomplished at the price of too many other even more important values. What they want is a state with economic justice and order, yes, but a state with far greater intellectual freedom and with the exact rule of law rather than the capricious rule of strongmen.

But if, in looking at this generation of Russians, one can see, hear and sense quite clearly these new ideas about personal and national freedoms, to understand the changes one must also look at two other closely allied and also highly important developments: the changes in the concept of the collective and a slow but marked tendency toward greater individualism.

It is difficult for Americans, raised under the Sign of the Individual, to understand the power of the collective spirit in Russia — a spirit that permeated the veins of Old Russia just as it permeates the arteries of the New Soviet Union. In tsarist Russia, the collective could be seen most clearly in spiritual form in the peasant masses, who considered themselves all common children of the tsar, who saw the land as belonging to "the people" and who felt a psychic unity among themselves, particularly in the Orthodox church. The intelligentsia recognized this, looking at the peasant masses with awe and foreboding and eulogizing them in some of the finest literature the world ever knew.

There was even an old folk legend that was current long before the revolution, which told of a time when a "nameless beast" would take over Russia. The beast was nameless because it would be composed of everyone: the collective, which rules Russia today.

It was natural, therefore, that after the Bolshevik revolution this inherent traditional Russian collectivism (the individual is part of the mass and is valueless alone) should be transmogrified into Soviet collectivism. In the new state proclaimed in Leningrad in 1917, local soviets or collective bodies of representatives of the peoples were to be the basis of the new "Socialist" state which would eventually lead to Communism — that form of human development in which man would have perfect unity with his fellows.

In everyday terms since then, the collective has been the center of every Soviet citizen's existence. The "collective" is his work group in his factory (from which he receives his salary and social benefits, to whom he goes with problems, with whom he shares almost every form of recreation). The "collective" is his housing project and all the people in it. Whatever he does, wherever he goes, he moves into a new "collective," with more meetings chaired by party chairman (on the local level elected, on higher levels appointed by higher party officials) and with more ties to more fellow Soviets. Ideally, he will never be alone or without support; if he is sick, his collective will even send him away for psychiatric help in a collective clinic, and when he wants to take a trip he almost always goes to his trade union collective's rest house somewhere out in collective Russia.

For the young people, this enforced collectivity is beginning to tear at their restless desires for great individual freedom, but for the older Russians it is a soothing, protective thing; they cling together, fearing apparently that, if society opens too much, they may fall out. Little can they understand the assertive loneness of the young, as dissident writer Andrei Amalrik and his wife found out when they were once asked by a puzzled policeman, as they attempted to picket for a civil rights cause, "But if you are going to picket, why don't you picket with your collective?"

Laurens Van Der Post, before his journey to Russia a specialist on African tribal life, concluded that the Russians were very similar to primitive peoples because "the primitive is the condition of life wherein the instinctual, subjective and collective values tend to predominate. The civilized condition of life is where rational, objective and individual values take command." He defined the struggle today as "the struggle of men who want to live individually and specifically rather than collectively and generally."

As with most Westeners, the collective spirit frightened and awed him. "The feeling of being together had an extraordinary, almost tangible power," he wrote. "I went to the circus where workers of a leather factory had taken over the entire circus. As the evening went by, this feeling of solidarity became so marked that I felt in danger of losing my identity."

I had much the same reaction as Van Der Post, but I also sensed a terrifying, frightened loneliness inside this vast society of sharing and enforced and often resentful brotherhood. I also soon came to realize that, among the young, the collective spirit was changing rapidly and that it was a trend they would talk about freely.

"The collective has grown," Tatyana Malnukova, a brisk, wholesome young editor at the Komsomol magazine "Young Leninist" in Volgograd told me, as a group of very bright, eager and thoroughly unhostile young people on the staff sat listening. "Earlier, it used to mean reading newspapers aloud for a group or gathering together to visit theaters. Now people read by themselves and go to the theater alone . . . but they still discuss everything. If, earlier, in a rural club there was a collective reading of a new book, now there will be a discussion after everyone has read it." She smiled. "I think in the 'States this is not well understood. You think of it as everybody sleeping under one blanket."

Kathy Boudin, the young American radical who went into hiding in conjunction with the explosion which destroyed a townhouse in

Greenwich Village in 1969, noted when she was in Russia for 15 months a year or so earlier that the young Russians were so skeptical about the old collectivist spirit that they were even "suspicious about participating in the protest movement in the United States to make a better society." When she tried to talk to them about such things as "collective decision-making," she reported, "a tense silence would fall on the conversation." She adjudged that, to them, the "judgment on the collective" signified the pressures of "conformity and even repression." They submitted to these pressures in silence, she said, for that, at least "separates them from those who lie."

Probably the final word on this entire subject came from Valerie Melko, the young psychicist-psychologist from Kiev. "The ideology is changing somewhat," he reflected that day as we sat in the university chatting. "Such features as were ideal for one generation — collectivism — are changing to solidarity. But this excludes individualism. It means that, when deciding the problems of all the people, we must pay special attention to the individual needs of everyone in the group. In addition, such features as discipline from outside now become internal discipline."

These are provocative thoughts and thoughts that are widespread among Russian youth. For if collectivism is changing to "solidarity" — or a "sense of community" as some Sovietologists assert — and if Russian human beings are beginning to see themselves as more individual and less interchangeable in their society, then Soviet society is beginning to develop beyond its fearful, fanatic stage and toward the kind of patriotic and loyal but more normal and less excessive attachment to the state that most peoples have.

Moreover, this new trend towards individualism is bound to continue, for all of the "objective conditions" are rooting for it. As cars become available to a greater percentage of Soviet citizens, they are starting to go off in private little sorties of their own, *not* in those endless busloads of Russians traveling everywhere in their factory or school collective (680,000 of the new Zhiguli cars alone were rolling off the assembly line by 1975).

To get around the shortage of cars, innovative young Muscovites have done something else that proves their budding individualism — they have gotten motorcycles when they could and literally constructed their own cars around them. They call them "sami-delnii" or "self-made"˙cars. These miraculous montages of pieces and bits of tin, wood, string and spit riding about on two wheels masquerading as cars have to be seen to be believed.

They are individualistic in terms of spirits, too. A good amount of liquor in the Soviet Union is "self-made," too. They call it "samogon." Usually, farm families brew this on their own little stoves, and city people insist it tastes like Western Scotch. One couple I knew refilled an empty bottle of Western Scotch with samogon and was told by its friends that "That was the best Scotch you've ever served."

As fewer Soviets have to live in communal apartments, sharing baths and kitchens, they are going more and more to seek out being with their own chosen friends and not with whomever the state sees fit to throw them in with (40 percent still lived in communal apartments in 1971 and it was estimated this number would be down to 25 percent by 1975). Soviets are beginning to take vacations on their own, even to the extent of staying in barns for one ruble a night, and, in order to escape the boredom of always going to one's union's rest house, they are now switching with friends at other unions.

More and more Soviets are uprooting themselves, changing cities (except to the major cities, to which immigration is controlled) and changing jobs. And one of the greatest examples of the regulation of self that is proceeding apace across the face of Russia is the extent to which the peasants are flocking to the cities.

Whereas in tsarist times 90 percent of the population lived in the physical beauty, but human squalor of the countryside, today half of the citizens are city-dwellers. And, among the young people it is apparently difficult to keep any "back on the farm" — an example of the exercises of self-will that will change the country beyond recognition. *Or*, as the magazine "Village Youth" commented in 1969: "We used to think that when things got straightened out on the collective farms, the young people would no longer be eager to get away from them and go to the city. Now that time is upon us. Yet the young people do not remain in the villages."

In the factories, competitions have come down to the individual and how well he does his work, in place of the old system of competition between factory collective groups. In the economic world, there is *not* the kind of "Capitalist resurgence" that many Western observers mistakenly read into the liberal economic reforms of the mid-1960s, but there certainly *is* the fact of greater decision-making on the lower levels. As well, there is a measureable tendency, encouraged from the top, to improve efficiency on the rank and file level by giving the people more power against local "bosses" in terms of electing their own leaders and providing an alive and creative local cadre.

The late Maurice Hindus, perhaps the best writer on the Soviet Union over the last 35 years, also noted these trends: "To my mind the growing individualization of the citizen, though of course within the framework of public ownership, is one of the most significant features of the new Soviet epoch." He went on to note "the growing urge to privacy, away from the 'socialist togetherness' which the party has been zealously promulgating to the cultivation of personal self-assertiveness and an inner personal life." In effect, young people would no longer be the "screw" in the state machine, as Stalin once so aptly described his idea of the human being.

Hindus was told by a Moscow psychiatrist as early as 1965 "You must remember that the age of Stalin was an age of brawn; man was simply a tool of production and only his muscle counted. But the post-Stalin age, especially since the 20th party congress and Khrushchev's denunciation of Stalin, opened up the age of the mind: self-annullment gave way to self-awareness, and the citizen again began to feel like an individual."

In this new period of greater, though not total, individuality, the Soviet state has had to face the reality that, as people become more educated and aware and as "the thaw" makes progress more dependent upon persuasion than terror, many of their programs and much of their propaganda is backfiring. This happened quintessentially with the Soviet Jews, who have grown, since the 1967 war, into a particular thorn in the side of the state with their demands to emigrate to Israel. Why did this start? "Many young Jews of my generation actually learned to love Israel from the Soviet Union's anti-Israeli propaganda," Anatole Dekatov, a young Soviet Jew who escaped to London, commented. "It was this anti-Zionist campaign which converted many Jews to Zionism. Before then, they had not thought much about it; now they became enthusiasts." This is considered an accurate reflection.

There is also the "infection" to stolid, unsmiling Muscovy from the outer rims of the Soviet state, from the more free-thinking, free-wheeling peripheries — from areas like Lithuania and Estonia and Georgia and Moldavia. When one goes to Estonia, for instance, one soon finds that Tallinn is no dark and forbidding city, even though, when I was there in November, the dark Baltic winter had set in and the neon lights were burning brightly at 9 a.m. On the contrary, it is the one really "swinging" town in the Soviet Union.

The other Soviets look sometimes humorously, sometimes jealously, sometimes hopefully, at Tallinn. They know they could never get away with what the Estonians do, and no one exactly knows how *they* get away with it.

Here you can buy Scandinavian newspapers on the street, and there are posters advertising trips to Sweden, Finland and Denmark — trips that Estonians are regularly permitted to take. In fact, the Estonians and the Finns exchange boats nearly every day in the summer months and wave at each other in the Gulf of Finland as they cross to their respective "foreign shores." Since the Estonians can have only 5½ rubles changed into Finn Marks, they can't exactly set the town on fire with wine, women and song, but the several thousand who make this trip every summer do see, first hand, a European country — something no ordinary Soviet will ever get to do in his lifetime — and they report back.

Tallinn's nightclubs stay open to 4 a.m. and if the dancers continue to pay 2 to 4 rubles a song, most bands will play until the cat drags in. Estonian jazz is famous, and the famous (in the Soviet Union) Voice of America jazzman, Willis Connover, visited the Estonian jazz festival, becoming a hero to millions of Soviet jazz-lovers. Economically, there is more individualism in these areas as well. In the 9th of May fishing cooperative, for instance, which is situated in a beautiful pine forest outside of Riga, fishermen get higher wages according to the value of the fish they catch — hardly a pure socialist idea. An an estimated 40 percent of the population is still Lutheran.

The party chieftains are quite well aware that all of this has an effect, and one way they are attempting to deal with the changes, ironically, is to insist that this more sophisticated idea of the collective and this new interest in the individual was always part of the Soviet system.

Fathers and Sons

One very strategically-placed man who believes and will argue that the individual is simply coming naturally into his own and that Marxism always foresaw this is Dr. Vladimir Kolobkov who is head of the Chair of Scientific Communism at Kiev State University and who advises the party at its highest levels as to how to deal with modern youth. I found him extremely amiable, willing to consider any opinion and remarkably free from the programmed hostility and viciousness of other top party members. Indeed, he seemed the closest to a genuine scholar that I have found.

He argued that what is happening today among Soviet youth is a simple outgrowth of the development of Communism from a dictatorship of the proletariat to the time when all workers will be intellectuals; at the moment, they are marooned on a way-station.

"I think that many are becoming more involved in the person and in psychology," Dr. Kolobkov told me in the summer of 1971, when I had my second long interview with him. "This is my formulation and theory, too. It is connected with the personal mind. When a person, growing, becomes more complicated, his mind is growing too. A man with four years education thinks flatly. He is one-dimensional. A man with 15 years education thinks in many dimensions. His thinking becomes more complicated. He thinks much more about himself and his place in society. He is still connected with society and depends upon other people. He can be an individual, but psychologically, not socially."

We were sitting in the parlor of my "suite" in the Hotel Dnipro, I was sipping cognac, he did not drink because of a heart condition. Suddenly a mammoth thunderstorn gathered and flung itself ferociously upon the great outcropping of hill and rock upon which the lovely city of Kiev sits. Rain and sleet attacked the front windows savagely, and bolts of lightning streaked across the sky in the rich Ukrainian prairies below.

"Many Soviets have told me they see the collective changing . . . from formal collectivism to a kind of sense of community," I suggested.

To my initial surprise, he agreed. "Yes, with the transformation of personality, you can see the change from formal collectivism to — let us call it — conscious collectivism. And this is what we want." He also agreed that the young Soviets were becoming much more "relativistic" — that is, they saw the world in more relative and less absolute terms. "This is because they are more educated," he said. "It is the same in the U.S. The older generation is more rigid because it is less educated. The many-sided approach of the younger generation can be explained in the fact of higher education."

Still, one has the feeling that the currents at work are not at all those which theoreticians of Communism expected from their hothouse experiment. They wanted to create a "new man," and, in ways never dreamed of, they have. But he is a "new man" far closer to the Western World and to the open road than they really wished.

The masters of Soviet Russia have no intention at all of letting these individualistic impulses go unformed, expressing themselves in free-form as in the West. They are slowly liberalizing, yes, but this only means they are searching now for new, more sophisticated methods of dealing with developments and writing post mortem into their theory new ideas which, at base, unquestionably threaten the rigid original form of their state.

When I left Dr. Kolobkov that day, I asked if I might get anything for him in the 'States.' "Well," he said, wrinkling his brow, "perhaps some books . . . What I am interested in now is the manipulation of the mass mind."

✿ Chapter Seven
Class, Status and Privilege
— The Two Worlds of Russia

"Many, even as they sought to approach the masses,
felt an obscure foreboding that the
entrance of this million-headed actor upon the stage of history
might crowd the intelligentsia itself forever off that state."

Bertram D. Wolfe in "Three Who Made a Revolution."

𝒯HE Chekhovian woods are dark and moody, with legions of pine trees standing close together to keep out the sun and the prying eyes. There is no equivalent word in the Russian language for the Western conception of "personal privacy," yet here, in the woods between Moscow and the nearby village of Uspenskoye there is privacy — for the privileged elite of Moscow.

The Russian countryside is different, even from the American Midwest, which it most closely resembles. It is wild and brooding, unmanicured, an uncombed vastness. Here there is an imminent sense of doom, even on a sunny day; and when it is dark and cold, a suicidal air hangs over the Russian land.

The great and often effective myth of Soviet society is that collectivism calls everyone to live together in brotherhood and harmony in those huge, tiresomely-standardized apartment buildings that are mushrooming everywhere; but the fact of life is that the Russians do not really spontaneously communicate with each other. At the first chance, they are escaping into the woods all alone if possible, because that has been throughout Russian history and is today the one place where they could be alone with themselves; within their own private forests of the soul.

No wonder, then, that here, protected by trees that turn black in the heavy shade and protected by roads that are tightly closed to all except those with special passes, live the 40,000 members of the elite party, intellectual and scientific community of the Soviet Union. Simple wooden huts or "izbas" with sloping roofs surrounded by tangled gardens and berry patches — these belong to middle-level bureaucrats, scientists and intellectuals. Modern ranch house "dachas" with picture windows and swimming pools — these belong to men like party chief Leonid Brezhnev. And all are hidden, even from each other, by forests.

What they have, materially, is not exceptional compared to the average of material goods coveted and often gained by even middle class people in the West. Rather, it is what they have in terms of class privilege that is so exceptional here.

In a country which has made a sacred ideological fetish of grouping everyone together in anonymity, in a country where collective concern and not one's own personal life was supposed to be the arbiter of human thought, in a country whose holy tenet is "to each according to his needs," the Soviet elite is living like rampant individualists. Alone and apart, basking in the pleasures of much of the worst and most self-serving of the burgeoise world.

While this has been occurring for some years (Stalin had nine dachas and used to pay his top men "extra salaries" which he handed to them in sealed envelopes), it has been increasing recently. For one thing, the material well-being of the Soviet Union has substantially increased. For another, consumer goods take on an added importance because they are, for the first time, even remotely within reach.

But the dangers of the creation of such a privileged elite, particularly when the great mass of people is still called upon to make continual sacrifices, are only beginning to show now, for only now is the country opening up enough so that more and more Russians are coming to know of these practices and coming bitterly to resent them. It is particularly galling to the young, who tend to be more idealistic about Communism. It is telling that many of them, again reflecting the deep desire for honesty, resent most not the fact the leaders *have* privileges, but that they *hide* their privileges. It is also telling that the sons of this elite, experiencing the hypocrisy at first hand and at the same filled with guilt from benefitting from it, are the most alienated of all.

"Sure, we know about these things," a young man named Volodie in Moscow said, "everybody knows about it. Taxi-drivers talk about it, and there are plenty of jokes. But what can you do about it? I once went with a group of students to Bokhara and we slept in sleeping bags in the museum. But there was nothing *in* the museum. The director told us that party officials had taken all the treasures — rugs, coats, pictures — to use in their own homes. But he said he had vouchers. Great! A museum full of vouchers!"

Some young who consider themselves real Communists grow openly angry about it. "We see them (the top officials of the party) sweeping into the Kremlin every morning in their Rolls Royces and Mercedes-Benzes and we wonder: 'Is this what Communism has come to?' " asked a student named Oleg, his eyebrows arched. "We always believed that Communists were supposed to live and eat and suffer with the people. Nobody even knows who they are. Why don't they let people go if they want to? Why are they so lacking in confidence?"

But though many of them know that these things exist, most of them have never actually seen a special store or a private professional club, or — the most rare — a top-private Communist party nightclub. I, in fact, may be the only Westerner to have seen such a club.

I was having dinner with a high-level party official one evening in a central Russian city and, after dinner, he suggested we go dancing. At first, when we walked into a nondescript building with a public restaurant in the front, crossed through the dining room and came into another building in back, I did not know where I was. But when my escort flashed his party card at the door and we entered a type of nightclub which was about as common in the Soviet Union as a stock exchange, it was with no special insight that I immediately suspected something.

"Can anyone come here?" I asked, as we sat down at a table in a discreetly-lighted room with candles and a large dance floor.

"Why, yes, of course," he said. Then he turned to order some Scotch for us — another un-Russian thing.

When a floor show came on after midnight (also so un-Russian) and when girls in typically Western nightclub costumes began dancing to the theme from "Dr. Zhivago," and when couples began doing a clumsy Russian version of the twist without anyone coming over to them and telling them it was immoral (*even more* unRussian!), I could guess that I had, indeed, penetrated some curious inner sanctum.

Others joined us, and though the people I was with continued to deny that it was anything more than a typical "restaurant" for "everybody", I knew well that no such nightclub as this exists for the "masses" in Russia.

At the end of the evening, I turned to my escort and whispered again, "*Who* can come here?"

He smiled broadly. "*We* can," he whispered back.

The story of privileges is getting out, of course, for Russia is no longer one huge locked safe. In 1971, the popular German magazine, "Der Spiegel," detailed for the first time in great length the economic, material and social privileges of the elite.

This irritated Soviet officialdom so much that copies of "Der Spiegel" usually reserved in libraries for use by only a tiny circle of privileged readers — professors, top teachers and journalists — was put on a 2-star rating. That meant, according to a teacher who generally would have access to it, that "only Victor Louis (the famous English correspondent reputed to be a special KGB agent) and a dozen KGB men can read it!" However, dog-eared copies of it continued to pass from hand to hand in the Soviet Union, and a lot of Soviets already have also read it in samizdat, the hand-typed, underground literature.

What is it, precisely, that constitutes the "privileges" of the Communist elite?

First, it is material privileges, but material privileges in the sense of being able to acquire goods from the West. While the average, hard-working Soviet citizen is standing in endless, exhausting lines every day and night to buy the expensive and shoddy Russian-made consumer goods, the Soviet elite is quickly and efficiently buying foreign goods at its own shops.

Politburo and Central committee members buy in "spetsmagaziny" or special stores where all possible Western goods are available. Since these are located in the private, heavily-guarded apartment buildings where these men live, few Russians and even fewer foreigners ever see these stores.

They work in a way that would certainly benefit big eaters. On the first of each month, the official pays a fee of 50 rubles or $56, and this enables him to buy food for his family in any amount.

There are, as well, special stores for middle-level bureaucrats, army officers, and intellectuals. A few very top level people even have "open accounts" in the State Bank, where they can withdraw any amount in rubles so long as it is spent only for personal needs. This represents as close to a checking account as the Soviet Union has come.

In addition, many artists and performers who earn foreign currency abroad are permitted to use 40% of their earnings in "valuta coupons" — coupons issued by the State Bank, which allows them to buy foreign goods in the Beriozka foreign currency shops usually reserved only for foreign tourists.

Because of a difference between foreign "prizes" approved by the government and what they consider "cash gifts." Alexander Solzhenitsyn, having won the Nobel prize for literature and thus having incurred the severe displeasure of his government, had up to 1971 received only $5,000 of his $70,000 in valuta coupons. His was considered a "cash gift," which brings with it fewer privileges in terms of foreign exchange.

There are many other accoutrements of privilege. Only the elite have the "dachas" or summer houses in the countryside, where they get fresh vegetables and fruit from a special state farm reserved just for them. Only the elite drive into town in Mercedes-Benzes, Chevrolet Impalas and Rolls Royces. Only the very top Kremlin elite is directed into the central lanes of the big thoroughfares — the lanes are reserved for them and this is enforced by the police. Only these men have permission to hunt in a specially reserved forest, Zavidova, 100 miles North of Moscow.

Then there are the other privileges that accrue to people because of advanced professional standing, in particular the "clubs" where the only really excellent food in Moscow can be had. These include the Journalists' Club, the Writers' Club, the Architects' House, and — the most elegant and fashionable — the Movie House.

This is all a long way down the road from the Revolution. One of the first decrees written after 1917 by Lenin cancelled the law of inheritance, and the Council of People's Commissions at the same time decreed that no party official could earn more than the average skilled worker — this was known as the Party Norm. In the early '30s, Stalin cancelled both of these decrees in a deliberate move to create a privileged class loyal to him, and the process of creating this new elite has continued, unabated, until today.

Perhaps the most questionable part of the present-day post-revolution elitism is the fact that these prizes of the Socialist society are inheritable; they accrue to the children of the elite, who need do nothing to deserve them. When the poet Voznesensky's wife, Zoia Bogoslavskaya, wrote a novelette that was published in the youth magazine "Yunost" in 1971 about a young man from an important family who bought his thesis in the University and went on to buy everything in life, she was bitterly attacked in other magazines. This type of situation simply did not exist, the other writers said.

And then there are the privileged foreigners — strange, never-never world characters who live in a shadow world in Moscow, blessed with the best that the Soviet state can bestow upon them. Some take on the role of newspaper correspondents, which is always a good cover since so many evils can be explained away by the vagaries of our curious profession. The most noted of these is the ubiquitous Victor Louis, a British "correspondent" who is widely known to be a very special type of KGB man. The little, dark-haired, innocuous-appearing Louis, who complains of lumbago and is always traveling hither and yon in the world in search of treatment for it (all the while he is actually performing highly curious missions for the Soviet secret police), lives in an elegant dacha outside Moscow, with two swimming pools, a tennis court and half a dozen foreign cars. He is crazy about gadgets and, to hear him talk, the only reason he always wanted to come to the 'States was to roam through Hammacher and Schlemmer. But then, he's been everywhere else: from Easter Island (when the Americans were getting ready to abandon their base there), to Taiwan (when the Soviets were trying to make a deal with Chiang behind Mao's back) and even to Israel (when the U.S. was wooing Egypt in its 1971 attempt for peace). Lumbago can be a terrible ailment.

I telephoned Louis one day in Mosciw and found him in his dacha. I told him simply that I would like to see him — because I thought he was interesting (which was somewhat understating the case). "Oh, my dear," he said in a piteous tone, "I would like to see you, but you know my lumbago is very bad. Besides, I've always been extremely kind to visiting journalists. I've picked them up down at the National Hotel and brought them out here and entertained them at the dacha. Then what did I get for it? One asked me for a Coke, so I gave him a Coke. Then he wrote me up saying I lived so luxuriously in Moscow that I even had Cokes. I feel like I've taken advantage of. And, besides, there's the lumbago."

What all of this shows, is the tremendous duality about everything in this society and the enormous dichotomy between what is supposed to be and what is.

Why should this be so? The Marquis De Custine attributed it to their consuming inferiority complex regarding the West, and he observed in words that still apply today: "I don't reproach the Russians for being what they are; what I blame them for is their desire to appear to be what we are. They are much less interested in being civilized than in making us believe them so. They would be quite content to be in effect more awful and barbaric than they actually are, if only others could thereby be made to believe them better and move civilized."

Today you find this duality everywhere — not only in the chasm between the privileges of the elite and the sacrifices of the masses but in the structure of the new class system, in the persistence of racial prejudice, and in the nagging persistence of the idea of two cultures, one for the intelligentsia and one for the people.

Everywhere you look, in Russia there are two worlds. *At least two*. Take class, for instance. Class feeling was supposed to disappear in the "classless society." Yet today, a highly rational man like the famous Soviet physicist Andrei D. Sakharov, father of their H-bomb, will state categorically that the class system, as illustrated by economic and privilege factors, is about the same in the U.S.S.R. as in the United States. As he wrote in his "Manifesto," "Forty percent of the Soviet population is in difficult economic circumstances. In the United States about 25 percent of the population is on the verge of poverty. On the other hand, the 5 percent of the Soviet population that belongs to the managerial group is as privileged as its counterpart in the United States. The development of modern Society in both the Soviet Union and the United States is now following the same course of increasing complexity of structure and of industrial management, giving rise in both countries to managerial groups that are similar in social character. We must therefore acknowledge that there is no qualitative difference in the structure of society of the two countries in terms of distribution or consumption." This is considered by Western scholars to be about right.

But for the new generation of Russians, this class system, like the economic system, is largely "given;" they do not feel the need for the old passionate classlessness of the early days of the revolution for the simple and obvious reason that they never lived through it. The new class system — plus the new elitism — has led to new class problems that run deep in this generation and are more similar to problems in the U.S., where the educated young become more and more removed from physical labor, than to other socialist countries, such as China.

Such popular papers as Komsomolskaya Pravda or Komsomol Truth, for instance, are filled with letters from workers complaining bitterly about students who make fun of them or won't talk to them. Some young people use the word "meshchanye," which used to refer to the very small bourgeoisie, to characterize the small mentalities of the present day small bureaucrat or worker. These class problems are a subject of novels as well. In 1970 novels such as "Love and Hate," published by the Military Publishing House, the rightist author Shentsov was accused by none other than Pravda for "inciting workers against the intellectuals." The intellectual class was not disloyal, Pravda declared roundly, only individuals were.

Moreover, when I visited the Leningrad offices of the historic youth newspaper, "Smena," founded by Lenin himself, and asked the editors what problems of their readers they were dealing with, they were very forthright.

"Who will be the worker in the original sense?" Alla Beljakova, the attractice, crisp young editor of the magazine said, sighing and looking for just a moment perplexed. "Graduates today dream of individual creative work as an independent worker or research worker. They think that is more romantic than being a shop steward. Another problem is that everyone wants higher education. We are trying to develop the idea that it's not necessary to get higher education to be an intellectual.

"It's not a question of money," she interjected hastily, "for workers get the same money" (this is true — and important). "It's not a question of social equality. It's just a question of the diploma."

"A matter of prestige?" I asked.

She nodded. "Yes," she answered, with surprising candor. "It's very boring to be a factory worker. But we're trying to make it more interesting. We're trying to tell people that they can be just as intellectual being a machine operator. The paper is stressing the fact that there should be no disappointment for someone who doesn't get a higher education. He still has many ways open for development. Maybe it is better to be a good machine operator than an ordinary engineer. Our motto is from each according to his ability — each should do what he does best.

"We are trying to show that all work can be creative. For instance, it is a most prosaic job to drive a tramcar. But one driver wanted to do better work, so he would say, not only 'This is Nevski Prospect . . .' but 'this house is famous for . . .' He became a guide to the city. This is what we call creative."

Surveys continue to show, however, that, despite well-meaning exhortations such as these, the most popular professions among Soviet young people are not those of creative tramcar conductor or zealous machine operator but those of cosmonaut, theoretical physicist, test pilot and physician. Among high school students, graduates want to become doctors, chemists, physicists and engineers. It is interesting that most of these are professions having to do with the sciences and that political jobs, such as party work, are never mentioned, despite the power that accrues to a person through them.

Nothing is quite so despised, however, as the service professions, despite the fact that trading and catering services now need four times as many young workers as agriculture and twice as many as industry. When, in 1971, a young man named Sergei Skazkin, who had straight A's in high school, chose waiting on tables as a profession, his comrades were aghast. Writing in the youth newspaper, Komsomolskaya Pravda or "Komsomol Truth," Sergei said, in pique, "I don't know about you fellows, but I don't see why someone who can make a tasty borsch and hamburgers should not be treated as a participant in a great construction project." Then he noted something highly important — the fact that young engineers and workers could not be kept on remote mining and building projects because of the absence of services.

In many ways, the Soviets can still legitimately take pride that the classes are closer together than they are in the West. After a long critical discussion we had about the country, one of my best friends, a very attractive young woman in Moscow, made out a list of things that the Soviet people *liked* about their way of life. One of the points on the list was the fact that the intellectual class is genuinely part of the working class, that they live in the same buildings (not in different apartment buildings or even neighborhoods, as in the West) and that they are often paid the same salaries. Another point was the striking overall attempt of Russian society to bring people to culture and culture to "the people." And this is true. Writers and artists often go to address gatherings of workers or farmers and — on this level — there is a genuine exchange between them that is largely absent in the West. But . . .

Despite these very real advantages, there exists in the young as well as the old — running on a parallel level and made possible by that particular Russian obliqueness that permeates everything — a derisive duality: one culture for the "people," one culture for the elite. This reflects the deep chasms between the two. Even though they may live next door to each other, there is a tremendous anti-intellectualism on the part of the masses — a resentment that often takes the form of "the people" supporting Stalinism, for instance.

On the other hand, everywhere I went in Russia, the feeling of eliteness — of superiority — in being an intellectual permeated everything. The same young who resented the material privileges of the party elite thought the cultural privileges of the intelligentsia were quite normal. One evening in Riga, a group made up largely of visiting Moscow journalists sat with me for upwards of seven hours drinking and eating heavily. These sentiments emerged quite clearly.

"Many young people here about the 'States and listen to the "Voice of America," one of the journalists was saying to me — in a low voice because one of the group was an insensate hard-liner. "They know about it . . ."

"And love it," another one whispered, with a devilish look in his eyes. The hard-liner caught this and threw him an angry look.

"Of course, the workers don't know these things," the first whisperer said. "They only read the propaganda in the papers. But *we* know . . ."

In Kiev, when my sculptor friend Nikoroyan introduced himself, he always said, typically, "Nikolai Bogratovich, sculptor . . ." He would not have had his prestige and identity without the "sculptor." When he appeared out of nowhere, with no warning and no reservation (an unheard-of thing in Russia, where everything, but everything, is planned and programmed) and couldn't get a room, he proclaimed angrily and archly, "An *artist* and no room reservation!"

In a country where a unitary culture under the banner of socialist realism was proclaimed to the world, intellectuals see banned movies such as "Bonnie and Clyde" and "Who's Afraid of Virginia Woolf?", foreign movies which are permitted in their own clubs (in particular the Movie House or Dom Kino) because they can "understand" them, whereas the people cannot. In a country where manual labor is extolled, intellectuals think it is beneath their dignity even to paint a wall or fix a pipe in their own apartments. The wife of a writer I knew had no hot water in the kitchen for years because her husband refused to put the necessary pipe through from the bathroom. "Well, next year we'll get a better apartment," she said resignedly.

"The intellectuals believe that the masses demand a certain culture that is appropriate for them," said one Western diplomat who long had mixed with the Soviet intelligentsia and had carefully thought this through. "They can create this for the workers with their left hands, and meanwhile, they devote themselves to real culture. This creates a strange condition in which the intelligentsia is living in a special world where things are okay for them but not for 'the people.' When they think about the 'people,' they think about giving them more materially, not liberating them."

"It is closer to the French intelligentsia than to ours, except that it is subsidized by the government. Moreover, they have a view of the intelligentsia in the West in which anything can destroy them. There's a great fear of the businessman. Writers here do not really want an open competitive system. They'd rather make a good movie and have 20 people see it."

Or, as an artist friend in Kiev said, "One of the artists in the union went to Mexico last year and he was perfectly enchanted with it. All he did was rave about it. Finally we asked him, why didn't he stay there? What? he said, Stay there? I saw how the artists live there — working like dogs and doing everything on their own. Here I have my studio supplied by the state and everything else; I have no worries."

What all of this means in practice, however, is that culture for the masses is dull, didactic stuff which purports to teach them socialism in the most simplistic manner possible, while the intelligentsia reserves for itself innumerable privileges — in culture, as well as in material things.

Sovietologists estimate the "in-society" at about 500,000 members — writers, artists, playwrights, actors, party officials and scientists. They call themselves "the one percent." For them, everything is possible: plays not approved by the censors are given nightly, sometimes for several years, in closed showings; forbidden manuscripts are passed from hand to hand around their inner circle. One of my friends, in 1967, had a copy of "Dr. Zhivago," then totally forbidden. He had got it from his boss and he could only keep it two days.

What would happen if "the people" — that abstract, always threatening mass — saw these things? Like a dark current running through all of Russian history is the fear that too much freedom, too much stimulation, too many unassimilable new ideas might make of this mass an anarchistic, hysterical animal. Ironically, this is much the way it is today, and the Soviets have still to come to grips with the new problems of class, elitism and education.

The Russian intelligentsia, of course, has always stood apart from the intelligentsia of Western Europe, just as it stood apart from its own "masses". One reason was that it came, not from the the bourgeois class but from the working class itself (perhaps this is why, on one level, it so despised the working class, for it knew it) and from the aristocracy. Another reason was that, in a vast country of untouched darkness where none of the ideas of the Western Renaissance or Enlightenment ever reached, it was only the intelligentsia who thought at all in terms of ideas and theories for change — but they had no way to apply their ideas and dreams and they lived in total separation.

Today this same intelligentsia, just like the country's mentally less agile leaders, has even failed to come to grips with new problems of class, elitism and education. It is perhaps one of the most interesting predicaments that, while the Russians deride the idea of the "classlessness" of the West — where a workingman is not frozen in his class but can rise to the middle or intellectual or entrepreneurial class — they are themselves creating such a society. How can the dictatorship of the proletariat continue while the management of the state is rapidly passing to the new class of second generation workingmen's sons who are highly trained managers of socialism and not workingmen at all? In publications scattered around the tourist waiting rooms, the Russians deny that the United States has or can absorb the working class into the middle class. Yet this is basically what is slowly happening here.

Attempts to reform education in order to mix the different classes of young people at an early age simply did not work. Russia is ripe for no "Cultural Revolution" ("We are not Chinese," one friend told me huffily.) Krushchev's 1958 "reforms," in which university matriculation was delayed for two years so that students could work and live with the workers during that time, apparently had more deleterious than good effects and they were soon abandoned. "There is no evidence that the working class had a particularly salutary influence on the political outlook of the student-workers," Dr. Jeremy Azrael, Sovietologist at the University of Chicago, says, "If anything, closer contact with 'real life' heightened awareness of the gap between ideology and actuality and turned credulous schoolboys into critical realists and cynics. There is little question that student radicalism actually increased throughout the entire period."

Soviet ideologists scorn and scoff at the Marcusian (a "werewolf," they like to call him) ideas of the student class and the intelligentsia becoming the revolutionary cutting edge, in place of the disinherited proletariat, but, in fact, they have no answers to this new phenomenon. Nor do they have answers to the basic dilemma — the basic class dilemma — of Soviet life, which is that Communism deals only with what man does manually, not with what he *is*. They have made a theory of creation out of ephemera, out of a passing stage of man's life, and now the educated young are asking, "Where do we go next?"

❧ Chapter Eight
New Theater, New Arts

"The poets of Russia were always warriors for the future of the native land, for the triumph of justice. The poets helped Russia to think . . . The poets helped Russia to struggle against her tyrants." Yevgeny Yevtushenko in "Precocious Autobiography," in the early 1960s.

"The public . . . looks upon Russian writers as its only leaders defenders and saviors against Russian autocracy. The title of poet and writer has eclipsed the tinsel of epaulets and gaudy uniforms."

Vissarion Belinsky, the famous literary critic, in 1847.

THE Sovremennik or Modern Theater, and thus much of the new-style young theater in Russia, sprang to life in 1956, that watershed year when the Soviet Union sprang back to life in the wake of the passing of the dark ships of Stalinism. The relief and light that flowed from Khrushchev's courageous step of de-Staliniization flowed out and over much of the Soviet Union like an epic mental and spiritual wave. Nowhere were hopes higher than in the Russian theater, once a spiritual gem of the world but, under Stalin, reduced to callous cowering.

That year, a group of the most talented young actors and directors from the once-great Moscow Art Theater, sick unto death of the bans on performing any decent play except the classics, grasped the moment by actively beginning to plan for their own, "modern" theater.

"The Sovremennik was created by a group of enthusiastists," Oleg Tabakoff, the immensely talented actor who rose to become

97

director of Sovremennik, recalled one day in Leningrad, as we sat in a theatre, chatting, "and this meant certain things. It meant, for instance, that the first year and a half we could only work at night time. At that time, there were problems in the Art Theater. You had to follow a certain line in the repertoire. What was wrong was that at the same time you could see on the stage such great plays as works by Tolstoy, Ibsen, Shakespeare and you could see the plays of authors so much lower. First of all, they had no respect for the visitors — a play might give advice on how to clean your nails, for instance, or tell you it was useful to clean your shoes. The modern plays were somehow not serious. But when you were in the theater, how could you protest? The only way was to do something different."

In the suddenly open and momentarily honest mood of the country, the young actors found many kindred spirits among themselves. Working late at night after their performances at the Art Theater they began to practice Victor Rozov's "Life Forever," later to be made into the internationally-shown movie, "The Cranes are Flying."

Tabakoff is a sandy-haired young man. His eyes are mischievous, not a common trait among Russians, and his whole manner is jaunty and filled with charm. He was wearing blue jeans and a simple beige shirt, and he looked much younger than his 40 years. Now, in June of 1971, he sat in the back of the darkened Theater of the Five Year Plan where Sovremennik was summering, and reminisced:

"It opened at 1 a.m. and we felt that the audience took it very naturally. We finished about 5 a.m. The audience was a mixed one — students, workers, parents, artists. They didn't want to leave the theater, even though it was 5 a.m. They demanded a discussion of the play and to know the future of the new group." He laughed. "Maybe they weren't really struck by the skill of the actors, who were young and not perfect but loved what they were doing. Somehow this crossed over to the audience, and this was the main feeling that brought together the company and the audience."

The group of young actors, heady from their first success, decided they must have a theater and that they must pioneer modern plays in a country that at last seemed ready for them. In the exciting course of the next few months, everybody did everything. Oleg Ofrimov, a brilliant man, was both performer and first director. Igor Kvasha was one of the actors. Tabakoff was actor and manager. He laughed about this.

"Even nowadays, I look too young," he said. "I had to collect money, and I bought a very big, very thick briefcase that was also very yellow. As manager, I carried it and sometimes it gave the impression of moving all by itself, it was so much bigger than I."

And now 15 years had gone by. Sovremennik had become so popular that it had a theater of its own; all of its performances were sold out and a good number of the best young playwrights wrote only for them. "What kind of plays are of interest to us today?" he said. "Modern and talented ones. It is not of interest to us that a play is just about peasants or writers or intellectuals. We are interested only in plays which deal with some problems — plays which touch problems of great interest and importance for the whole of society."

But what kind of plays? I pressed him, trying to break down the typical Russian obliqueness. What had they done with "socialist realism," the only form of art expression that was to be permitted under Stalin?

"We are concerned with the branch of the tree of art that is realistic," he said, as stagehands noisily moved the seats on the stage. "We call it psychological realism." A slight ironic smile touched his lips.

How did *that* relate to "socialist realism?"

Now he grinned. "It is the very best part of socialist realism," he said, irony now in his voice.

And Stalin? Did they perform any plays about his era? For the first and only time a spark of anger touched his otherwise amiable features. "We know all about these things," he said testily. "If it deals only with them, it is not interesting for us. You like to deal with our problems, but, believe me, it is much harder to live through them than to write about it. People in the West who do this are not responsible for it — for them, it is just a curiosity."

This is not true, of course — the Russians do not "know all about these things" today at all — but since you can never know what pressures a man like Tabakoff is under to say certain things, I left this matter and went on. What did *his* theater teach about why man lives and for what? I pressed on, for socialist realism still *is*, despite all, the only form of art officially permitted in the Soviet Union.

"If I knew for what we must live," he said, to the echo of the stage-hands' clatter, "I'd be a new prophet. I'm not." He paused, then added quickly, "We work for the sake of love — for the sake of real love. Does that answer your question about what we teach people?"

In effect, he was talking about giving new and fresh plays — plays that dealt, not with the hackneyed questions of the "classes," but with real and vivid problems of live, thinking, suffering, laughing, crying individuals — a tendency that filled out still further the "new individualism" observed elsewhere.

He paused, then went on. "There is such a thing as truth in the theater," he said. "We are not interested in just reality or just comedy or tragedy or satire, but in a certain character of human feelings and conceptions."

One of the Sovremennik plays that has most illustrated these expressions — and that, in a sense, represents somewhat of a rewriting and certainly a deepening of Bolshevik history — is the historical saga, "The Bolsheviks, by the young playwright, Mikhail Shatrov. While the Bolsheviks are all presented as heroic people, they are also represented as *real* people, which is a sharp change from the past. "This represents a new trend," Victor Rozov had told me the day we talked in the Writers' Union Cafe, "a new and much more truthful way of relating historical events and a more complicated and honest way of representing history."

When I asked him if Soviet writing was tending toward more psychological interpreation, he answered quickly, "Yes. The psychological documentary is popular now. I myself am one of the 'psychologists.' I am even going to write an article called 'The Untruth of the Fact — the Truth of Things Imagined.' "

Truth, yes, that is the important thing. That is what the great men of literature of the last century lived and died for, that is what they dreamed of seeing the New Russia personify and that is what Soviet Russia, replanting the dark Russian soul in modern times with an obsessive total ideology has least stood for since the revolution.

In the fall of 1971, in New York City, ironically, I was finally able to meet the great young poet, Andrei Voznesensky. Probably no writer in the Soviet Union today better exemplifies the unending search for "truth." In 1967, I had attempted to see him in Moscow, but, having just had a trip to the United States cancelled because of official outspokenness, and having just written a letter to Pravda about the devious circumstances of the cancellation, and having just had Pravda editor Mikhail Zimyanin say of him that if he ever did it again he would be "ground to dust and I myself will see to it that not a trace of him remained," Voznesensky not surprisingly was "not available" to foreign journalists.

Now we sat in the incongruous setting of the coffee shop of the Picadilly Hotel in New York as the baby-faced, winsome, sad-eyed, 38-year-old poet alternately ate scrambled eggs and talked in a low, singing English. A double irony was contained in the fact that he had finally been allowed "out" because Brezhnev, Kosygin and Podgorny had just embarked on whirl-wind tours of their own. The poets could be their international shadows, they evidently decided, because how, otherwise, could they show how advanced and "respectable" and "open" the Soviet Union was becoming?

"This generation is more free," Voznesensky started out. "It wants to find answers, and it needs philosophical answers. They're reading the old philosophers. Before they were reading only popular writers. Now they're reading Marx, too. In our generation, not many read Marx. They read about Marx.

"In poetry, too, they want something more deep. Mandelsham (Osip Mandelsham, the poet killed by Stalin) is popular. It's instinct — poetry has to be complicated because life is complicated. Some poets simply give the political slogans of today, but this it not the aim of real poetry. Vietnam is okay, but in this generation you need more complicated poetry."

Russia has always had special regard for her poets, even as she killed them — or perhaps because of that, she killed them. In the darkness, poetry was the illumination, the vehicle of truths otherwise not to be spoken. "You stimulate with poetry," he went on, "and people find their own answers. Poetry should make us blush with shame. There is sense in writing political things, in writing about Robert Kennedy, but there is more — we should be shameful in our blood of not saying words against crime. What is shame? Our lost sense!"

To Voznesensky, as to most Russians, poetry and art were no

peripheral thing, no amusement; they were at the very center of life
— which is precisely why work has to pass the board of censors. "Is
poetry an instrument to change reality?" he cried at one point,
putting down his fork and scrambled eggs. "If something changes,
poetry has to do it. Who else? It connects people with people. What
else would do it? The trade unions? Who? Who?"

Then, more calmly, he gave a strange benediction. "Certainly
Russia will change. Even now . . . we have the year of the Fiat. But it
won't be the same as in your country. You do not have the same
interest in art. We are more mystic, we are more solid and deep."

What gifted writers and performers like Voznesensky and
Tabakoff are reacting against, first of all, are the strictures of Soviet
society, particularly as shown in the statute of the Union of Soviet
Writers, which regulates and passes on the work of every writer.
Passed in 1934, it defined "socialist realism": "Socialist realism is
the basic method of Soviet literature and literary criticism. It
demands of the artist the truthful, historically concrete representation of reality in its revolutionary development. Moreover, the
truthfulness and historical concreteness of the artistic representation
of reality must be linked with the task of ideological transformation
and the education of workers in the spirit of socialism."

What was behind this was nothing peculiarly Bolshevik, for, all
through Russian history, art had been tied to the truths of the
absolutist state of that particular moment. When Orthodoxy was
proclaiming Muscovy the "third Rome," only church art was
permitted. When religious beliefs were breaking down in the 19th
century, the famous "Traveling Artists" broke away from the
Academy's strictures and exhibited "revolutionary art" — pictures
of a desperate peasant guarding the wood of the aristocrat, and a
lascivious upper class man interviewing a humble servant girl. Art
was never, as in the West, doubt-filled, explorative, "decadent."
Art was never relative to life. Art was never "formal," that is
dedicated mainly to style. Art was content — teaching.

When the revolution came, a great conversation ensued among
the Bolshevik hierarchy. Should art be free . . . and the tastes of the
people be lifted up to the highest? Or should it dip down to the
simple but honest tastes of the masses?

The decision was not long in coming, and it turned out to be a
purely Slavophile type of answer. As the infamous A. A. Zhdanov of

the Politburo, the man entrusted by Stalin with enforcing Socialist realism, said at the time, "We are to teach the decaying West, not vice-versa."

Art was to be of the people, for the people and, if not by the people, at least approved by the people. It was dipping down.

In Riga, I got a look at this curious business when I visited Maxla, the state union of artists and they explained the concept of "People's Art." "If only one (print) is sold," Maier Furman, director of the plant, explained, "It will cost 350 rubles. If it goes to the people, the prints will cost only 2 or 3 rubles." He insisted that "the people decide whether it is good for our time or not."

How do they do this? Through exhibits. People come and write down what they like or don't like. The organization will not give an opportunity to the artist if the people say it's bad. For all the artists, it is necessary to make an art work in such a way that the person who looks at it has an idea of what it is."

This "theory" is easily manipulated by those in power, of course. And, whereas in the 19th century, aristocratic art was removed from the people, what has happened today is that socialist realist art has also been removed from the people. In both cases, what it purported to represent of the inner life of the people was largely false, giving to most of the vaunted Soviet culture an overwhelming element of dishonesty and alienation from the real things in life.

This began, but just began, to change with the Khrushchevan thaw. Artists began to paint more personally, realistically and abstractly ("daubs of an ass's tail," Khrushchev called this, in his expressive way) and writers began to express what so many of the young people were thinking. In the sudden euphoria over the new freedom, Yevtushenko was heard to remark, "Suddenly I somehow found that I must answer all the questions on my own." In the play given then, "Ominous Days," the author, G. Mdivani, has a character say, "I am not a microbe but a man. Let my conscience be my guide. I have ceased to be afraid to tell the truth." (Truth was nowhere in the society, but, among the intelligentsia, everywhere in thought). And in Vasily Aksyonov's "The Colleagues," the wildly popular, interestingly vague and wholly non-didactic novel about young people muddling through life with little purpose about them, one character says: "I am responsible to my conscience alone, not to some verbal ideologists. All they do is interfere with my work of seeing life."

These innocent expressions, then rampant among the young, early evinced from the party an abiding concern over the dangers of the "emotional self-expression of the new generation" and a return to "useless subjective emotions," or, in general parlance, personal feelings. Then it got worse, making it clear to the hardliners (Stalin might be gone, but Stalin's men were still in power) that the "thaw" was applying the warmth of free expression not to a snowball but to a glacier.

The glow lasted until 1966, when the first trials of young writers for publishing "anti-Soviet propaganda" abroad began. Suddenly some of the best poets, like Voznesensky and Yevtushenko, had trouble being published and were refused permission to go abroad. Alexander Solzhenitsyn, the man who kept trying to tell his countrymen they must deal with Stalinisn, won the Nobel prize for literature, thus becoming an "out" and "un" person in his own land. The liberal editor of "Novi Mir" or "New World," Alexander Tvardovsky, was replaced and died.

Many of the worst Stalinists, like Anatoly Safranov, editor of the conservative "Ogonyok" or "Mirror" made it clear that this time they didn't care what the West said about their cultural problems. Reminiscing tenderly about Stalin in 1969 to Frank Hardy, an Australian Communist whom he horrified, Safranov recalled the "good old days" in the '30s. "Stalin liked to watch films alone late at night in his cinema in the Kremlin," he said. "On one occasion not long before his death, he invited the director of a new Russian film to a private screening. While the film was running, Stalin's secretary came in with a letter. Stalin looked at it and said, 'No good.' The director fell down on the floor in a faint. Stalin watched the film to the end, then asked, 'Why is this man lying on the floor?' 'He fainted, Comrade Stalin; he thought you meant the film was no good.' Stalin revived the director and said to him, 'Your film is not bad. Don't be afraid, Comrade. Half the world says I am no good — but I do not faint.' "

Unquestionably, in the mid- '60s there was a halt called to the great leap forward in the arts; unquestionably, there was a regression. But it has not in any way been so all-encompassing or so total as then it was feared. There has been what amounts to a temporary halt in many of the more daring publications and productions, but most books, plays or poems are being published or produced somewhere. The culture of the country, out of the necessity of beating the system, has been spontaneously decentralized. More and more, off-beat or questionable literary pieces came to be printed in magazines in outlying cities, such as the Russian language magazines "Prostop" in Alma Ata and "Zarayevostoka" in Tashkent. And, in fact, everything is livelier and freer and more humanized in the non-Russian parts of the U.S.S.R.

"Censorship breaks down in the provinces," a Western diplomat in Moscow said, describing the new way. "One play might have many cuts in Moscow and few in Leningrad and none in Frunze. In the Baltics, plays are performed that are unthinkable here. Yevtushenko's poem, 'Under the Skin of the Statue of Liberty,' was not published in Moscow but was published in Minsk. It's a patch-work kind of thing and there's a great deal of sabotage on all levels."

When you get out in these outskirts of the Soviet state — whether in Central Asia, Georgia or the Baltics — you find literary themes talked about and written about that are unthinkable in Moscow, and you also find a far more intense interest in the individual man. This, for instance, was the conversation one day in the Estonian Writer's Union, a big, modern building in downtown Tallinn where writers live and work (in this case, totally cut off from "the masses"), in addition to talk.

As we sat in an attractive modern room, Scandinavian in design, looking out over the old rooftops and winding, cobble-stoned streets of the medieval city, the conversation soon got onto the forbidden theme of man's "alienation" — from his work, his society and his fellow man — a theme that is not supposed to exist in Communist society.

"Some years ago, there was the tendency to write only social prose," a rather posed, pop-eyed and very popular young poet, Rudolph Rimmel, said. "Now some changes have taken place. It is not printed in such big numbers. Now, literature deals with people — their feelings, their thoughts. Perhaps the most interesting thing today is people and a man and society, and how the soul of the man reacts to the pressures of society. The vulgar socialist point of view is passed — we look at things much more broadly. We do not consider 'sozialnost' (concern for the community) as part of education. It's the same all over — man is less generalized."

"That's the same topic our writers are exploring," I said.

They nodded. "It's the same problem all over," one writer said.

"In my recent book," novelist Vladimir Beekman interjected, "I deal with the problem of alienation."

Alienation? "Yes," said Rimmel, "We can say that technology and science develop more than the consciousness of the people — it brings conflict."

How do Soviet characters react to alienation? "One person can show conflict in pessimism, another may fight, some may surrender," Beekman said.

In his book, "Transit Passenger," which immediately sold out 32,000 copies, an Estonian from Tallinn and an Estonian living in the West meet, talk deeply and part.

What does the book show? "It compares two alienations," he said. "It does not give any final salvation. The reader must find it, if he wants to."

And in the Vilnius, Lithuania, Writer's Union, the beautiful old house originally occupied by the Counts Trshkevich, Oginski and Sniadecki and filled with elegant carved wood on the staircase and walls:

Algis Chekoulis, writer: "We're not afraid now. You know, we've been going through a process. Russia has always been very isolated. You don't find this in Czechoslovakia or Poland. You find it even more in China."

Another writer: "Little by little we're coming out. We read foreign papers now. You remember Chekov's story about the man with the shell around him?

Algis Pocius, union secretary: "Well, we still have men in shells, little bureaucrats who are afraid to break out."

Everywhere you go, particularly in these areas, the themes of the new plays deal not with ideological problems but always with the human being. One of the most wildly popular plays of the Sovremennik in the early '70s, for instance, was "One's Own Little Island," by an Estonian writer. It dealt with a group of young miners who had flunked their exams and were searching for meaning in life (every once in a while one of the young people snapped on a tape recorder and music from "Hair" blared forth). Finally they meet an elderly nature-lover who shows them the beauty of the forests and the land they're destroying with their strip mining, their bureaucratic snafus and their production quotas. "In the end, they realize it's their land," said Tabakoff, "they become the masters of it." But not before they keep asking, throughout the play, "What are we living for?"

Another new play, "Justice is My Vocation," published in the popular Leningrad magazine, "Neva," deals with a journalist who makes a serious mistake in a story, accusing a doctor incorrectly of not saving a man's life. Traumatized, he attempted to get his editors to run a retraction, but everybody tells him, "Just forget about it, it's not important." The play ends with his leaving the paper — hardly a positive ending for a non-positive hero.

Much the same is true in literature. After the thaw, the most popular books of that coming-of-age generation were the ones by men like Aksyonov, who created the Russian version of the "anti-hero." And a new author like Chingiz Aitmatov, the highly popular Kirghiz writer, has created considerable stir by writing non-positivistic novels like his "The White Ship," which deals with the suicide of the hero, a 7-year-old boy, because he is so disillusioned by the evil and hypocrisy of those around him.

"Where were his school friends," one engineer demanded, typically, of the magazine "Literaturnaya Gazyeta."

Much the same thing is occurring in films. In one recent popular Soviet film, often compared in the West to "The Graduate," a youth, Alik, comes to hate the compromise and mendacity used by his friends to "succeed" in life. "Every day should be lived without telling a lie," the boy says, and then everything in life goes wrong for him, as all the hypocrites blithely move on ahead. Interestingly enough, some critics greatly praised the film. "Soviet Screen's review dubbed him a "positive hero who can tangibly express the conflicts of youthful idealism versus the ability to adapt."

And much the same is true in painting, art and sculpture. In these areas it is not that they still don't employ approved styles, because they do. "Painters have to do certain things for public consumption," one artist told me. "So you go before the committee and every one changes things so much you wouldn't recognize your mural design as yours." But in the privacy of their own studios and in the privacy of their own souls, they create what they want.

Today many, many of them are creating, not only the long-forbidden abstract paintings and sculptures, but madonnas, icons and suffering Christs. "Socialist realism," scoffed one artist in Odessa to the other. "I don't know what that is, do you?" His friend guffawed. "We create many styles," the other man said, "We don't use that word any more because nobody knows what it is." He had a studio filled with things he had painted for himself.

Of course, they cannot sell these art works to the state. However, today they can sell them to private parties and they can sometimes exhibit them in outlying buildings of the cities — a remote technical institute, for instance — where their friends and other interested persons can see them. And, of course, they hang what they want in their homes. Which means, in a strange way, that here, too, what really means something to people is what they do privately — on their own and in their own homes. By its inability and unwillingness to keep up with the sophisticated interests and passions of its best people, the Soviet state has driven them into privatism and individualism and, in culture particularly, made the collective aspects of the state irrelevant to its most creative people.

In effect, the new and original literature and art, while still proscribed officially, is housed within the individual, and, as well, is moving slowly in from the edges of society to the center of society. It is that anomaly, a noose of free expression, that is sure to draw tighter and tighter around the old, hard socialist realism core, until it eventually leaves it for what it always truly was: a dead and lifeless corpse.

It seems impossible, too, that there could be more than a temporary regression, for styles are changing rapidly in everything, including the public arts like architecture and design, leaving a people on all levels with a much higher standard of taste which will affect all areas.

In 1967, for instance, the only good modern architecture and planning I saw was in the Vilnius, Lithuania, where a new section, Girmunai, was done in exciting modern architecture; there were even special coop apartments for "singles" and a 22-story new Hotel Letova with a distinctly Caribbean look about it and a real old-style sauna for tourists. When I returned in 1972 Kiev had built an entire new city across the Dnieper of stunning new architecture, complete with arms of the river carved out to give each apartment complex its own beaches and boatstalls. All over the country, I was surprised to see the sudden fascination with design. Whereas, previously, never a picture was hung, now there were good new restaurants with charming variations on traditional designs, beautiful murals and sculptures in public places and even whimsical menu covers and "koktails" of cognac, liquor, syrup and *ice!*

The older Soviets seemed to me a people almost totally without any sense of fantasy in their lives and wholly without any visual sense. Art to them was either sheer virtuosity, like the Bolshoi, and thus politically and socially harmless, or else lesson-giving, like the approved socialist realist novels, plays and paintings, and thus politically edifying.

But the new generation is filled with both fantasy and a much more sophisticated visual sense. Before, they had some fantasy on the stage; now they were beginning to have it in their own lives, and to mix it with the pangs of truth as well.

As the Soviets face their next half century, some strengths and some weaknesses inform the prognosis for the future.

They live with the clear danger that most modern art and literature has been so inane, so burdened with admonishments, and so irrelevant to real life that many young Russians have lost interest in it. Over and over (the return to the past again!) young people told me, when I asked them their tastes in literature, that they were interested only in "facts" and in the 19th century writers—by 1970, a Dostoevski cult had risen to gigantic proportions. (One must remember that Dostoevski was a proscribed author during the first few decades after the revolution.) Worse, they know in their own hearts that they have given the world very nearly nothing in the arts during the Soviet period.

Their ignorance of world culture, moreover, is often so startling as to be breathtaking. Even the sensitive Tabakoff at one point said to me, "And you Americans have only two writers." He looked triumphant. "Only two." He had only been permitted to read Edward Albee and John Updike, so this brilliant actor honestly thought there were only *two* American writers.

On the positive side, there is none of the slick, sick stuff — plus the cultural relativism — that is degrading much of Western culture. What's more, they at least have a positivistic, optimistic base of ideas about man's life on which to build.

Is there going to be productive change? Is the "two cultures and two worlds" syndrome — one for the elite, one for the people — going to fuse in the future? I think so.

For despite everything, there is the undeniable march of time, which is what most of the "thaw generation" is now counting on. Russians are becoming increasingly better-educated, which makes the old, instructive stuff of art unacceptable; more and more Soviets are being allowed to open their ears and eyes to the culture of the rest of the world and, once that happens, you can't keep them down on the kolhoz. The U.S.S.R., like so many countries in the world, is still being run by an elderly generation born in the last century, but they will not live forever.

When Yevtushenko gave a speech to the quadrennial Congress of Writers in the Spring of 1971, he complained that, "My contemporaries are at the controls of cosmic ships, but the only controls they are not trusted with are our literary magazines. Everybody (who runs the Writers Union) thinks we are still children and cannot be trusted with the toys of grownups, which we may break because of inexperience."

He concluded with a thrust at relativity, by ridiculing those "who write bad poems about Vietnam while ignoring the moans of their next-door-neighbor who is ill." He was referring to Czechoslovakia, and he ended it with, "This is flight from reality and bad citizenship."

The Congress then went on to elect the Union's new leadership — a 226-man board of directors, most of whom were over 60. The 79-year-old conservative novelist, Konstantin Fedin, again headed the 45-man secretariat, but he was so feeble that week that he could not deliver the keynote address.

Time will pass. The men who fainted before Stalin will die off, a new generation will come to power, and perhaps even the dreams of men like Tabakoff will be fulfilled.

Like most young intellectuals, he thinks it is time to move on. He dreams of starting another, even newer theater in which deep psychological dramas would be given by such presently forbidden playwrights like Strindberg, Becket and Pinter. Getting to the very psychological guts of things, in effect. In the process, he might even muddle around and find a No. 3 or a No. 4 among the Americans.

He is convinced that, in the wake of Stalinism, Russian theater is about to bloom. "Due to the fact that during Stalin's leadership the intelligentsia was destroyed physically, we believe that the time for harvest has not yet come. But it will come soon."

The young Russians who are turning to the past for sustenance because the culture of the present is so dull and vapid, who worship everything Western because everything Soviet is so tiresome and who snap up theater tickets for even moderately interesting plays like "One's Own Little Island," are desperately hoping he is right.

It's well past time.

✺ Chapter Nine
A Day With Joseph Stalin

*"Paper will put up with anything
that is written on it."*

"I trust no one, not even myself."

Joseph Stalin

*9*T IS well past Joseph Stalin's time, too. It is over 20 years since
the man who ruled Soviet Russia with a hand and heart of steel died
in his Kremlin apartments, as paranoically filled with fear and
retribution in the hands of death as he had been in life. A whole
new generation has come to maturity since Nikita Khrushchev told
the world, with such astounding candor for Soviet Russia, that
Joseph Stalin had been, not the "Little Father" that the peasants
worshipped, but a macabre, maniacal figure filled and brimming
over with the "dark" qualities that have infected so much of the
spirit of Russian life since the bloody early Russian peasant
uprisings, the Mongol invasions, and the isolation of Great Russia.

Still, to understand this generation it is still crucial to understand
the life, times and spirit of Stalin — and Stalinism today. For it is
his death and the destruction of his myth that stand as the
watershed for the currents that have begun to wash clean the spirit
of *this* generation. More than anything or anyone else, it was Stalin
and his actions that have formed, contorted and to some degree
burnt clean the character, hopes and fears of the Russian youth of
today.

In the end, all their counter-ideas — their passion for the
spiritual life of man, their quest into the past, their ideological

indifference, their deep desire to know the outside world, their rewriting of the spirit of collectivism, their new individualism, their psychological bent in the arts — can be traced directly back to the influences of this one man.

Stalin, therefore, is a man who must be known and understood, and to do that one must understand Russia, for Stalin came to be the greatest 20th century advocate of the historic, ideological and spiritual mission of the Great Russian people. But to do that, one must also understand the republic of Georgia, that wild, mountainous republic where that wild mountain man was born.

The first reaction of many foreigners when they first visit Georgia is how different — how very much more pleasant — it is than Central Russia. Tbilisi, the capital, is a city that hangs, often precipitously, over a dashing Caucasus river that pours down from the mountains in a swirling cascade of foam. On the sinuously winding streets of the city, one is easily caught up in the fast tempo of the place. The people are outwardly gaier and they walk faster than persons elsewhere in the Soviet Union, who seem to move, perhaps with an accurate assessment, as though there were no place to go. Conversation is easier, and very nearly non-ideological. The mood of the streets is southern, almost Latin. There is raucous chatter and there are constant shouts in the snaking lanes of the old city, with its mottled wooden houses built in the early centuries after Christ — and this, too, is in sharp contrast to the sullen silence of most Central Russian cities.

Historically, everyone has been here at one time or another, and seldom as tourists, Turks, Persians, Mongols, Tartars, now Russians — all invaded, occupied, left their mark. The Turks had the most obvious architectural influence on the city, just as the illegitimate child always testifies mutely to the vagrant father in his face. Indelible proof of the invasion of the Turks centuries ago may be seen in the old houses of Tbilisi of the same, many-windowed woodwork as Istanbul.

But the Turks were only one of many invaders who turned the Georgians into fierce resisters and, very often, brutalized people. In the Middle Ages, in order to bury their famous Queen Tamara so that no invaders could find her body, a group of Georgians somberly accompanied her body into the mountains where another group took it, killed all the original mourners and moved on. The same strange, sanguinary "ceremony" was repeated over and over until it was certain her body would be safe. It has never been found.

But today's two and a half million Georgians — the men with long black mustaches and languorous eyes, the women with sleek, feline reticence — have lost some of this intensity. They like to enjoy life. A typical Georgian story has a husband staying out all night with "a friend." She sends cables to ten of his friends asking each one if her husband spent the night with him . . . and each one wires back quickly, "Yes."

The Georgians are also rich, because they work hard, cheat, and do things no other "socialist" would dream of. Making use of the low internal plane fares and the free markets where peasants can sell what they grow in their own private plots, Georgian farmers take their blooming fruits in bags, hop a plane to Moscow or Leningrad, sell them at exhorbitant prices ($2.50 a lb. of strawberries, $1 a head for cauliflower, $1 a lb. for old green apples), catch a plane home the same day and still ring up a tidy profit.

Beneath the undeniable charm and the public good humor and joking of the Georgians, however, are darker traits not always seen by the average visitor. Alongside the good workmanship, the affluence and the independence of the people, is a great deal of corruption and an unnatural violence that explains a great deal about the last 50 years. For instance, a major problem is how many Georgians attack policemen to steal their guns — guns are everywhere, and often used. Women still are often "kidnapped" by their fiances as part of the marriage ritual. There is an "Asiatic" (a word often used by Lenin to describe a deep depravity but never used by Stalin, who *was* "Asiatic") brutality underlying the colorful, innocent surface. And it is this pervasive brutality, exemplified in the person and mythology of Joseph Stalin, that many young Soviets are attempting to rise up from in Russia today.

My story involves one young woman tourist who saw this peculiar savagery that informs Georgian — and then Russian life — in a particularly personal way. She came to Georgia to see the historic sites and instead spent a day with Joseph Stalin.

The young American woman — Barbara Dumont — stopped for three days in Georgia on a lengthy tour throughout the Soviet Union. She was well-read, an historian, and thought of Georgia both as an historical curiosity and as a place to rest in between the difficulties of trying to work elsewhere in the Soviet Union. It seemed an interesting place to spend a long weekend. After all, it was a country that was Christianized in the 4th century — 500 year before "holy" Kievan Rus gave up its pagan gods. In its great gorges and mountainsides even today live such curiosities as the Circassian Moslems and even such peoples as the Svanethians or Khevsurs, numbering perhaps in all 8,000 and still dressing in chain metal with helmets adapted from the medieval crusaders who passed this way once on their way to Jerusalem.

Much, much later, another Georgian also started on his way through religion. In his early years, Stalin, then Joseph Djugashvili, studied with the Jesuits and was destined to be a monk. In an interview much later with the noted historian, Emil Ludwig, he was asked if he had found any good qualities among the Jesuits. "Yes," Stalin answered, "they are methodical and persevering in their work. But the basis of all their methods is spying, prying, peering into people's souls, to subject them to petty torment. What is there good in that? For instance, the spying in the dormitory. At 9 o'clock the bell rings for tea, we go to the dining hall, and when we return we find that a search has been made, and all our boxes have been turned inside out . . . What is there good in that?" Later in life, he was to find a great deal of good in that.

On her first afternoon in Tbilisi, Barbara was shopping on the main street of the city not far from her hotel, the old Hotel Tbilisi. Her blond, wholesome looks attracted men accustomed to black-haired women and several tried to induce her to stop to talk. Pleasantly but firmly, she rebuffed them all; she knew enough to be extremely cautious in a place like Tbilisi.

But once she came near to the Hotel Iberia, an elegant new hotel which she wanted to see, a nice-looking young Georgian — heavily-built but attractive in his manners — started walking alongside her. At first, she paid no attention to him and waved him away. Then he made a joke. "You should get to know us," he said, jogging to keep up with her fast pace. "We're nice. The Russians don't like us because we're rich and they're jealous. They say when a Georgian goes to Moscow and goes to the checkroom to get his coat he puts down a 20 ruble note and says, 'Never mind the coat.' " Despite herself, she smiled. Then, when they approached the hotel, he was hailed by several of his friends, who soon surrounded her in a good-natured manner. "But we're okay," one said in very American type English. "We're all journalists." At this, they took out their journalists' cards, and knowing Russian, she was able to read them. "If you don't believe us, we'll take you to see the television studio," another suggested, in an attractively innocent and open way.

Finally they convinced her to go only to the hotel coffeeshop and she and two of them sat at a table having coffee, champagne and caviar, while two others sat at the next table. It all seemed quite harmless, and the conversation was interesing. George Sulkhanizhvuili, the burly young man she had met first, had a good sense of humor and seemed to her besides to be a good example of the more open-minded, non-ideological Georgian.

"He's nice but too big," the other Georgian — a small, little man with bright black eyes, a look of continuous surprise, and a devilishly pointed chin, said once of George, shaking his head. "You should see him on television — he's all head. That's all you can get on the little tube."

George seemed to her to be unusually fair-minded. He talked very emotionally about the two Soviet astronauts who had just been killed and then said, "But I felt the same when your astronauts were killed. We are all human beings — I do not feel any differently about our people or your people."

He did, like perhaps most Georgians, seem to be very anti-Russian, and one time he even grew quite prudish about them. "They are brutes," he said, with his lips twisted in distaste. "You hear them all the time making dirty jokes about their mothers. No Georgian would do this.

"I suppose I could go abroad now," he went on, "but I don't really want to, the way you have to go. You march around in a group and sit in a bus and someone says, 'There on the left . . . and there on the right . . . ' I'd rather stay here."

After an hour and a half, the two young men walked her the two blocks to her hotel, still laughing and joking, and George suggested he drive with her, her Georgian woman guide Ia, and their chauffeur the next day to see Gori, Stalin's birthplace. "Why not?" she thought to herself, "He's good company." Besides, Ia, a slim young woman geography teacher, with dark glimmering eyes, assured her that she knew him "well." "He's very well known here as a television commentator," she assured Barbara, "A fine fellow,"

The next day the tour group started out at 10 o'clock across the lush Georgian countryside — over golden, close-cropped mountains and valleys carved by meandering streams. The villages were picturesque, the orchards pregnantly heavy with every kind of ripe and robust fruit.

After two hours' driving, they came to Gori, an industrial new town of 200,000 people. It was almost indistinguishable from all the other patterned cities of the U.S.S.R., except for the central square. That, like so few things in the Soviet Union, was unique.

In the midst of a long parkway which stretched out half a mile, with low pine trees forming a parade line on both sides, stood the tiny wooden hovel that was Joseph Djugashvili's birthplace. You couldn't see the roof of the house because the entire remembrance was covered with a second roof of yellow stone which was held up, somewhat in the manner of a very poor man's Greek temple, by pillars all the way around.

Created many years ago by Lavrenti Beria, Stalin's loathed secret police chief, this odd superstructure reminded Stalin's daughter, Svetlana, when she saw it in 1951, of one of the lesser underground railway stations in Moscow. As for Stalin's mother, when she was brought to see it, she is said to have uttered a vulgar but precise Georgian word and to have quickly returned to her simple home in Tbilisi.

Inside the house, Ia pointed proudly to the simple accoutrements — a bed, a table, a stool, a chair — for Stalin's father had been only a simple cobbler. There were pictures of Stalin as a young man, when he was a seminary student and when his natural fanaticism was steeped in the passionate peasant Catholicism of the Georgian church. He was handsome, dark-eyed, terribly serious, this Joseph Djugashvili. It was later, during the revolution, that he abandoned his real name and took the name Stalin, which means in Russian "man of steel." The aptness of *this* designation is one of the few things about him that no one has argued.

Behind the house, they entered the Stalin museum, a huge, two-story building made of the same golden-colored stone. A curious building — Oriental-looking, with its Venetian windows and its ornate crenelated trim. Coming in the front door, they faced a huge statue of Stalin at the top of the entrance stairs. Visitors had brought small bouquets of flowers, which they placed around the feet.

Looking above the statue, Barbara saw engraved Stalin's words: "I have always been a student of Lenin's, and that is all I ever want to be."

(But no where in the museum was there any note of Lenin's warning in his final "testament", written in 1923 before his death, in which he recommended Stalin be brought down as head of the party. "Stalin is too rude," he wrote, "and this fault, entirely supportable in relation to us Communists, becomes unsupportable in the office of general secretary of the party. Therefore, I propose to the comrades to find a way to remove Stalin from that position . . . " Nor did she find anything about the months when Lenin lay dying and Stalin held him and Krupskaya, his wife, virtually prisoner in the Kremlin, while he destroyed all of Lenin's plans and persistently telephoned Krupskaya, berating her with foul curses.)

Inside the museum, there were letters, photographs, school records, pictures of the war, and many, many pictures of the man of steel. There were photos of him heroically side by side with Nikita Khrushchev, his successor as leader of the Soviet Union.

(But nowhere could Barbara find even a mention of Khrushchev's denunciation of Stalin at the 20th party congress and his documentation about the millions Stalin killed.)

At the end of the museum, there were gifts to Stalin from leaders and countries all over the world — huge plates, gifts of silver, rugs with his cunning Georgian face (which seemed to grow more like a jungle cat's as it grew older) woven into them by loyal Central Asians. Many of these, curiously enough show him shoulder-to-shoulder with his "close friend" General Sergei Ordzhonikidze, the handsome, well-loved Georgian Bolshevik.

(Barbara knew that most Soviets still did not know that Stalin had sent several NKVD men to Ordzhonikidze with a revolver — either commit suicide at home or die in the cellars of the Lubyanka prison! After bidding farewell to his wife, Ordzhonikidze shot himself in the presence of the secret police. But nothing was left to chance. A Kremlin doctor was waiting in the next room to certify the death by heart failure, and Ordzhonikidze was buried with full honors, while a "stricken" Stalin looked on. And of course, he was not alone. In the last years of the 1930s, two thirds of the top officers of the Red Army were killed in purges directed by Stalin, thus leaving the country at an unspeakable disadvantage when the Nazis invaded.)

As they left the museum, Barbara fell silent, and this seemed to disturb Ia. "We think he did more good than bad," Ia said suddenly. Was even silence in the face of Stalin's memory not enough?"

George had been quiet all day. He was well, even elegantly, dressed, with a Western-style wide tie, a striped shirt and a suit that was in good taste. He had gone his way, studying everything with an apparently unfeigned interest. It occurred to Barbara once, as they looked at the house, that he was probably the best-mannered young man she had met in Russia.

But now he had an idea. "Let's go to the country," he said. "Let me take us to dinner . . . "

Ia's cautious eyebrows rose for just a minute. But George said appealingly, "It's my friend. I'm the god-father of their child. He is chairman of a kolhoz and they'll be happy to have us for dinner."

They drove into the Georgian countryside, into that robust abundance of apples, grapes and peaches, to a typically huge and even affluent Georgian farmhouse. The orchards were heavy with fruits of every kind and frangrance, and the houses were the largest Barbara had seen anywhere in the Soviet Union. They were perfectly square, made of plain brick and wood. Nothing very decorative about them, but the size was impressive. Inside, there was some heavy, nondescript furniture scattered around a front room big enough to be a ballroom. The walls were painted an eye-shattering bright red. There was an upright piano and on it stood . . . the omnipresent picture of Joseph Djugashvili.

Dinners like this in Russia, even outside of Georgia but particularly inside it, take on a peculiar rhythm of their own. There is a point-counterpoint of eat and toast and drink and joke and eat and toast and drink that leads ever on to a higher level of joviality. But it was always forced joviality and it was always forced drinking.

After the dinner had started, the husband, a husky, swarthy farmer, introduced the counterpoint by raising a toast of home-made wine "to the friendship between Stalin and Roosevelt." "They greatly respected each other" he said, and "that shows the Americans and the Georgians are friends," He raised his two-foot-long animal's horn that Georgians so love to drink from, filled it with home-made wine and passed it to Barbara.

But don't you know, she wanted to ask, that he killed up to perhaps 10 or even 20 million people? She looked around the table.

They were all staring at her expectantly: husband and wife and five little pairs of children's Georgian eyes. She decided only to refuse the large horn. "It would make me sick." She pointed to the end of the table. "Please, the small horn."

So they drank to Joseph Stalin and Franklin Delano Roosevelt, but she drank from the small horn — thus satisfying those curious purposeless moralims that Americans so often cherish.

At 7:30 p.m. the group left the farmhouse for the two hours drive back to Tbilisi. For a while, they sang recent, popular American songs, and in the quiet of the moonlit night Barbara thought about many things. For all of her traveling in the Soviet Union, the "Stalin question" remained constantly in the front of her mind, nagging her thoughts and casting a shadow over the things she admired in Russia.

Some were talking about a "return to Stalinism," but she did not think this was an accurate description at all of the present state of affairs. She agreed more with a well-connected Western diplomat in Moscow who had told her, "The very idea is ridiculous. Stalinism was the absolute rule of one man, backed by a ruthless police apparatus. Today, on the contrary, we see much more of a collective rule and a gradual loosening of the reigns."

Yet, she knew, too, that there had been no real decision on the place Stalin would occupy in Soviet history.

In the philosophical faculties of the universities, they spoke, and this only occasionally, of the "oshibki" — the "mistakes" — of Stalin, using the same word one would use if one misjudged how long it would take to drive from Leningrad to Novorod.

Certainly the state and the society itself had come to no conclusion whatsoever about where his spirit should stand in their memories. "I think to this day people are still seeking new ways of development after the death of Stalin," Victor Rozov had said, always thoughtful. "This is still underway. Some people, especially in the West, thought after the death of Stalin that everything would change magically, but, to be serious, it will be very long. I personally do not believe in magic."

Certainly Stalin had been reevaluated upwards since the seismic cultural shocks of the Khrushchev revelations — recent movies had portrayed him as the pipe-smoking, benevolent father figure, always asking advice from his trusted assistants. And there still existed, among many, an unquestionable resentment of Khrushchev for his demythologizing of Stalin. The workers — the Russian "hard hats" — tended to yearn for the days of Stalin, when there was order and when the "intellectuals" were not allowed to "raise hell."

To the common people, Stalin was their "vozhd," their Russian "fuhrer." He was the non-lineal but directly emotional successor of the czar, their Communist "little father," who would save them from error, protect them in war, punish them for their own good and take care of them just as the czar had . . . and just as the czar had *not*.

Who would not resent and even hate someone like Khrushchev, who destroyed the security of fealty to the "vozhd," who demanded the rigors of knowing the truth, and who tore away the comforting curtains of the past, even if they were a shroud? Discarding Stalin meant having to grow up into thinking, individualized, self-regulating human beings.

So when it got down to an argument over how many millions of his own people Stalin had murdered — after bringing many of them out in court to force them to admit even to Stalin's own murders — no one cared too much except the small, self-exacting intelligentsia. To determine whether he killed (between the purges, the destruction of the kulaks and the deportation of minority peoples) 1 million or 5 million or perhaps even 20 million of his own best people is, to the common and not highly-principled Russian mind, about as edifying and worthwhile as trying to count the angels dancing on the head of a pin.

They reached the capital about 10 p.m. and dropped Barbara off at her hotel. George walked her to her door, said he would call the next morning, and left. As she prepared for bed and packed some of her things for the trip back to Moscow in another day, she felt, despite all, that it had been a pleasant and (unusual for Russia) an uncomplicated day. Finding her phone not working — a common thing in the old Soviet hotels, at one point she went out to the floor woman's desk to make a phone call to her Moscow guide downstairs. They chatted for a few minutes, rather animatedly, and she returned to her room.

At 10:30 p.m., there was a knock on the door. First she called out, "Who is it?" But sensing that she couldn't hear through the heavy doors and thinking vaguely it was probably her Moscow guide, she opened the door an inch to see who was there.

The person at the door was George Sulckhanizhvuili. But just as she saw his face — in that single moment — he also pushed the door inward, violently, pinning her behind it. "Nyet," she cried out, angrily, "nyet . . . nyet . . . " Within seconds, he had locked the door behind him and stood facing her.

At first, Barbara was unable to speak, partly from astonishment at the extraordinary change in his appearance. Half an hour or forty-five minutes before — what was it? — he had been as he had been all day: tastefully dressed, a perfectly decent young man of 28 with impeccable manners, totally in control of himself and blessed with a rather fey sense of humor.

And now . . . now his face was contorted. Now his skin was flushed. His jacket was slightly askew, and his tie and the top of his shirt were open. His eyes, which were large and which he often purposefully crossed when he told jokes to give himself an absurd and mischievous expression, had taken on a strangely savage look. His mouth was set in a cruel expression that was so different from the slightly bemused and tolerant expression it had had all day that she wondered if she were seeing the same man.

She thought, for a moment, that she was seeing a man who had snapped — who had suddenly switched into another person. Later she would remember an Austrian officer from World War II, one who was anti-Hitler, say of the Slavs: "They're like that. Suddenly something snaps and they become raging beasts. During the war, they were very kind to children — they never fired into children, as the Nazis did. But they were terribly brutal with women."

He held her tightly by the left wrist, simply staring at her. Though she was not in any way a hysterical woman, she began to feel a hysteria rising within her. "Get out, go," she said, still calmly, in Russian.

"No," he said, with a determination strange for the wildness of his expression. "No, I have come to stay." Then he ripped her nightgown down the front.

Impressions and questions flew through her head, one after the other, in the few moments before he began to hit her. How far down the hall was the floor woman? Why had she allowed him to come to the room, when no one is supposed to be allowed onto the floors?

Could she get to the window, which was open? What then? Jump two stories? There was a bottle that the farm family had given her. It was on the table — could she get to it and hit him with it? She knew you could kill people with bottles and she wanted to kill him. Was there any way to trick him into leaving? Was this a provocation — a setup? The Russians were known for doing this to visiting professional women . . .

Then, almost without thinking, because there seemed nothing else to do, instinctively she began screaming. She screamed as loud as she could scream, which was loud, and she saw the rage rise until his large face had turned an engaged purple. Then she didn't see but felt his hand come down on her face. The blow was so stunning, it knocked her glasses off (they careened like a spinning coin across the shiny floor) and he threw her hard against a desk, while he continued to hold onto her wrist.

When she was able to see him again, she saw and felt the excitement rising in him. He liked this. Perhaps this was what he had come for?

"I want a drink," she said. Perhaps he would let her go to the table and she could get the bottle.

A deep, knowing growl came up from his stomach. "Oh, no, oh no," he shouted, "*I'll* get it for you." Still holding her tightly by the arm, he moved the two of them a few feet across the room, poured a few sips of the sickly sweet green liqueur into a glass and offered it to her. She took a few sips and he put it down.

Then she screamed again and he hit her again. This time nearly knocking her unconscious. She was growing desperate and he was growing enraged at her resistance. "Pig," he started to scream at her in English and then in German "pig . . . " "schweinehundt."

"Tomorrow the police, tomorrow the police," she repeated.

"What police?" he said, laughing a nasty laugh. "I'm with the television."

Once more she screamed, now hardly thinking what she was doing, and he hit her half a dozen times, spinning her body back and forth, hitting the desk and the table and the bed, wrenching her head, until she could barely see the room or him, his teeth bared like a wild dog's and his eyes heavily dilated. He had clearly reached a peak of emotional and physical excitement. "This," he shouted, showing her a fist that could easily break open her skull if he hit her with it.

He forced her to sit down on the bed, but he didn't touch her. Strangely, he said, almost appealingly, "You want me."

"I don't want you , I don't want you," she spat out in Russian.

Then, almost rationally he asked, "Why not?"

"I don't like you."

For a moment he seemed to be thinking. Or was it that whatever liquor or hashish he had had was reasserting itself above the other passions. Finally, he spurted out, almost sleepily. "If you don't want me, I'm going to go."

"I don't want you," she said softly, in order not to break the mood or irritate him.

He stood up and pulled her by the wrist. "I'll go if you promise me two things," he said, as if they had been having the most casual of conversations.

"Of course," she answered.

"If I come to the United States, you'll sleep with me? And tomorrow we'll go swimming?"

"Of course," she said, as if it were the most natural thing in the world.

"You promise?" His eyes were getting heavy.

"Yes, of course. Tomorrow at 3."

"Tomorrow at 3," he repeated, like a parrot. Then he let go of her wrist for the first time since he had entered the room a half hour before, unlocked the door, and, without another word, left.

Unbelieving, she stared at the door. Then she ran to it, sprang upon the key and relocked it. She want to the window and, though it was warm outside and no one could climb up two stories, locked it. For a few minutes she sat on the bed and tried to breathe again. Then she got dressed and went to the room of her guide from Moscow and told her the whole story. The guide was enraged; she had been with Barbara for weeks and knew she did not invite this sort of thing. "Tomorrow morning we'll decide what to do," she finally said, choking on her fury. "We'll get this man's job — that's the least thing."

By morning, Barbara's ankle and leg were swollen to twice its size. They were bruised so much she could not walk on them. She didn't remember where, in the melee she had hit them — or on what — but it would be a full month before she would be able to walk again.

Her Moscow guide, who was Jewish, was still infuriated . . . but others did not feel the same.

Ia appeared and sat in the room with "I told you so" eyes and pursed virgin's lips. "I'm sure he is sorry," she said to Barbara, her eyes veiled and accusing. To the Moscow guide, she said privately, "She deserved it. She brought it on." Why? "No, she didn't *do* anything but she talked to him and she allowed him to buy food for her — in Georgia, that means a woman has agreed . . . Then when he came to her room and she rebuffed him, he had every reason to be angry." And to act as he did? "Yes."

The few other Russians whom Barbara related this story to, mostly in order to get their reaction, all agreed that it was a common thing. Why, after all, are Voznesensky and Yevtushenko always writing poems about wife-beating? It's an old custom, even more fun if the woman is not your wife, and one of the few that have with no modifications survived the Soviet period. The Moscow guide finally advised Barbara that, despite her physical wounds, nothing could be done. "They will turn it against you," she said, speaking with considerable honesty. "Obviously he bribed the floor woman and others, so you will have no one on your side. They will make something dirty of it. You are better not to carry it through." American officials were interested in hearing the details of the story, but they, too, advised against action.

Nor did George apparently think he had done anything untoward. The next afternoon, he telephoned at 3 p.m. He wanted to know if she wanted to go swimming. She didn't.

In retrospect, she began to see and to understand several things. She began to realize that what Westerners think of as crime is often seen by the Russians simply as folk custom and that it is thought of as quite natural behavior. Violent physical misuse of others is as Russian as Chicken Kiev.

Then, in the midst of her disgust, she began to have a strange, even somewhat mystic feeling about that day, as if she had seen in one brief, intensified vision what was behind all the brutality, grossness, falsity and hypocrisy which is Russia at its worst: the dark butcher which the old are trying to forget and the young are trying, not to forget, but to rise phoenix-like from.

Perhaps I should add that I know this story to be true. Barbara was me.

❧ Part II
The Young Russians

❧ Chapter Ten
The True Believers

"Russia is a village. Moscow is the facade;
we have always needed facades. But the truth of this country
is still in the village."

A Moscow historian quoted by "An Observer"

$\mathcal{M}$ OSCOW University is the palace where the Kremlin dauphins are brought from all the muddy, snowed-in villages and dingy, cabbage-reeking communal apartments and brightly-colored and carved wooden houses of the world that is Russia to be trimmed and tailored for the court of the Communist system. Standing imposingly on the gentle slopes of the Lenin Hills on the outskirts of the city of Moscow, it overlooks the city — and the world — with a haughteur as powerful and as amusing as an iron anvil.

Nowhere is there a university quite like Moscow University. Its towers piercing the sky, built in the wedding cake style of late Stalinism, and housing up to 15,000 persons, it is a world and not simply a school: the symbol of the new state. It is also the place where the most ambitious, blinkered, unquestioning, authority-accepting young people of the Soviet system come to get started on their own peculiar stairway to the stars.

Perhaps nowhere is the isolation of Russian youth from the youth of the rest of the world more notable than here; it struck me like a lightning bolt one afternoon. I was catching a taxi at the "cabstand" near the American embassy in 1967 when two rather obviously American girls, dressed neatly but with a harried look in their eyes, suddenly appeared beside me. "Come along," I said, and soon we were all careening through the streets of downtown Moscow.

They were frustrated and they were angry. Their disgust with the society they were leaving boiled over and out of them — They simply could not contain it any longer. It was their last week and the Russians were making it as difficult as humanly possible for them to leave. Like so many foreign students, whether from America, Africa or Asia, they had come to Russia leftists and were leaving rightists.

"This is the worst society you have ever seen," the girl named Peggy said, with a stunned look about her. "The students at M.U. are so vulgar — they push, they shove, they grab you in the halls. The only time they laugh at anything is when they're making fun of someone."

"The drinking . . . " Marilyn inserted, as our cab hurled itself around a corner. "They drink to gain unconsciousness. There is no sense of social fun in our sense. Either there's this grim sadness of Russia or this flight to oblivion." She hmpphed, "I can't stand either one."

"Do you know there's no word in Russian for privacy," Peggy went on, "or for efficiency. They don't know what either is. In the university our rooms are 6 by 9, with two beds. Some house couples with two children. There are only supposed to be 11,000 there, but probably 15,000 live there. All the babushkas, too."

It was apparent that I had caught them, after a year studying in Moscow, at precisely that moment when all their frustrations were erupting in one mammoth explosion. "And the corruption is incredible," Marilyn interrupted. "Everywhere you go sales people in the shops and restaurants are selling food out the back door. One doctor told a foreign student he wouldn't treat him except for one of his art books which cost . . . " She paused for emphasis and continued, "*fifty dollars* in the United States and sells for *four hundred dollars here.*"

"The Russian students," the other girl went on, her face contorted, "they know what's going on. But most don't care. They don't want to do anything that might harm their chances within the system. Oh, they say the system needs changes, but they don't want to rock the boat. My roommate has a suitcase full of forbidden books and manuscripts. But she really still thinks that Moscow is the center of the world. Do you know that she stops talking to me if other Russian students come in our room — she tells them she never talks to me."

"And what they think of America! The ignorance is unbelievable. They think all Americans are either racists, millionaires or hungry. They think we're exceptions. They can't understand how we could be excited about individual candidates in elections. Their Supreme Soviet is so high no one knows them. There's really nobody to attack — there's no place to start."

"And the classes . . . It's virtual chaos. Everybody talks at once and nobody listens." A spirit of intellectual inquiry? "Ha! It is so ridiculous, you can't even think about it . . . "

The conversation went on like this, with both girls venting their anger and disgust, pent-up for a year, to a countrywoman met at random in a strange and in many ways devilishly difficult country. When we reached my hotel and I got out of the cab, I watched their two brown-haired heads disappearing toward Lenin hills in the taxi. I was struck more even than previously by the multiple and wondrous ways the Russians have of antagonizing nearly everybody.

A few days later I went out myself to take a first-hand look at the "big U."

Because absolutely no outsiders are permitted inside without permission, in order to get in, I walked, my head high, my gaze haughty, past the guarding "babushka" at the gate as though I belonged — as though I were a Russian. Luckily, there's a good deal of sloppiness in Russia. She didn't question me. Inside, the mixture of styles and smells struck me like those of a damp, musty Middle East Marketplace. There were vast inner rooms with fluted columns and there was a maze of dark, dingy hallways smelling of cabbage. The basement housed a delicatessen, a shoe repair shop and a laundry room, where an eternally querulous babushka vented her wrath on anyone who wandered in. There were movie theaters, where even old American films were shown, and bulletin boards where, in 1971, petitions to "free Angela Davis" were hung. Two Americans signed one of them that year, creating a tremendous row with the embassy.

In this cafeteria of services for the privileged young elite of the Soviet Union, "everything" is available, but the students do part of the job. In return for their 30 to 40 ruble stipends each month, they are expected to take turns at monitor duty in the halls and at cleaning the kitchens, where they can cook their own food. They are expected to attend Komsomal meetings on their own floor, and they are literally dragged out to them if they forget.

Then, when exams come after four or five or six years, 70 questions are given to them beforehand. They have several days to prepare these before, dressed in their best suits, the girls carrying flowers, they go in to take their oral exams before a panel of professors. Beforehand, there is panic. When they come out, they shout out their grades; and everybody shouts in answer — either in glee or in condolence.

As I wandered, alone *and illegal*, through the halls, as the students of old M.U. — the elite — bumped and pushed and shoved and jabbed me in the ribs without ever so much as a word of apology, I was thinking to myself of how dull even this was, to our Western taste. Yet to the Russians, this was the most fascinating place in the world.

This — Moscow — is the center of the world to these young people on the way up, and most of them particularly look down on Leningrad, for it is "not really Russian" and "not really Soviet," like Moscow. They know that the vast, all-encompassing city plan of Moscow, which before 1980 will clear away much of the charming old part of the city and replace it with vast symbolic open spaces and huge monuments, will mark Moscow forever as the epi-center of Communism. Even so, there is a strange spirit about Moscow — an anti-metropolitan spirit, a spirit still of the village. Perhaps that is the key to the odd, unfinished air that hangs over Moscow University. Perhaps that is why, too, in the winter there are so many suicides here — young people jumping from the high tower.

In the years 1961 - '62 - '63, M.U. had been the center of the new boldness and the expression of the new euphoria that bloomed in the wake of de-Stalinization.

In those years, the school was alive and abuzz with student clubs — ostensibly it could be a music club, a gardening club or a literary club. But all, in reality, were, to one extent or another, political. Students spoke up freely about anything that was troubling them, even going so far as to put on the spot with the most irreverent challenges members of the party's Central Committee who came to answer their questions.

William Taubman, an American student who attended M.U. in those years, described one of these meetings in his book, "The View from Lenin Hills." The member of the Central Committee opened the meeting, saying, "I want to speak with you tonight frankly and objectively about whatever is on your mind."

Soon the students were asking whether a group of prominent artists and intellectuals had sent a petition to the Central Committee "opposing any rehabilitation of Stalin at the 23rd Party Congress." When he denied it, a boy cried out, "If the aritsts didn't sign it, let them deny it publicly themselves." The questions came hot and fast. "Do party officials get special privileges that ordinary citizens don't receive? Don't they . . . buy special goods in special stores." The more the speaker denied what everyone knew, the more riotous, undisciplined and openly disdainful the audience became.

By the end of the '60s. most of this was past at M.U., if not at other universities and institutes. As one embassy official described the state of M.U. in 1971, "the heavies are in control again." They were, indeed.

The controls were reinstated with full force after this brief period of laxity. These "controls" were aptly described by Maria Vovchok, a 22-year-old who defected while on a cultural exchange trip to London. "There were ten people in my group at the university," she said, "and we not only had our own informer, but we knew exactly who he was. With such a system, the authorities know all about any protest long before it gets organized." The student informers had no real choice about it, she went on. "If a student is 'invited' by the KGB to collaborate, it is difficult to refuse. Such a refusal would arouse suspicion in itself and might harm the student's academic prospects. On the other hand, collaboration may help a student's career and may even get a mediocre student through his exams."

It is highly doubtful, however, that intrusions such as this seriously disturb the great mass of students at Moscow U. For the careful selection process — Komsomol work, good grades, never a blotch on your political record — that brings a student here and dubs him party-bound, also weeds out the disaffected. What are the characteristics of this party elite, which is highly different than, say, the intellectual elite or the average young working group?

Perhaps Georgii Fedotov, the Russian philosopher, has given the best description of this type of Soviet man: "He is robust, physically and mentally; he lives according to orders, dislikes thought and doubt and appreciates practical knowledge and experience. He is very ambitious and rather hard-hearted toward other peoples' suffering, a prerequisite of a Soviet career. He is willing to work himself to exhaustion, and his highest ambition is to give his life for the community — for the party or homeland, as the case may be."

Who was Fedotov? That is the key: Fedotov was an Orthodox philosopher who, early in this century, went into exile in the West. After ennumerating these characteristics of the typical Soviet party man, he added, "All these features are reminiscent of the ruling class of Muscovy in the 16th century!"

Another outside and objective analysis of the types of young leaders the system chooses comes from a prominent Sovietologist in the U.S. who prefers to remain nameless. In characterizing the students he studied with at M.U. in 1958-59 — and these groupings seem still to hold today — he found "the satisfied"\ to be by far the largest, but he felt that "Their imaginative capacities have atrophied." He also found "the bored", who were "anti-social rather than political deviants"; the "political activist," nearly all of whom "seemed almost obsessed by some personally-experienced, war-connected, violent disruption of normal life"; "the discontented," who were dissatisfied with everything from "the inadequacy of consumer goods to job discontent to the rigidity of intellectual controls"; "the disaffected," who had "generalized and politicized their discontent to the point where only fundamental alterations in the Soviet political structure could satisfy them"; and the "inner-emigres," who were "wholly isolated" and whose views lacked "discipline, coherence and refinement."

Certainly the types of people who came out of M.U. — and other "top" schools like it — were often, to our way of thinking, cynical and abrasive. Alexander Backaloff, a journalist in Riga, was a typical case, as he insisted to me that movies of social protest were made in the United States only because they showed the way that everything really was. "If one person was poor and 20 million were rich, do you think the 20 million would fight for one?" he demanded. When I told him they often did, he looked puzzled, then cynically unbelieving. "Why should they?" he asked.

But — how prevalent is the "true believer" type in Soviet society today? How does his existence and how do his passions blend with or conflict with the other, *relatively* free-thinking and seeking types that are also growing in the U.S.S.R.?

My judgment — and, of course, any estimate is simply a limitedly informed and finally intuitive guess — is that probably 10 percent of the youth population is made up of this type of fanatic true believer. And it must be remembered that many of them become "true believers" not only out of faith but also out of the imperatives of ambition, for the system carefully cuts off from further advancement anyone who does not show the requisite enthusiasm and faith. Here, if you fail in the exams of loyalty to government, you do not fall back into private industry or go West or move to another country. To be thrown out of Moscow U. is to be thrown off the ladder·to the stars.

"The system not only picks people who play the game, but drives intelligent people into other areas. This is real control," says one Soviet specialist.

It would seem, then, depressingly clear that little will change with this new generation; that simply a new band of bureaucrats are being trained to keep their eyes straight ahead in the towers of M.U. But this is not true.

Even the disillusioned young Americans at M.U. admitted they saw a real generation gap even there "in the kids wanting to read books. They go to their parents and complain to them about not being able to read certain things, and their parents say those writers are traitors, that they shouldn't even want to read them. There's a real difference here. The older generation thinks it fought the war and rebuilt the country and that the younger ones don't appreciate anything they've been given."

What also gives me the feeling of slow but steady change, is that so many of the "satisfied" or the true believers" — the people at the very center of things in the U.S.S.R. — turned out to be, once they were out of M.U. and places like it, people who, while they continued to believe, were beginning to be far more complex and elaborated people than one might have thought at the time.

Take a man in his mid-30s, whom I talked with a good deal. "It is difficult for Americans to understand how we feel about Lenin," he told me one afternoon as we walked around Moscow. "Fifty years ago, this was the most underdeveloped country in Europe. My grandfather was a serf. Then after the revolution, my father was able to go to school and now I have a good position. Americans have a different history. You never had a war on your territory since the Civil War. You had a natural evolution, but we didn't."

This was 1967 and Voznesensky had just sent an angry letter to the government complaining he could not go to the U.S. "I think Voznesensky made a mistake in sending the letter," this man said, "but they made a mistake, too. They should have told him why he was denied a vista instead of just saying, 'No visa.' Of course, he is an intelligent man. He knows enough to call the embassy and find out. Most likely it was some little bureaucrat from old times. People don't realize it but it is often the party people who are very liberal. It's the little men who are holding things back." What is changing? "Minds," he said excitedly.

When we talked about "socialist realism," he said, "Formerly this meant only describing actions. It denied any psychological content. Now we say you have to relate it to man's work. If he's a millionaire, you have to show he's a millionaire, but he can also be a good family man. Now there are many kinds of realism."

And as to Russian inferiority, he maintained that "Russians no longer say we are best, we do everything best. This was very foolish."

But if we are to talk about the "true believers" among Russian youth, we have to note several other types besides the up-and-coming party men. There are, for instance, the innocent, wholesome young people who genuinely feel that Soviet society is inevitably progressing toward the perfect, Communist society. In a conversation with four Komsomol members at the University of Bokhara, Karen Saudovich Saidov put it this way: "Now we aspire to grow new men, new persons, a new Communist society and new Communist relations between people. Your papers say that the Capitalist and the Socialist system are very close, but this is not right. In the future in Communist society there will be no thieves, because all of future society will consist of new persons with new character. It will not be necessary to have a militia. Of course, we must have one now because we are surrounded by Capitalism.

Perhaps nowhere is the genuine idealism of this type of young person found, even today, more than in the new cities in the wilderness of Siberia and the far North. In the beginning, these challenges and sacrifices called for a type of young person who wanted to sacrifice himself for his faith. But even this is changing today. Today, according to Dr. Lisovsky's surveys, most young people go to the virgin islands or to faraway projects for adventure, for the extra money earned, to be with their friends and to get advancement and professional experience more quickly.

Perhaps Bratsk, a "new city" in the Siberian vastness just north of Irkutsk, represents this pioneering spirit better than any place, for here, from 1956 on, young Russians came by paths through the forest to live in tents while they built the largest hydroelectric dam in the world.

The town itself is a mixture of forms. There are shacktowns of wooden huts that look like "old" Siberia. Then you come to nicer little wooden houses with carved and painted trimmings in more traditional Siberian styles. And beyond, in several separate cities separated by forests, are the big new sections of the city with standardized, prefabricated, three- and four-story monotonously similar apartment buildings.

Bratsk, today with 120,000 residents of an average age of 27 years and the highest birth rate in the Soviet Union, is only one of 928 "new cities" built since the revolution — and the difficulties have been legion.

"There were thousands of snakes on the cliffs in the beginning," Elena Rogozinska, a young guide, said, reminiscing. "The bears kept coming in because they never knew people before and had no fright. But the biggest problem was the mosquitos. You couldn't sleep without nets. People even went to dances with nets over them. But when the rapids were covered with water, the mosquitos left."

"Why did I come to Bratsk?" asked Dr. Anatoli Verezuk, a big, handsome doctor from the Ukraine who now works at the Bratsk hospital.

"The romanticism of the city drew me there. Everybody wants to see Bratsk. But, also, you get much more practice here than in other parts of the country. You show whether you are capable or not. You prove yourself. Conquering the wilderness? We do more than speak of it."

"Ten years ago, we could only hear the noise of the locomotives," another doctor, Yaschenko Vladimir Georgievich, chimed in. "It was a very unknown place. Now when you go out, people always say, 'Are you from Bratsk? You are so far away.' They think you are heroes."

The idealism of Bratsk is nothing like the American idealism of fighting for free speech or thought. It is typical Russian idealism: the idealism of sacrificing to build concrete things — the idealism of bricks.

But besides these innocent, trusting, infinitely cheerful types of true believers, like the youngsters in Bokhara, and the "idealists of action" of Bratsk, there is another type of true believer who believes not out of love of his fellow man nor for the privilege of serving society but for hate of everything outside of himself and in order to facilitate his own aggressive desires for power.

The Russian I knew who most personified the obnoxious traits of this type of man was a Novosti correspondent named Yuri who saw me through Lithuania and Estonia, the two areas which still hate the Russians so much the Russians fear to leave visiting correspondents alone there for what they might find.

At first I thought Yuri, who was a tall, dark-haired man of about 30 with the pinched, tense eyes of so many Soviet bureaucrats, was just another thug. He hung about with a surly look and a snarling manner. But soon I began to wonder if he were quite sane. In a restaurant at the airport in Vilnius, we had stopped to eat on a delay of several hours and, when a man at the next table stood up to greet the headwaiter, Yuri said, with that peculiarly Soviet expression of sarcasm on his face. "You'd never see that in the 'States. It's 'get me this and make it quick.' "

Then he went into an odd story which, at first, I did not know how to judge. "I was in the hotel in San Francisco — the big one on the hill with the bar on top. The director had taken us up. Then the drinks came, he signed the check." He looked at me triumphantly.

"So what?" I said, trying to figure out what he was aiming at.

"He can go in any time and drink vodka and not pay for it. Then there were girls in scanty costumes. Very pretty. They don't get paid. They pay him — he told me."

When I tried to explain to him that everybody signs checks in the United States and that the part about the girls was ridiculous, he just laughed that sarcastic, knowing, ignorant laugh that this type of bureaucrat employes in place of rationality.

Then, suddenly, he admitted of his own accord that he had never been to the 'States. "But I know everything about your country," he said surely. "I can imagine everything. Just the way it is. I know more about it than you. Who are the five most powerful men in Washington? What is the highest building?"

Soon after this, I tried to ask our waiter to sit down, and have a drink with us and he grew furiously angry. "Never do that," he shouted at me. "The man's on the job. It wouldn't be proper."

Yuri, of course, is not one of the new leaders — he is a journalist — but he has considerable influence. What's more, even many of the younger leaders, while they might not behave in *quite* such a free-form vulgar fashion, are actually often much like him in their dealings with other human beings, Soviets as well as foreigners.

But who *are* the new leaders? Who will be chosen from the true believers at M.U., the center of the world? What will they be like?

The amazing thing is that, of the 20 million supervisors of the labor force, of the 600,000 in the government, of the 12.8 million members of the party, of the 300,000 apparatchiki, of the 24 on the politburo, no one, but no one, knows who or what is likely to arise from among them to be the new leaders of the Soviet state. "That level of leadership is certainly there, probably among the deputy heads of departments, but we don't even know the names of these men," one diplomat in Moscow said, simply.

A few Soviet specialists are outrageously optimistic. Before his death, the late Maurice Hindus wrote, "This writer is convinced that a new leadership, younger, bolder, more far-seeing than Khrushchev's successors, with an outlook at least as unorthodox as that of Tito and his like-minded associates, will come to power through a palace revolution, as did Stalin, as did Khrushchev, as did Brezhnev and Kosygin."

But most are not only curious but pessimistic. Many of the few presently visual "younger" leaders are also hard-liners. The next party generation is made up of 50ish men like: Alexander N. Shelepin, the former secret police chief and Komsomol leader; Dmitri S. Polyanski, party ideologist; wily infighter Kiril T. Mazurov; the fanatic puritanical Mikhail A. Suslov; and the 40ish Konstantin Katushev, known as a tough negotiator and the protege of Brezhnev. These men are called by many critical younger Russians the "ominous generation." Since most were in their early twenties in the days of the great purges, the young often argue that they are even more cynical and inured to suffering than the

Khrushchevs and Malenkovs and Molotovs, who at least were with the revolution in its early, more idealistic days.

This does not seem, however, to be true. Soviet specialist Robert Conquest has typified the new time and the new leaders: "The aim is different but above all the mood is different — a timid (although sometimes panicky) mediocrity has replaced a raging will." Young people talk about the beginnings of a "psychological breakthrough" — the gradual road up from the overriding fear of the Stalin years to a feeling that perhaps they can begin to affect events themselves.

What these leaders, or the men just behind them, or the men who might spring up one day from anonymity, are likely to do is wholly impossible to say at this point — although in a general sense at the moment the struggle seems to be, not between liberals and conservatives, but between old, partially rehabilitated Stalinists and the more dynamic, ambitious younger apparatchiki or technocrats.

What *is* clear, however, is that the changes that are occuring are more likely to carry the younger leaders along with *them* than are the young leaders likely to affect the changes. They will have to react to the masses. Individual leaders in the sense of chosen Western leaders are not at all likely to arise; what is happening is that the system is unquestionably developing from the one-man Byzantine dictatorship of a Stalin to a much more highly sophisticated and genuinely collective leadership where different power groups — the military establishment, the technocrats, the managers, the scientists, the party authorities — give and take, horse trade and even court public opinion from the floors of the Kremlin. This new form of system, of course, both forms and is formed by the new generation.

Many Soviets — and foreigners — will insist that the new leaders are "just as bad as the old ones." One Russian boy said, "I know some of these people. They're worse than the old ones, just as rigid and unthinking. They like the idea that they know something nobody else knows. They don't even talk to their wives about what goes on. Under Stalin, at least you knew exactly what you could do. Now there is much more guile in making you serve the regime."

But this is over-emotional. The new leaders *are* different. They are better-educated, better-mannered, and more apt to use incentive and pursuasion when they can (although they certainly are not incapable of using force when it is necessary). They want the Soviet Union respected — they do not want its world role sullied by overreactions and overrepressions at home. They are responsive to public opinion — local and world — to a limited degree.

In the spring of 1972, I watched a prime group of these new young party leaders when they visited a rock-style bar on Chicago's Near North Side. They were a little out of place, but not much. Dressed well in the newest Western fashions, they politely listened, drank beer and comported themselves with a moderate degree of sophistication that would have been impossible even ten years ago. They even went out into the city by themselves and didn't want to offend us by saying anything critical about the United States. "I've never seen a Russian group like this one, and I've escorted many of them," their tour leader told me, with an air of astonishment. "But this is the cream of cream. They ask what they want and do what they want. They don't even have to take another one with them. This shows the degree to which they're trusted."

Part of their sophistication can be explained by the fact that students show that, among members of the Communist party recruited since 1952, specialist education and experience, particularly economic, increasingly are criteria of greater importance than the political and bureaucratic skills that were almost exclusively the route to top level leadership under Stalin. As Dr. Frederick C. Barghoorn of Yale University has written: "This emphasis on economic expertise as a criterion of leadership contrasts sharply with the different and simpler requirements of earlier eras, when Soviet leaders were at first revolutionary ideologues, and then, under Stalin, politician bureaucrats untrained in engineering and economics and, as a rule, lacking in formal higher education.

What this means is that the "kadrovniks," the party cadres who in the past often had little education and many of whom were simple thugs, gradually are being replaced by the "apparatchiks," the industrial directors and managers of the economy who are far more sophisticated, scientific and broad in their thinking.

Citing all these changes, Dr. Barghoorn sums up that "today's Soviet youth, despite the determined efforts of the Party to fill their minds with a 'two-world' outlook, will be still less receptive to the fanatical aspects of Soviet Marxism than preceding Soviet generations have been. As time passes, the fantasy world of Soviet official propaganda should seem less and less believable to the upcoming Soviet generations."

❧ Chapter Eleven
The Dropouts

"Alienation," said the speaker, a lady professor of philosophy, "is a phenomenon of capitalist society. There can be no alienation in a socialist society where men are united by patriotism, internationalism, and the struggle to build Communism."

She spoke so earnestly that I was sure she believed every word she uttered.

At question time a young man, one of the few young people in the audience, spoke up. "Are you quite sure," he asked thoughtfully, "that there is no alienation in our society?"

William Taubman, describing a lecture in Moscow
in his book about student life there,
"The View from Lenin Hills."

T HE SOVIET UNION has its dropouts, too — many of its most able young men and women who have psychically "dropped out" of the mainstream of Russian life. With touches of irony, they call themselves "spiritual emigrants," "spiritual dropouts" simply "dropouts" or "inner-emigres". They stand at polar limits to the true believers.

While they do little immediate harm to the society, neither do they take part in it (this is the only rebellion many of them can show). Shunning the total Marxist involvement demanded of them, many of them more and more are retreating into their own dim little corners of life and into their own little circles ("krushki" in Russian) of friends. Often in order to individuate themselves and live pure and ethical lives, they have dropped out of the mass and hidden in dark corners: individual atoms who cannot understand why they can't live in the sun. These young people frighten and disturb the old because they face their elders with, if not anarchy, the implicit threat of a disintegration of the mass and the destruction of the collective.

In many ways, they are the 20th century counterpart of the 19th century's "superfluous man," yesteryear's hero who lived without purpose, without roots and without faith. And they are much more dangerous to the system than the open dissenters. "After all," Andrei Sinyavsky has written, "the (dissident) was like the positive hero — clear, straightforward, and, in his own way purposeful. Only his significance was negative — to hinder the movement to the Purpose. But the superfluous man was a creature of different psychological dimensions, inaccessible to computation and regimentation. He is neither for the Purpose nor against the Purpose — he is outside the Purpose."

Everywhere I went in the Soviet Union, particularly in 1971, when purposelessness had grown dramatically, I found young people who fit into this aimless category. An artist in Riga described the privateness of the phenomenon: "A person has to create a world, and man must have time to live with himself."

Yuri Ivanovich Bulgakov, a tall, blond-haired young mathematician in Leningrad, the most "superfluous" city in Soviet terms, is one of this group. Once — in the early '60s — he was at the top of his class in the mathematics institute. Today he has taken a third rate job in a government office, and he will probably have it, and nothing more, all his life.

"I'm a simple man — a small, simple man," Yuri said one evening, as we sat in one of the parks along the Neva watching the sun set behind the waterways of the lovely old city. "I don't take part in politics. All I want to do now is to go to the forest and live there simply."

Summer was ending, and the beautiful "white nights" of the city of Peter were fading into the black days of winter. The sun, which had hovered uncertainly just behind the horizon from midnight until morning since June, was leaving the genteel old city to the growing darkness. But while it lasted, walking through the white nights was like walking through a thin veil of gauze. One didn't think about ideology here, only that there is beauty in the world . . .

and that winter darkness irrevocably followed it. Yes, it was still possible here to think of just going out into the forest . . .

"I'd build my own house with an axe." He paused and took a drink from a bottle of wine which we were illegally drinking in the park. "The problem," he began again, "is I do like minimal comforts, too, but only minimal. Many of my friends already have done this."

Why do this? I asked him. And I reminded him that all of them had highly-prized university educations, that they were therefore among the elite and that they could certainly get good and lucrative posts.

Yuri was 29 then, with restless, searching, and sometimes troubled eyes. He slouched and walked in a dreamy, unplotted way. A gentle man. Now he drew a circle in the sand of the parkway and then drew an X over it. He stared at it.

"There's no target for my life, no target for anything," he said finally.

It was in the early 1960s during the post-Stalin Khrushchev thaw that Yuri's disillusionment began. "The 20th congress was a terrible shock to my generation," he said. "We admired Khrushchev for doing what he did, but we know he was one of the worst butchers. What he did in the Ukraine — oh, it was horrible. Even in 1955 — they urged us in the institute to criticize things. We did, and then we found it was just a provocation, a way they could find out which of us were critics of the regime."

Not surprising, it was poetry that came to symbolize the vital, vibrant dissent of this period, just as it has always through Russian history. Even while working class Russians may mistrust much of the intelligentsia, they still respect the poet. Josif Brodsky, the prominent young metaphysical poet sent as a "social parasite" (what, indeed, are metaphysical poems good for?) to Archangel to work in the fields and eventually deported to the 'States, found that the peasants adored him. He was a poet. "It was a fruitful experience," he told his friends when he returned, "and, really, I enjoyed it. The peasant in whose house I lived treated me like a son. The local officials and, indeed, the whole community were good to me. I think of these people with love. They were happy to have a poet in their midst and they tried in all possible ways to help me so that I could write."

The night Yuri made his "great mistake" he had been to a poetry reading in a park while visiting Moscow — a poetry reading the police broke up.

"When I saw them beating up young poets, I just couldn't believe it," he said. "I didn't even know what I was doing. But suddenly I stopped and started yelling at the police. Seconds after I had done it, I knew that was the end. The next day I went up before the Komsomol at the institute and resigned. They would have kicked me out anyway.

"I was lucky, I guess. In my prayers, they said I had done things 'against Soviet man,' but they also allowed me to resign, so I could still get a job, albeit not a very good one."

Yuri suddenly looked very sad, as a small boat plied by us in the Neva — past the old palaces and toward the fortress of Peter and Paul, where the early political dissidents, who were also dissatisfied with their society but who took an activist way out, had been imprisoned.

"Sometimes, particularly when I listen to some sweet Western jazz, I feel so sad," he said then. "I know there will never be any place for me."

Still, despite this desperation, Yuri wavered back and forth — typical of the irresolution of the dropouts. He loved the Russian people. "The government is not the best in the world," he said, "we all know that. But the Russian people is very good. I love them. But they're too meek. When Russians drink — have you seen them? — they don't drink like Americans. You drink to express yourselves. Russians draw into themselves and start to cry."

He had a certain hope. "We don't have democracy unless we have economic improvement. And it's coming. That's why we want progress. Then things won't stay the same. But if there's war, we won't have progress."

And occasionally, despite a near despising of the system, he was passionately, defensively Russian. "It's a dictatorship," he said at the end of the evening, "but we have to protect ourselves in the world, and if it weren't us, it would be you. I would never go anywhere else. I would never be happy away from Russia.

The next day, ironically, I saw him in the Beriozka shop downtown, where the best Russian goods are sold only to foreigners and only for foreign monies. I didn't speak to him, as he looked yearningly at one thing after another that foreigners, but not he, a Russian, could buy in his own country. It seemed to me at one point that he was a head floating bodiless atop a milling crowd. I thought then to myself about how unattached so many young Soviets are, how they seemed to be floating weightlessly through such a heavily weighted society.

By the 1970s, I met Yuri's type of dropout everywhere. While the Soviet officials, always said flatly that no such phenomenon existed, every young Russian and every foreign observer I knew was talking about the "dropout development" with considerable interest.

"Among the young intellectuals and scientists, there is an increasingly privatistic attitude," said one Western diplomat who had studied in Russia and also served there. They want a pure personal life — they don't want to be compromised by politics, so all their acts are aimed at their personal life. There's a lot of withdrawal, a lot of inward-looking. It helps the regime by removing prospective dissidents, but it is not what the regime wants. It means a lack of spiritual spark from much of the group that should be the creative guiding force here."

"They just like being with their friends," said another Western diplomat "and they speak with utter frankness within their own group. After their families, most important is their 'Krushki' — their circles. Here there is an enormous amount of closeness and trust. One circle, for instance, might have a military man, an architect, a poet, a salesgirl, an engineer, maybe some parents. They drift together. What makes living here bearable for an intellectual is this great liberty a man has among his friends. In one's personal life, it is a fairly libertarian atmosphere. You can wear long hair, sleep around, drink. Here there is a great tolerance, although there is this terrible comformism on the surface." Or, as another observer put it, "Russian repression is even worse than we think in the West but we much acknowledge that it does not affect or touch most peoples' daily lives."

I met so many dropouts that I was soon able to compile a list of certain of their characteristics.

Almost all, for instance, were originally disillusioned by the revelations of the truth about Stalin — and then twice disillusioned when the promise of the Khrushchev "thaw" was thwarted by the renewal of a hard line. Just as, in the 19th century, the majority of revolutionaires were sons of priests or aristocrats and in the U.S. the young radicals came from the upper middle classes, so now a disproportionate number were from the families of active old Communists — probably they saw the hypocrisy more vividly and took it more personally than others. Many reacted, at one time or another, by "taking off" for one of the remote areas of the U.S.S.R. to do manual labor of some sort — an escape to the far reaches, where one could live a pure and simple life.

"My father was a big Communist in Leningrad," one boy told me. "Boy, would he be disgusted with me today. But my mother really nearly disowned me when I went to the Far East and dug ditches for six months. I just wanted to get away from everything. My parents' generation — *they're* the real lost generation. They gave in to everything. They were afraid of everything. They did everything awful under the sun in the name of humanity. I don't believe in humanity. I believe in one other person.

"You know, I think I have a great well of tenderness that I could give to someone else. But I don't know if I can even do that, this society is so awful."

Even among these young people, there is almost no counter culture, not because there is not an intense yearning for one but simply because it would not be permitted to exist. There has been, in recent years, a more tolerant attitude toward dress. Miniskirts for girls and longer hair (but not too long) for boys are accepted, and more open-minded men like Sociologist Vladimir Lisovsky in Leningrad says simply, "It is not miniskirts we should worry about but minibrains." Western music is craved for with an incessant lust — a craving partially filled by the enormous underground in western records — perhaps because its uproar breaks into the quiet boredom of Soviet life. There is a fascination with hippies, probably because, in this society so ordered outwardly to the point of sterility, the hippie is a symbol of the free spirit and a total unconcern with money and ambition, two elements that obsess older Soviets.

"What about hippies?" Alexander Ostrovsky, an engineering student I met in Novosibirsk demanded to know. "The government here tells us they're all bad. But if it's true that they don't care about money and just want to live, then I don't see why it's so bad. When I get my degree, I'd like to go to Vladivostok and . . . just live. I'd really like to drop out . . . " Then he paused and other thoughts came into play as in a point-counterpoint of statement-contradiction that many young Russians feel. "But you know, I'd also like a new car and a flat." He smiled — a beguiling, mischievous smile.

"You're no hippie," I said accusingly.

"I'm half-hippie," he said, still smiling broadly. Then he took the napkin on the bar where we were sitting and doodled on it. "Our two countries, he said, drawing two circles. "Both peoples are exploited, you by the capitalists, us by the party. But way up here . . . " He marked a spot at the top of the napkin, "We're coming together. We're going to be all the same. What we have today — it's all right for the people, but not for us, not for the intelligentsia."

While many dream of hippiedom, outside of enjoying rock music very few go so far as to try to embrace it, particularly in terms of taking dope. I met some students who told me that there is some hashish or marijuana grown by farmers in Georgia and Uzbekistan and some that comes from border countries like Iran and Afghanistan, but they were not forthcoming on the subject, except to say they got it "from the judge's son." Certainly, compared to the problems in the 'States, the drug problem here is miniscule, although it is growing in Kiev, Astrakhan and Tbilisi. It is dealt with harshly and unsentimentally.

The salient fact about almost all the "dropouts" was their inward-turning. Take a young couple I met in Odessa, Galya and Nikolai Soloukhin. What was astonishing about them, at least to a Westerner, was the lengths to which they had gone to arrange their lives in order to live in their own way.

They had one room in one of the old, Frenchified buildings built in the early 1800s near the port by Count Richelieu, the founder and designer of Odessa. But what a room it was!

It was lined with books in all languages — books they had bought, borrowed and sponged from tourists and sailors and got out of the black market. They had a good selection of Western jazz records — records apparently got through the inexplicable underground in Western goods. Besides these luxuries, a modern pull-out bed, Finnish cabinets, Western posters and a small bar gave the tiny room the air of a concealed den or lair far away from the utilitarian drabness of ordinary Soviet life.

Nikolai, son of a party leader who had risen from being a port worker and thus was *the* ideal and model for Soviet society, had wanted to be a painter and was doing well enough in his institute until he insisted upon painting abstract pictures. Unable to develop as he wished, he dropped out.

But what really shocked his parents, who had dreamed of his going into party work, was when he suddenly took off for Central Asia to dig ditches.

Today, married to a sprightly, gay, dark-haired girl, Nikolai works in a factory. Galya wanted to be a composer but, also unable to do things the way she wanted, she does nothing — except live within the four protective walls of their strange little room.

Each "dropout" is different. There are genuine "hooligans" who roam around the big cities, sometimes in gangs; in Moscow, these have become a problem for their attacks on African diplomats. These are black marketeers, who work in that strange underground of foreign money, icons and rock records. There are "bichi" — semi-hooligans or "no-goods" who go out to the labor-poor Siberian cities, work at daily rates, live in tents and raise hell on these frontiers, which are some of the few places left in the Soviet Union to raise hell. According to Komsomolskaya Pravda or Komsomol Truth, bichi include "former bank directors, builders, disappointed artists, metal workers, graduates of circus schools and piano tuners." In short, everybody and anybody. "as painful as it is to note," the journal continued, "these people exist who have isolated themselves from society, from its moral principles, ethical norms and also its laws." No one can estimate how many there are, but in one small village several hundred had appeared over a four-year period.

This was singularly striking, that Komsomolskaya Pravda should acknowledge the existence of these "nuisances," because Soviet officials still generally make it a political point not to acknowledge that there is any such thing as an alienated young person, much less a dropout. The only times a recognition of such shame is shown is in certain novels, plays and movies, such as "Julski Dozhd" or "July Rain," in which two people fall out of love, thus symbolizing a typical story of alienation. And Khrushchev himself denounced another movie, in which the son asks his father, "What do we live for?" and the father answered, "I don't know.'

Nor is there the slightest recognition of another form of dropout — the scientific and technical dropout who goes into theoretical work to avoid political and ideological interference in science.

But, basically, whatever reason for the dropping out, these young people first saw two choices — give in to the system, a choice which many of them see as ethically intolerable, or fight it, like the dissidents do, and go to jail or give up every chance of developing one's life to the fullest. And then they saw a third — simply refuse to take part. Many of them have reached a kind of peace with themselves through this curious compromise of resisting the strictures of society. But it is the peace of the dead.

This "peace" was exemplified perhaps most dramatically by a book by the young Russian author Yuri Kuper, "Holy Fools in Moscow," published in 1974. This is the way Harrison Salisbury reviewed it in the New York Times:

"Day after day. Drinking vodka. Drinking wine. Young men and young women, pairing off, now with one, now with another. Coupling, uncoupling. Night blending into day and day into night, weeks to months until no one knows what month, what week, it may be. Or hardly his or her name.

" 'What difference does it make?' one of them asks. And finally we ask the same question. This is the crespuscular insight into young Russia today, 57 years after Lenin proclaimed that heaven-on-earth would replace the ugly structure of Czarist Russia, that comes to us through the candid eyes of Yuri Kuper, a young Russian artist and writer who only a year or two ago was part of the scene he now re-creates in 'Holy Fools in Moscow.'

"Now, a new vein is being tapped of which Mr. Kuper is the most dramatic example — raw, realistic, brutal. There are no redeeming characteristics in his young people. No heroes. No villains. These are the same kind of dead-eyed men and women we meet in 'A Clockwork Orange' or, perhaps, 'Last Exit to Brooklyn,' drained of emotion, drained of life, knowing no future, cut out from the past, existing — barely — in a totally banal present.

"These are not young Americans or English or French. These people live in today's Moscow and Siberia. And in the Workers' State none of them work. Some have jobs — but none labor. They are time-servers who draw their pay, hardly knowing the name of the office they report to. One has himself certified as a psychiatric outpatient. He draws a pension and is free to spend his time drinking and picking up girls. Another is a book thief. He has developed his technique to a high art. Day after day, he wanders from bookstore to bookstore, stealing from one, selling to another. He earns more in a day than most Russian factory workers in a week. Each night the money dribbles away in vodka."

The only "moralists" among the "Holy Fools," Salisbury says, are the prostitutes who ply the railroad stations at night. "Any unconventional demand outrages their moral sense. 'Don't think that just because I'm 'that kind' that I'll do it,' one responds. 'I still have some shame left,' " he writes. And:'

"Mr. Kuper's Russians simply say: 'Tak Skuchno zdes — how boring it is here.' So boring that anything, the dregs of a vodka bottle, a night with a sick factory girl, an endless hangover, is to be preferred to the cardboard reality of Soviet life today."

To the parents' generation, of course, these young people represent an unholy problem. Before, Russia could punish her sons by sending them to Siberia or giving them a lowly job. What do you do when they go to Siberia themselves and spontaneously settle for the poorest jobs? When they *choose* Magadan over Moscow? And wht do you do when they drink themselves to death?

Oleg Alexandrovich, a young Soviet Jew I knew is one of these lost souls. I met him once one Monday and asked him casually what he had done all weekend. "I drank," he said, with a slightly dazed look. "I drank." How much? "Two thousand kilograms of vodka." Oleg always had red eyes and was slightly unshaven. He didn't know who he was or why. "Why do I drink so much? There's only drink where my heart was."

One night we were walking along one of the Kremlin bridges and the lighted towers of the Kremlin created a fantasy in the sky — a beauty and lightness that was totally unlike the Soviet Russia you see every day. "Fifty years of Communism," he said, scoffing, as he looked at some lines of people waiting, even in the early evening, "and we still have lines."

'I'm a Zionist at heart," he said once. Then, "no . . . no . . .I'm not anything." Then, "but don't worry about me. Nothing will happen to me. I'll just never go abroad."

But to me the most gnawing case was a student from Irkutsk who was studying in Moscow and wanted desperately to meet with Westerners because he wanted to know "the truth about the world." He hated hypocrisy with a white passion. "Even Yevtushenko," he spat out one evening. "He wants to be the international editor of 'Novy Mir.' He's trying to ingratiate himself to the establishment at the same time he maintains his image as a rebel. To us he's not a rebel anymore." He told jokes about Lenin — an unpardonable crime. Typically, he was not interested in modern literature, he was interested in facts — in "truth." The thing he seemed to like best about his country was the Moscow Film Festival, where, through connections, he could get tickets to see Western films otherwise forbidden. Once he had seen six films in one day — a matter of great pride. He hated people who "believed." Once when I praised the Russian Baptists for their honest and courageous faith, he got angry. "I can't stand anyone who *believes* in anything," he cried.

He was a brilliant boy, and he was sorely vexed and confused when I met him because he had been warned by his friends — and, I suspect, by the police — that it was not "wise" for him to see Westerners.

One night we were talking, and he was saying to me, with a kind of Russian quiet depression, "If we're afraid, then we're giving in to them. The one thing we can't do — we can't give in." The only way he could see of confirming his integrity was not to give in.

For just a moment, I must have made some involuntary movement or betrayed some expression that made him think I was suspicious of him — or thought him perhaps a provocateur — both things that were quite untrue. For he looked at me with that Russian passion in his face and in his voice and said suddenly, "*you're* afraid of *me*! I can see the look of dread on your face. Do you think *I'm* one of *them*? Oh, God, do I have the mark of Cain on my forehead?"

I will never forget this flash of underlying desolation and hopelessness, never. Then he put his head down in his hands and said, softly, "Will I never be able to live?"

✨ Chapter Twelve
The Dissenters

"The thinking generation of the 1960s calls upon all people of integrity to support these two courageous individuals by signing their names to our letter. He who keeps silent commits a crime against his conscience and against Russia. We who are just emerging into life are already fed up with hypocrisy and deceit — we want truth and justice."

Letter signed by 24 students to the Soviet government
on behalf of Pavel Litvinov and another dissenter
before their trial.

*9*T WAS mid-summer, one of the nicest times in Moscow, with fresh breezes more usual for autumn blowing across the river. As we walked on the corniche along the water, the city — so heavy, so grey, so Muscovite — seemed, for a few hours, to be a friendly, open, normal, human, even Western city.

The man walking beside me spoke constantly. He was a rotund little man with dancing eyes, an unbridled Dostoevskian beard and a mischievous expression that belied the truths of his past. For Pyotr Yakir was a man with memories that would spiritually paralyze most normal men.

"The Russian people have always been a people used to praying to God," Yakir was saying, as we strolled through the cool Moscow night. There was the bitter-sweet touch of an ironic smile on his lips. "Moscow was the third Rome. When this is in your blood, God can be anybody. Mao Tse-tung once said about the Chinese that they had a long tradition of bowing to the emperor, now bow to me!"

Yakir, a historian by training and then, in 1971, a dissident by choice, was in a philosophical mood. "There was a tribe of Chechens in the northern Caucasus," he went on, "and they always hated the Russians. It was in their blood. There is an old story about a Chechen and a Russian raised in the same village. They played together and they were like brothers. One day they were going to a wedding and the Russian was walking behind the Chechen on the path. Suddenly the Chechen said, 'Oh Vanya, I think you'd better walk behind me. It's in my blood to kill you.' "

Again the strange smile. "Well, it's always been in the KGB's blood to hate dissidents," he went on.

"Recently the KGB warned me again. They told me, "We're good people, but if you continue what you're doing, we'll be forced to arrest you." He smiled, more somberly now, and added, "It's in their blood."

Yakir was 14 when "they" — Stalin's henchmen — arrested him in 1937. That was the same year that his distinguished father, Major General Iona E. Yakir, was arrested in Stalin's purges of the leading officers of the Red army. These purges destroyed 2/3 of the officer corps above the level of colonel, leaving the country helpless and supine before the Hitlerian invasion. "I sat for a long, long time in the camps," he went on, remembering. "Sixteen years. I saw many horrible things with my own eyes. I saw many good honest people die in the camps, and those people died not because of anything they did wrong but because of an arbitrary government."

Yakir, like many of those unjustly imprisoned under Stalin was "rehabilitated" — pardoned, forgiven, exonerated — during the first years of the Khrushchev "thaw." It was too late, of course, to "rehabilitate" his father and all the others who had died.

He went to Moscow to live, got an apartment and a job as a historian at the Institute of Historical studies at the U.S.S.R. Academy of Sciences. In those halcyon days, when Soviet intellectuals believed that a true liberalization was finally proceeding, Yakir was one of those picked by the government to travel all over the Soviet Union telling the truth about the Stalin years. In two years, he gave 300 speeches — nearly one every two days.

Then, as suddenly as had come the thaw, came the new winter. Khrushchev was replaced. The new men in power, while by no means carrying the country back to Stalin's time, were Stalinist hard-liners. Then, in 1966 came the trial and conviction of Andrei Sinyavsky and Yuli Daniel, two independent-minded, critical young writers, for publishing "anti-Soviet materials" abroad.

"When I saw people arrested again for what they thought, I protested against it," Yakir went on. "It was a new process, with new people. I wanted to see a society based on genuinely democratic principles. It is complicated, but necessary."

He and his "democratic" group of dissenters soon began picketing and demonstrating and publicizing the political trials that followed the Sinyavsky-Daniel trial like falling dominoes. Their main method of operation was a curious one — they would compile all the information possible and get it to the Western news agencies; once published in the West, it would be sure to be broadcast back to the Soviet Union through such vehicles as the Voice of America or the B.B.C. — and it must be remembered that there are 86,500,000 radio sets in Russia, 27 million of them which receive short wave.

"Why do we reach across the border in this way?" he asked rhetorically. "We know very well that in other countries there are many problems. But the Voice of America and the B.B.C. are a kind of bullhorn for us. Our job is to get as much information to them as we can. Then it comes back here, and people from Siberia to the Urals know about it. They may not know us by name, but they are listening to information sent back to us." He smiled, momentarily pleased with himself.

But his rationale for why this curious operation might work - today - was not so curious at all. Times had changed; the government was, as strange as that sounded, more vulnerable. "Under Stalin, we called it the Iron Curtain," he said, "but now is a different period. Now, regarding us, the KGB occupies itself with one goal - to see that information does not go out to the West. They are trying to squelch any sort of contacts with the West. Why is the government afraid now? Because at this time in the country's history it is trying to put on a facade of complete democracy, of freedom of the press. It is trying to take its place among the countries of the world, and anything that destroys that illusion is dangerous."

I thought that night how these dissenters insisted upon living openly, as free people, and insisting upon challenging society's fears. I thought that they were presenting Russia and its dark, secretive nature with some strange and tormenting choices for its future. And within a year, we had Russia's answer.

In June, 1972, Yakir and Victor Krasin, another dissident, became the protagonists of the KGB's famous "Case 24". They became the two symbolic figures in the new crackdown on dissent, a crackdown that illustrated all too clearly the strains within the Soviet system. These strains had been transformed and exacerbated by the budding detente with the United States, and to a great degree men like Yakir were paying for detente with their lives and freedom. As with a seesaw, when relations on the diplomatic level improved with the West, personal freedoms within Russia got worse. The Soviet leaders were trying — and trying hard — to buy off the dissatisfaction of their people with material goods. Detente was designed to serve that purpose, so, when detente appeared to be working, they could tighten up inside . . . and they did.

The two men were tried in September in a five-day "subversion trial" that took place in the drab stone courthouse building in Moscow's southeast Lyublino district. A tall, green wooden fence surrounded the building, where several uniformed policemen and a handful of civilians with red arm bands blocked the main door. The courthouse was in a factory district, and freight train whistles occasionally pierced the air.

The government made the extraordinary announcement that the trial would be an "open" one, but Western correspondents soon learned this meant only that they would be given a daily briefing in the courthouse. "It's not in our tradition to invite foreign correspondents to trials involving internal affairs," Nikolai T. Khudin, the "briefer" smilingly informed the correspondents in their first meeting. Yet, the names of the correspondents often came up in the trial, whenever it was alleged, as it often was, that the men had passed information "injurious to the Soviet Union" to these correspondents.

In the end, both Yakir and Krasin were sentenced to three years' confinement and three years' deportation (probably in Siberia) for "anti-Soviet activities" and they only received this light sentence because they cooperated with the court. How the Soviet officials got the two men to cooperate, to give names, to tell how the "Chronicle of Current Events" was published, no one will be able to know for a long time. This trial, though on a very minor scale, was frighteningly like the '30s purge trials where the old Bolsheviks came into court and confessed massively to crimes they had not committed.

However it was done, once they were permitted to see the Soviet and foreign press, Yakir declared, "I certainly don't intend to engage in anti-Soviet activities. I'll work honestly, just like all Soviet citizens."

And Krasin said, "Anti-Soviet activities made me interrupt my research work, and I intend to return to my candidate's thesis on the rate of economic development in the U.S.A."

But under questioning, Yakir regretted, he said, that, in a private conversation with British Correspondent David Bonavia, he had said that people should not believe him if, in the course of the investigation, he disavowed everything he had done. And so it went, until the Soviet news agency, Novosti, put the final touch on the entire dark charade: "These two men now give the impression of people who have been freed of an enormous burden. And although there is punishment awaiting them, they do not consider their life as ended. On the contrary, in a sense it is only beginning. They will be working, working like all Soviet men and women, like all the 250 million-strong Soviet people."

It looked, then, as though the dissident movement which had flourished in the late '60s and early '70s was all but dead. Its membership revealed, the Chronicle shut down, its leaders imprisoned, the movement must be finished. Yet, even while Yakir and Krasin went to prison, others started reorganizing . . . once again. With a year, the Chronicle was printing again and new groups were clandestinely forming.

The average observer, accustomed to the "Old Russia," in which no voice of questioning, much less protest, was allowed to be raised, might well ask: What is happening? Is it possible that a genuine dissident movement might actually survive, much less be able to influence, the Soviet state?

Without being sanguine or childishly optimistic, one can say cautiously that, for the first time in Soviet Communist history, an underground dissent movement — made up of Soviets on all national, professional and class levels exists in the Soviet Union. In terms of numbers, it is miniscule. The groups are as fragmented as the most complex crossword puzzle — a structural form they often resemble. Most Soviet citizens do not even know they exist. But these extraordinarily heroic people refuse to give up, and they refuse to give in.

As new ones go to prison, old ones come out to fill the empty places. Knowing they will be arrested immediately and pitting themselves with a dour inner courage against an ingrown world that constantly cries at them, "Traitor!", they nevertheless go on picketing, demonstrating and writing petitions. With the innocence and joyous hope of the early Christian martyrs, they are convinced that by their own individual actions they can transform their totalitarian society — and the amazing thing is that in many and mysterious ways, they already have.

In trying to judge the importance of the movement, Yakir told me before his trial that is was "like an iceberg" — that you see only the few at the top but there is a huge mass underneath that to one degree or another sympathized with them. And this is probably about as good a description as you are apt to get. For while there are at any one time only a few hundred committed activists who go out and picket and demonstrate (and then promptly go to jail), there are certainly tens of thousands huddled underneath the water's surface, *sullenly* and often *hopefully* waiting for a change.

The first "truth" about the dissident movement is that it has no real organization, although the various individuals are in a loose and nebulous contact. Indeed, none would be permitted in a tightly controlled society like Russia's. But, in much the same mystical manner as the dissenters of the 19th century, there are mystical bonds that unite them in what they consider to be their "purifying mission." It started when, after Stalin's death, all over the country, unofficial (and illegal) "student organizations" sprang up spontaneously, and often they made contact with each other. Occasionally, one, such as "Progressivnaya, Politika, Pornografiya" or "Progressive Politics and Pornography," a dissident student movement which began in Kiev, spread and developed independent chapters throughout the country.

In the early 1960s, Peter Sadecky, a Czech scholar and son of a member of the Czech Communist party, was invited to give some lectures in Kiev and, by the way, found himself enrolled in this secret group.

Describing the first meeting he attended as an initiate, he said when he defected later, "There wasn't a scrap of fresh air in the room. The windows had been pasted over with several layers of newspaper painted in black lacquer and then boarded up to make doubly sure that no chink of light could show thru. Over the boards a layer of corrugated cardboard, then a layer of sacking and then, on top of the lot, an incongruous lace curtain. My throat was attacked by smoke, my nose by the pungent smell of a mixture of drinks. The room was packed." Some of the group apparently already were in a state of undress.

These types — and many others — come together not only at meetings like these but also more informally to protest trials and other infringements of human rights and to try to force more precise observations of Soviet law. They support each other on these major issues, even when their real interests differ.

They communicate with each other through some astonishing underground publications, such as the "samizdat" (literally "self-published," since all are hand-typed carbons); magazines for elite intellectuals such as "Political Diary," which has been printed since 1964 and deals with very advanced political and economic themes: a fantastic satire magazine called "Mtsyry," which features the buxom otherworld heroine "Octobriana;" and, most important, the "Kronika" or "Chronicle" which has been mysteriously published bimonthly since the spring of 1968. All these publications are uncannily similar to the underground revolutionary publications of the 19th century, and hand-typing them has become such a routine job that one popular Russian joke has a husband asking his wife why she has been retyping "Anna Karenina" for a week. "The children won't read anything unless it's typed," she answers wearily.

Kronika, which Sovietologists estimate is put out by a group of prominent writers and scientists, since they're the only ones who would be privy to much of the information it contains, began publishing literature and soon switched to documentation — expressing the same fascination with "facts" that seems to run like a pulsing vein across the face of Russian youth. It is published in such a rigidly non-polemical, straight-news style that is has, on occasion, apologized for some slip into subjectivity.

Everything from thumbnail sketches of dissenters to reports of political trials to news of new underground organizations are included. For instance:

— "In the village of Zarechanka . . . the Catholic church was closed on the instructions of the local authorities. It was turned in to a grain store.

— "In September, 1970, Sinie Mustafeyva (a Crimean Tatar) was sentenced to three years in labor camps for putting up black flags on the premises of the police and the district executive committee on May 18 (the anniversary of the Tatars' deportation from the Crimea is on May 18).

— "Leonid Naumovich Kolchinsky was expelled from the ninth class of secondary school for speaking in defense of Sinyavsky and Daniel and against the invasion of Czechoslovakia."

The quickness with which Kronika moves astonishes many Western observers. When one Pimenov, a 30-year-old mathematician from Leningrad was sentenced to five years of exile for "spreading falsifications detrimental to the Soviet system" in the fall of 1970 the trial was held in the provincial town of Kaluga, 200 miles south of Moscow. Despite the fact the judgment was delivered at midnight, Kronika got the word and, by 10 o'clock the next morning the latest issue of the journal was out with the news in it.

How do they do it? Apparently Kronikas are always moving around the country on the persons of sympathetic bearers. And apparently, in terms of information, the idea is that you are to give news to the person from whom you got the Kronika. If you attempt to go above this person, you will be taken for an informer. This procedure makes the whole "happening" of Kronika even more impressive, because it means all of these people have come to feel many of the same things through some sort of psychic process of spontaneous combustion that reaches across the entire personality structure of the country.

"If you look at how quickly and accurately Chronicle publishes information, you see they are building the sense of movement," Harvard University Soviet specialist Dr. Edward Keenan said in a recent interview. "This conception of a movement is entirely new. It is also important that there is a kind of cooperation among the various national and religious groups, for Chronicle has information on Orthodox, Baptists, Jews, Old Believers and others.

A national approach in the past has been unheard of. People now have a sense of being together with their countrymen. They are trying to think things through. Some of their ideas are pretty zany, but still they are not giving in when the cops knock at the door."

Moreover, it was revealed in late 1971 that the dissenters were not only hand-typing and hand-delivering their missives, some were going the ultimate road — a group of reform Baptists announced in a declaration to Kosygin that they had formed a "publishing house" and that they were operating their own secret printing press, "Khristyanin" or "Christian." Very few things are more prohibited and illegal than maintaining any type mimeographing machine or printing press in the Soviet Union. Yet they even ran the declaration off of the new press!

The rundown of dissenting groups — actually they are more like cells that come together, part and meet again — begin with Yakir's "democratic" group, which was of course decimated by his trial. This group, whose vague ideology hinged on generalized efforts to democratize Soviet society, was the core group for all the others and bended to coordinate them very loosely. It was also the activist arm. Or, as one member said, "We do the dirty work."

Behind them, doing much of the thinking, was the large growingly vocal and extremely important group of scientists who are disgusted with Soviet ideological interference in scientific research; religious dissidents such as Baptists, Evangelicals and groups of Russian Orthodox who cannot get permits to build churches; thousands and thousands of students and young people who read samizdat, listen to foreign music and yearn to travel, read independently and live in a state that will not embarrass them by its heavy-handed oppressions; increasing numbers of serious and loyal people fighting on various levels for a just application of Soviet law; and some dissident groups, like fascists and old "blood nationalist" Slavophiles, with whom the rest cooperate only on the principle of civil rights. Very important are the 2.5 million Soviet Jews, an estimated 10 percent of whom would leave for Israel if they had the chance and who have been stunningly successful in their sit-ins and demonstrations in getting permission for 14,000 Jews to emigrate in 1971 alone. The Jews are joined by such nationality groups as the always restive Ukrainians, Armenians, Moldavians, Georgians, Turks and Crimean Tatars, who are the descendants of the Golden

Hordes who were deported by Stalin. Approximately 50 percent of them died in the deportation to Siberia, and the survivors are waging a bitter fight now for a return to their Crimean homeland.

There are many ways to characterize the dissenters. In temperament, seriousness and degree of normalcy, they range from the very best-adjusted and the most brilliant to the totally maladjusted and rabidly neurotic. Sociologist Lewis S. Feuer sees two major groups: "the Literary Opposition, which rejects the Marxist-Leninist notion of class ethics and class morality and holds that there is a universally moral law binding on every man, and the Scientific Opposition, which rejects dialectical materialism in favor of the logic of science."

But perhaps the best characterization of the types of oppositionists comes from imprisoned dissident writer Andrei Amalrik. He sees three idological viewpoints around which opposition has crystallized: genuine Marxism-Leninism, (or liberal Marxism, which attracts the greatest number), Christian ideology and liberal ideology. "Genuine Marxism-Leninism contends that the regime, having perverted Marxist-Leninist ideology for its own purposes, does not practice real Marxism-Leninism and that in order to cure the ills of our society, it is essential to return to the true principles of that doctrine," he has written. "Supporters of the Christian ideology maintain that the life of society must return to Christian moral principles, which are interpreted in a somewhat Slavophile spirit, with a claim for a special role for Russia. Finally, believers in a liberal ideology ultimately envisage a transition to a Western kind of democratic society, which would, however, retain the principle of public or governmental ownership of the means of production." As to the Democratic Movement, which brings all these together, it "has no clearly defined program," although "all its supporters assume at least one common aim: the rule of law, founded on respect for the basic rights of man."

The story of how the dissident movement began tells a great deal about the deep changes occurring within this new, post-war, post-Stalin generation.

It grew, ironically, from the event that was designed totally to discourage young Soviets from any thought of dissent — the 1966 trial of Daniel and Sinyavsky. It struck not only the outside world but also much of the thinking part of the Soviet Union like a thunderbolt, for, after a period of ten years in which not one person had been imprisoned for what he thought, these two young men were sentenced to five and seven years each in Siberia. They had gone too far, and the state — jarred by their determination — reacted with the old Stalinist fist. They had criticized not only social ills, they had come close to hitting at the fundamental tenets of the ideological creed itself.

"So that prisons should vanish forever, we built new prisons," Sinyavsky had written in his iconoclastic "On Socialist Realism." "So that all frontiers should fall, we surrounded ourselves with a Chinese wall. So that our work should become a rest and a pleasure, we introduced forced labor. So that not one drop of blood be shed any more, we killed and killed and killed."

The 1966 trial was designed by the Soviet government as a warning that the euphoric feelings of openness and freedom coming in the wake of the Stalin years were going too far. But if the government expected a quiescent or even a groveling response to the "warning," it was mistaken.

Fearing a return to Stalinism, yet coming from a generation which had not known at first hand the horrors of Stalinism and thus did not know their attendant fears, young Soviets reacted in an unprecedented way.

The only witness who had been permitted to speak for the defense at the trial was Victor Dmitrievich Duvakin, a professor of Russian literature at Moscow University. Almost immediately afterwards, he was dismissed from his post. The students' reaction was outrage. Approximately 200 of them pushed into the office of the university rector and demanded a public explanation. This was followed by a meeting of more than 3,000 students in the university auditorium where a party hard-liner harangued them on "anarchism" or "pseudo-liberalism" before he was shouted down. Duvakin was reinstated, at a lower level, but it was still a victory of sorts.

These astonishing events were followed by demonstrations in Moscow, "white books" of trials and interrogations which soon were published underground in the Soviet Union and publicly in the West and in unpublicized (in Russia) petitions and letters which were sent by liberals to the highest organs of party and government.

Soon these actions generated new trials with new names: Ginzburg, Galanskov, Khaustov, Bukovsky, Litvinov, Larisa

Daniel, Marchenko, Belgorodskaya, Kravchevsky, General Grigorenko . . . Strange little student organizations blossomed: a "Party of True Communists" in Saratov, a "Marxist Party of a New Type" in Riasan, a group in Gorky who wrote an analysis of the Soviet system. "All this suggests," Peter Reddaway, the London School of Economics' specialist on the dissidents, wrote in 1970, "that heterodox political ideas are now circulating widely in the U.S.S.R. and beginning to find a serious, calculated response among a section of young people."

What's more, instead of the groveling, self-inflictive attitudes of the Russians tried in the '30s, these new rebels of the '60s reacted with courage and defiance. In no way would they be cowed.

In August, 1936, the two old Bolsheviks, Zinoviev and Kanev, though innocent, agreed with Stalin that, in exchange for their lives, they would plead guilty to killing another famous Bolshevik, Kirov, although it was Stalin himself who had had Kirov murdered. After the two men had got up in court, and purgered themselves in the most maudinly self-effacing manner, Stalin calmly had them executed.

Now there was none of this. Said Vladimir Bukovsky, a handsome young Soviet Jew who was one of the most courageous of the dissidents, in his defense speech before his sentence: "I absolutely do not repent having organized this demonstration. When I am free again, I shall again organize demonstrations." Said Andrei Amalrik, after a long period in which, inexplicably, he was not arrested, "If I have enjoyed more freedom than many Soviet citizens, I have only myself to thank, because I have acted like a free person."

These were among the first people in Soviet history not to condemn themselves, despite the fact they were innocent.

Many of them tended to be — compared to the masses of dour, suspicious, fear-ridden Russians who, in their fanatic group orientation, deeply resent people who go off on their own like this — blithe spirits. There is often an incongruous spontaneous joyousness about them. Giselle Amalrik, a beautiful Tatar girl with huge, almond-shaped eyes, is like this. When she and her husband Andrei met, they had run away together to Siberia, where they worked in the fields to get the 2 rubles for the marriage license. In the spring of 1971, she went to Siberia again — outside of "visiting hours" — to try to see her writer husband, who had been sentenced to three years in a prison camp for publishing in the West his "Will the Soviet Union Survive Until 1984?" When she was not permitted to see him, she rode away from the camp in a truck, shouting, "Andrei . . . Andrew . . . " And her voice echoed across the silent Siberian plains.

(Russia is usually such a quiet country.)

If they seem at times, like a modern reincarnation of the old Christian martyrs — a type that flows like a weeping river throughout Russian history — it is because perhaps they are.

But to the great majority of Russians, in particular the officials, the dissidents are "traitors" or "hooligans" or worse. When I even so much as mentioned them to V.P. Filatov at the U.S.A. Institute in Moscow, the institute which studies the United Sates for the academy of Sciences, he shouted at me that "Our constitution is respected more than yours. These demonstrators here are just hooligans. They disrupt traffic. Our constitution is for 250 million people, not 20 or 30. Not for Solzhenitsyn and his group. We say to them, 'Leave if you don't like it.' We offered Solzhenitsyn a visa to Sweden to pick up his Nobel prize, but he didn't take it." He smiled a sinister smile. "He knew we would not let him come back."

To the working people, with their dark anti-intellectualism, there is good cause to resent these "intellectuals" and "snobs," to whom everything was given and yet who spit in the face of orthodoxy. How deeply they resent the dissenters' "spontaneity" — their free and open response — just as Lenin resented it!

And to many other free-thinking young people who don't take part in any of the dissenter activities and who never speak out, the dissenters present them with a tormenting sense of guilt. Their sense, too, of desperation was perhaps best expressed by a young man quoted by "An Observer." "Everyone's having a grand time," the young man told him at a party in Moscow. "Yes — but don't let that fool you. Inside, we're all sick, full of hate and disgust. We hate those bastards at the top, those Brezhnevs, those Suslovs, hate them with all our might. And hate ourselves, too. A handful of martyrs are brave enough to protest openly — and we don't even lift a finger for them. We have parties like this to try to forget them. They're our heroes, the Don Quixotes of Russia. Ninety percent of our people are happy to see them squashed. And we stand by while they're sent to their camps. That's what's inside us, behind the merry facade: pain and disgust and guilt and hate. Inside all of us, every moment of every day. I drink to the real heroes of this country, the people in the camps. But that's all I do about it: drink."

Lewis Feuer, professor of sociology at the University of Toronto and a deep student of Russian student militants throughout history, finds on the part of today's dissidents, a "philosophy of eternalism." This is in total opposition to Marx's dialectical viewpoint that ethical truths are relative and affirms to the contrary that there are ethical truths which are eternally valid for all men. Or, as Solzhenitsyn's protagonist puts it in "Cancer Ward," "There were greedy people before the bourgeoisie, and there'll be greedy people after the bourgeoisie."

Still, there is evidence to believe that the dissidents have some friends even "up there," on the level below the Central Committee and even in the hated KGB. "Actually," said one young man who was not a dissident but who was unhappy with the regime, "the ones who go into the KGB may turn out better than those who go right into party work. Police work inevitably involves much contact with the real problems of society. The KGB man, whether he is benign or nasty, gets a much better idea of how things really are and how people in this country really feel."

Anotole Shub, the correspondent of the Washington Post who was thrown out of Russia because of his close contacts with dissidents, noted that "There is sufficient evidence to suspect that top intelligence and security officials — probably in the KGB and MFD, but perhaps also in the GRU (military intelligence) and "special" department of the party secretariat — may be protecting and abetting oppositional movements under the classic guise of infiltrating and 'controlling' them. There have been numerous episodes, involving collaboration between Soviet and Western intelligence agents and informal understandings between police and dissidents, which seem to come straight out of the pages of Dostoyevsky and Conrad." Others have reported a secret policeman concluding the search of a samizdat fan's premises by saying, "This item is quite harmless, so I will confiscate it, but this one is really important — take it back and hide it well."

But this is only one side of the moon. The dark is black indeed. In investigating the authorship of samizdat texts, the KGB now uses computers to establish the frequency of words or the rhythms of style in a given piece in order to prove the identity of an anonymous author. (This, they say, is how they caught Sinyavsky and Daniel). Though dissidents now seldom are killed, they are sent to remote and brutalized Siberian concentration camps. It is estimated there are 1,000 camps holding 1 million men, tens of thousands of them political prisoners (0.50% of the Soviet population in captivity as compared to 0.2% in the U.S.). Terms range from three years for Amalrik to an extraordinary twelve years for Bukovsky, who was tried again early in 1972.

Conditions in the camps, particularly the infamous Mordovian complex, several hundred miles southeast of Moscow, are often inhuman. If you are under the "special regime" treatment, which is considered the worst, while performing heavy labor you receive only 1,300 calories of food per day — enough for a three-year old child. Beatings are common.

But to many dissidents, particularly intellectuals, the most chillingly awful thing is to be confined in a psychiatric or mental hospital. In notorious places like the Serbsky Institute of Forensic Psychiatry some 250 or more political prisoners are put in the same wards as mentally deranged patients. They are treated with drugs such as sulfazine and aminazine (a 1% sterile solution of purified sulphur) which brings on fevers, comas and often, derangements. Scientists who have been so incarcerated have testified in the West to watching their colleagues gradually fade away mentally. The intellectual cut of their minds becomes dulled, they forget who and what they were, *they become vegetables and, thus, in official Soviet eyes, far more normal* than when they are dissenting.

In a letter smuggled out of a Leningrad insane asylum, Vasili Chernyshov, formerly assistant lecturer in mathematics at Leningrad's Institute of Technology, wrote that "I fear death, but I will take it. I am horribly afraid of torture. But there is still a worse torture and it awaits me: the injection of chemical substances into my brain. Perhaps I will remain alive. But after it I will not be able to conceive any poetry and I will not be able to think. Can you imagine anything more horrible?" He was committed for writing philosophical essays and showing them to a few friends.

In the same letter, he recalled seeing Vladimir Borisov, an engineer who had been incarcerated for having in his possession underground literature. "They are treating him with aminazine," he wrote, and as a result of it he is losing his individuality. His intellect is being blunted, his emotions destroyed, and he is losing his memory. But the most terrible thing is that the treatment is erasing all his subtle human characteristics. This means death for creativity. After receiving aminazine, one cannot read. Intellectually, they all become crude and primitive."

The point, of course, is to tell these questioners of the system that the Soviet state considers anyone who questions the system to be just that, insane.

Perhaps the most poignant insight was contained in a letter written by former Red Army Maj. Gen. Pyotr Grigorenko, a leading dissenter who was finally released from an asylum as a political prisoner in 1974. He wrote of a young engineer who had been incarcerated in one of these hospitals for seven years for speaking out at a student meeting. The general said he told him he would never be let go unless he admitted his guilt.

The boy so consistently refused to do this that the general finally said to him in exasperation, "Your reasoning is so unreal that I'm beginning to doubt your normality."

"He stopped all of a sudden," Grigorenko continued, "Look at me with an expression I shall remember to the day of my death, and asked in a barely audible voice and a tone of bitter reproach: 'Do you really think that a man can spend seven years in here and still remain normal?' "

The use of drugs on detained dissidents was also publicly decried by the famous Soviet Nuclear Physicist Andrei D. Sakharov in September 1973. He called a press conference with 14 Western correspondents to urge world psychiatrists coming to the U.S.S.R. for an international conference that October to demand the right to visit dissidents held in mental hospitals. Sakharov, father of the Soviet hydrogen bomb, said that Soviet psychiatrists were injecting a depressant drug called halopiridol into dissident physicists.

Despite these increasing "discouragements" to thinking and to expressing one's own thoughts, Soviet specialists do not see any end to the dissent; indeed, they see a probable burgeoning of it, even, perhaps, the slow and uneven growth of a "movement." For, just as they seem to be successfully snuffing it out in one area, it bursts forth with a new white heat and in new forms elsewhere.

In the last ten years, the Soviet officials must have thought they had seen every type of abominated Western method of dissent. But, no. In May, 1972, Roman Kalanta, a 19-year-old Komsomol member from Kaunas, Lithuania poured a gallon of gasoline on himself and burned himself alive. Shouting "Freedom for Lithuania," thousands of young people accompanied his funeral procession, and before the ensuing riot was over, 500 were arrested. This was only one incident in a series of bitter dissent problems in Lithuania, one of the always-smoldering Baltic republics. At the same time, there was the astonishing occurrence of 17,000 Lithuanians signing an open letter to the U.N. deploring the deportation of Roman Catholic bishops, the arrest of priests and the destruction of churches. All of which illustrates poignantly the indestructiveness and the flexibility of the entire dissident theme in the Soviet Union.

Is it possible that a real "movement" will come of it?

There are many negative factors, not to speak of the gigantic task of attempting to awake the still quiescent masses of Soviet citizens. 1972 saw a massive crackdown on the dissidents, with Yakir arrested, the Chronicle under strong attack, the mysterious death of poet Yuri Galanskov on a prison operating table, the arrest of five Buddhist scholars in the remote Buryat Autonomous Republic and the roundup of hundreds of Ukrainian nationalists and the harsh sentencing of at least eleven.

Still, despite this, there was hope. In one year, 14,000 Soviet Jews were permitted to emigrate to Israel — formerly an unthinkable thing. Despite its mailed fist, the government was obviously still public relations-conscious; it even went so far as publicly to deny there were dissidents in psychiatric hospitals — a subject it had never even discussed before. Kronika was not broken, and, more and more, literary dissenters, like Alexander Solzhenitsyn, were deported rather than imprisoned.

"Three factors would seem to point to the likely development of a youth movement in the future, Peter Reddaway has written. "First, liberal ideas are spreading fast throughout the country, and among students of the sciences and the humanities alike. Second, the courage, political moderation and readiness for sacrifice shown by leading young dissenters, whether in freedom or in the camps and mental hospitals, suggest an underlying strength of opposition greater than appearances show. And third, the general apathy and indifference among young people to the regime and its leaders seem to have reached a new high level, thus creating fertile ground for those who favor protest and change."

When I interviewed Dr. Reddaway, a tall, blond, forthright, quiet man sitting in the cozy, typically British and ordered backyard of his house in London, he predicted that for the moment the "mainstream" of the movement would probably go into any new stage. "What I think will happen," he said, "is that the field will become more differentiated.

"At the ends, groups will form that are quite differeing from the mainstream. Some at the 'extreme moderate end.' At the other end, there will be fully underground groups. Another aspect is there will be more and more national groups, who will vary in their political complexion and in their degree of nationalism.

"The democratic movement will be the mainstream, with fragmentation around the edges.

"There is bound to be an increase in the underground groups, and some are bound to be violent, because the government cannot possibly keep up with everything the young Russians want and because every society has certain violent proclivities which are not easily bought off by material changes. If there are not political changes, there are bound to be groups of violent ones."

❧ Chapter Thirteen
The Scientists and the Law

"Could you possibly think that, in the fiftieth year of Soviet power, a Soviet court would make a wrong decision?"

KGB official Gostov in conversation with dissident Pavel Litvinov over the 1967 trial of Vladimir Bukovsky.

𝒯RYING to make your way through the streets of Moscow that black night was a soul-invigorating affair. You could feel Dostoevsky's demons dancing about you in the blackness and Bulgakov's mischievous spirits from the underworld flying over you on their broomsticks. By 8 o'clock, rivers of rain, in places a foot and more deep, were racing down the old streets as thunder clapped and growled across the grey rooftops.

It is a relief to have a night like this in Moscow. Suddenly, in the bountiful life of the elements, the dullness and vapidity of everyday drops away. You feel alive.

Drenched to the skin, we came into the big old building — one of those rare Moscow buildings with rather elegant hallways — and up on the third floor we found Valerie Chalidze, the prominent Soviet scientist and prominent dissident. He struck me with much the same impact as the night.

Half Russian and half Georgian but raised in Moscow, Chalidze was, in 1971, a handsome, tumultous man of 32. He had long straight black hair that flowed and shook like black ink when he talked. His eyes were black and piercing. Moody and brooding, his dark moods interspersed with moments of great gaiety, Chalidze looked the part of the dreamer. He used to go out and live alone in a tent on the salt flats by the Caspian sea and just think. But he also had a smile that was pure, simple and innocent.

"Last Nov. 4 we started our Committee on Human Rights," Chalidze began, as rain crashed against the single window in his big old book-filled room. "We want to consult with government agencies on human rights, to study how human rights are guaranteed by Soviet law and practice and to compare them with international laws. We concern ourselves more with a broad study than with individual breaches of human rights. Any member might be interested in one breach and defend that person, but that is his own matter."

A committee on human rights in the U.S.S.R., where such voluntary committees have always been impossible? A group of individuals — scientists, moreover — who intended to *recommend* things to the Soviet government, which had never exactly shown itself open to suggestion?

Yet, it was quite true. Moreover, they had carried it one step further and allied the "committee" to two international groups, one the International Committee for the Rights of Man, a consultative body to the United Nations, the other a group centered in Strasbourg. Ironically (even totalitarian states are imperfect), the arrangements had to be made by long-distance telephone, because mail does not go through on matters such as this.

Why, I asked, as the thunder rattled the skull on his bookshelf, again, should it be the Russian scientists who are leading this fight for human rights, whereas in other, western countries it is the scientists who are accused of being soulless, technology-mad automatons who led us to Vietnam and will lead us to 1984?

He thought for a moment, tossed his floating black hair back, and answered, "Because science demands an exact logic. We feel that the study of human rights also demands an exact logic. I and the committee feel that law should be based on law alone, with nothing ideological to precede the law.

"As scientists have logical minds, they are used to dealing with absolutes. They bring a special expertise and a special knowledge to the study."

Of all the varied dissent groups in the U.S.S.R., no group is so important as this scientific group. For one thing, its members and supporters are all highly respected men in their society — it is hard to call them "hooligans" when so many are recognized as brilliant and are laying the basis for the whole future industrial development of the country. For another, their society needs them so much it cannot afford to move against them as promiscuously as it has against other less essential, more "superfluous" men.

They are also enormously respected by the average person — there is, even today, a mystic faith in "science" which approaches the level of an alchemical fetishism — and many of the best young people go into science, believing it will eventually solve not only the problems of their physical environment but also their political and spiritual problems. "The great majority of young people express great interest in the technical sciences," the playwright Victor Rozov told me. "All the best ones go into them. This is testified to by the fact that the technical magazines have enormous circulations. You can't buy them after two days. If you compare the circulation of specialized art magazines with technical magazines, there is no comparison." He could have added, had he had the figures at hand, that circulation of the magazine "Technics for Youth," which deals with popular science and science fiction, soared from 500,000 to 1,700,000 between 1963 and 1967 and that library copies are worn out before readers on the waiting lists had a chance to get it.

Moreover, this almost mystical faith in science, which more and more is coming to be coupled with law, stretches far back in Russian history. The great critic, Vissarion Belinsky, the intellectual who, more than anyone, gave form to the 19th century revolutionary elan, observed over and over that what Russia needed was neither faith nor mysticism but a respect for law and individual rights. In 1855, with that strange hope that never dies in Russia, he wrote: "See how the new generation, disillusioned in the genius and immortality of our literary works, is avidly studying the sciences..."

"A field of study becomes an ideological one for students, when, under the given circumstances of time and place, it provides a fulcrum for the rejection of the older generation's standpoint," Lewis Feuer has written. "The actual content of the subject may be quite devoid intrinsically — that is, logically — of any ideological consequence." So it was with science. All through the 1880s and '90s, it was the students of the natural sciences and of medicine who led the strikes and drilled home the "social question." "Down with the Classics! Up with Science!" shouted the students, infatuated with the new ritual that was to save them and to save Russia.

Once the revolution came, Russia was the fifth greatest industrial power of the world, but her already-formed scientific elite was almost entirely destroyed by the ravages. As new scientists were trained, the favorite science soon became genetics — a dangerous science, as it happened, because it set the stage for that great evil actor, Trofim Lysenko, who, with his deep set, burning eyes and Rasputinian passions, with his strange attraction for Stalin, destroyed the next whole generation of scientists by marking out for Stalin those scientists to be executed and deported. Trying to prove that characteristics acquired by an organism in its lifetime could be passed on to future generation, Lysenko was the perfect — or, rather, the ultimately imperfect — specimen of the mating of scientific inquiry and ideology. Though his morbid power was finally destroyed (he still lives quietly outside of Moscow), the damage he did to Soviet science is incalculable: an entire generation of scientists wiped out and scientific inquiry ended for a generation. Those left in his wake are determined that anything even approximating "Lysenkoism" shall not happen again, and the only way they know to avoid it is to establish a more controlled society — not controlled by human or subhuman whim, but by law.

And, so, in the dissident movement, as they work quietly in the background, pressing forward on legal grounds and doing meticulous research into such areas as human rights' guarantees, the scientists shed an aura of respectability and solidity over the entire atomized and amorphous movement. They have been in close contact with the "democratic movement;" in many ways, the first is the brains, the second is the brawn. They also had as honorary members of their committee such writers as Alexander Solzhenitsyn (before he was deported) and Alexander Galich. It is widely believed that it is the scientists who edit "Kronika." Philosophically, they have tended to opt for the long run and to favor educating the people in the law, whereas the "democrats" of Pyotr Yakir tended to favor doing things "now." The scientists are the "respectable" dissidents, and, more, they are men obsessed with rationality, justice and the determination that their country shall diminish its dark, archaic, hysterical forces and take its place among the open, rational countries of the world.

The Russian scientists have what is often an advantage over the scientists of the West — or, at least, over the stereotype of the "dehumanized" scientist in the West. This is the fact that Soviet scientists tend to have as broad or broader an interest in the humanities as students of the humanities themselves. At Leningrad U., for instance, when Dr. Lisovsky did studies on what students admired as the "properties of a man of culture today," he found little difference between scientists and others. All marked "ethical relations with other people" as the first consideration. The second property involved a broad range of cultural interests.

This interest in the humanities has not, however, barred the development of a resentment felt by some Soviet intellectuals toward the privileged scientific and technical intelligentsia. The intellectuals of the humanities complain that the mathematicians and the men of the natural sciences have gained almost complete freedom from party thought control, while they are still forced to wallow in dogma. Still, the two areas — so often divided in the West — do often come together in the dissent movement.

With Chalidze, a respected physicist who was head of the polymer plastics group at the Plastics Research Institute in Moscow until he was put out of his office in 1971 and deported to the U.S. in 1972, was the illustrious Andrei D. Sakharov, the father of the Soviet H-bomb, and one of the most famous physicists in the world, Pyotr Kapitsa, the father of Russian physics, and many others. While they try to stay out of "politics" per se, everything they do is, of course, in some sense political.

The initial study of the committee was of the use of insane asylums and the rights of psychiatric patients, particularly with regard to political and literary dissidents. "If a person is sent away because of political beliefs," Chalidze said, with amazing candor, "it follows from the fact that human rights are not adequately protected."

Then the committee began studying such things as the place of and the right to defense attorneys in Soviet courts. But, more important, they are interested in the broader scope and purity of the law. Their passion is to avoid human interference in the law, to put law above ideology and political considerations. This is particularly difficult in the U.S.S.R. because Soviet laws states clearly that some laws apply only to the limits of ideological interest — only, in short, so far as Communism is being promoted.

Chalidze made this interesting analogy. "In Germany before and during World War II," he said, "the courts took it upon themselves to define the law. Some were sentenced and sent away because of the court and not because of the law. After the war, during the process of setting up the new law, there was a strong reaction to previous times. Now the law is followed very closely. In neighboring countries, the court still has more freedom of action in interpreting the law."

He gave an example involving Boris Tsukerman, one of the early members of the group who had by then immigrated to Israel. "Tsukerman was corresponding with an Englishman," he said, "and the letters always got lost in the mail. Tsukerman went to court and said that, according to the international postal laws, a person has the right to demand compensation if letters are lost.

"The court held that, since he wrote something against the government, that superseded other principles of law (such as his right to get his mail unhindered by government censorship). But they never even proved that he had written anything against the government.

"Operating on this principle, it means that Soviet jurists apply the law not as people who carry out the law but as those who have to think first if it is not counter to other interests."

But, very well, the skeptical Westerner may say, Chalidze and Sakharov and a handful of the young scientists may care, and care deeply, about legalism and scientific freedom from ideological control, but how deep does it go within the scientific community? Chalidze, after all, got himself deported because of it. More important, perhaps, how deep does the concern for legalism go in the broader Soviet community?

Of a Soviet scientific community estimated at 400,000, some generally conservative and fair-minded analysts estimate that perhaps as many as 60 percent sympathize with the dissidents. In a country without objective polls, a free press or freedom of speech, no one can really know, of course. But what is certain is that the Russian scientific community is becoming the most recalcitrant group in the Soviet Union in terms of individual rights and in terms of freedom from ideological interference.

And this is natural. Scientists, involved in a discipline where there is no room for lies and distortions, are particularly well-equipped to demand honesty on other levels of society.

Moreover, they are spreading their ideas constantly through their manifestos and manuscripts, usually published in the West but also spread around the Soviet Union through the underground press.

The most dramatic and, at the same time, lucid exposition of much of the prevalent thinking among the scientists has come to us in the basically social democratic and pluralistic Sakharov's 10,000-word treatise, "Thoughts on Progress, Peaceful Coexistence and Intellectual Freedom." A full member of the prestigious Academy of Sciences at 32, holder of his doctorate in his 20s (Soviet doctorates usually go to middle-aged men who have completed years of work), only 51 years of age in 1972, Sakharov made such shocking statements as:

— "Freedom of thought is under a triple threat in modern society — from the opium of mass culture, from cowardly, egotistical and narrow-minded ideologies, and from the ossified dogmatism of a bureaucratic oligarchy and its favorite weapon, ideological censorship.

— "What the demands that the intelligentsia subordinate its strivings to the will and interests of the working class really mean is subordination to the will of . . . the party's central apparatus and its officials. Who will guarantee that these officials always express the genuine interests of the working class as a whole and the genuine interests of progress rather than their own caste?

— "Facism lasted twelve years in Germany. Stalinism lasted twice as long in the Soviet Union. There are many common features, but also certain differences. Stalinism exhibited a more subtle kind of hypocrisy and demagogy."

But Sakharov's most cogently heretical arguments are reserved for his warnings that ideological interference in science has caused and is causing the U.S.S.R. steadily to fall behind the West. "We are now catching up with the United States only in the old traditional industries," he wrote. "In some of the newer fields, we are not only lagging behind but are also growing more slowly, so that a complete victory of our economy in the next few decades is unlikely."

This is not idealistic chatter about the rights of man, which moves the Kremlin not at all, this is the kind of expression from the scientists, who are also very close to the defense establishment, that the Kremlin all too well understands. Moreover, Western Sovietologists see clearly that Sakharov is right. Zigniew Brzezinski of Columbia University has pointed out that "The Soviet political system, which successfully stimulated the emulative industrialization of the country, is becoming an impediment to further social and scientific innovation. In the industrial era, growth was possible through centralism; in the technetronic age, creativity requires plurality. Key Soviet scientists recognize this . . ." Then he goes on to point up one indicator: the U.S. employs 70,000 computers, Japan, 7,900; and the U.S.S.R., only 5,000. Moreover, those they have purchased at great cost in the West are already out-of-date.

"What will happen," a Western diplomat in Moscow asks, cogently, "if, after all the Soviet people have sacrificed, Japan should become the second industrial power in the world, and Russia, the third?"

There is also the question that ideological interference in Soviet science pushes many of the finest young scientists into areas where the state needs them least. Pyotr Kapitsa, the elder statesman of Soviet physicists, wrote as early as 1962 that application of a strict Marxist philosophy to science would have made the conquest of space impossible because in the early days the Marxists rejected cybernetics as ideologically unacceptable. Later, he wrote that ideological anxiety was retarding the development of Soviet science since it leads young Soviet physicists, in effect, to drop out of the mainstream, avoiding experimental work (and thus collective political criticism) in favor of theoretical studies. There were three or four theorists to one experimentalist, he said, instead of the other way around. The state that had idealized science had also tried to make it conform to the ideology they were claiming *was* science.

But if these criticisms are prevalent among the older scientists who lived through the Stalin period they are even more prevalent among the younger scientists. With their desire to search out scientific and ethical truth in the world, wherever it might lead them, they are uniquely ready for scientific honesty.

Take, for instance, the story of just one prestigious scientific institution (a story now known in full in Western academic circles), the Institute of Medical Radiology in Obninsk, southeast of Moscow, where the bemused contempt of most scientists for the "science" of Marxist-Leninism was dramatically shown. Developed in 1954 because of a high-level decision to make it the site of the world's first atomic power station, Obninsk was to play a special role for both the society and for the young (Largely under 32) scientists who flocked there.

But by 1967, the Soviet press, which formerly had nothing but high praise for it, was "thinking twice" about Obninsk. Polls showed the young scientists massively shunned "public work" — which is a euphemism for ideological work. Some scientists who traveled abroad began to depict the Western Countries in a favorable light, and the magazine "Kommunist" or "Communist," the party's theoretical journal, criticizes the Obninsk establishment for becoming imbued with a "scientific" and not an "ideological" point of view.

Indeed, if further indicators of ideological lukewarmness are needed, Komsomol leaders and committees began to turn over so rapidly, as "political work" clashed with the scientists' irritation over political interference, that in 1967-68 there was a 70 to 80 percent turnover in the entire membership of the committees and bureaus of the Komsomol.

There is every reason to believe that the Obninsk struggle is, for Soviet scientists, a typical one — a struggle between ideology and science — but there is no assurance, yet, as to which side will win the struggle. Moreover, in some cases, recalcitrant scientists have been very harshly dealt with.

Zhores Medvedev, the prominent physicist whose twin brother, Roy, is also a well-known member of the Sakharov group, was taken away from his home and spent 19 days in a madhouse for a condition diagnosed as a "split personality" who had "paranoid delusions of reforming socciety." Eventually he was released, only after Roy mobilized a protest by such internationally known men as Solzhenitsyn, Sakharov, Kapitsa and Mstislav Keldysh, president of the Academy of Sciences. Noting the fear of "psychiatric" hospitals that is growing among the general public, Medvedev wrote, "If things go on like this, it will end with healthy, sane people sitting in madhouses while dangerous mental cases will walk about freely . . . "

As to the second question, there may be a substantial base among the scientists for a generalized desire for more freedom, particularly in their own work and research, and this may carry them into the areas of legalism. But is there, in the larger society, a deep enough base among the youth for the desire for a more real and just application of the law to make it an important factor in the makeup of the future of the Soviet state?

There is.

As Stephen M. Weiner, lawyer and specialist on Soviet law, has written, there is at least one significant difference between the political trials of the 1960s and those of the Stalin era and "This is the response of the Soviet citizenry itself to the legal proceedings. The purge trials of the 1930s . . . were received with passivity within the Soviet Union. No so the recent trials of writers. Resistance to political domination of the criminal process has now become a common and insistently articulated concern of a very wide spectrum of the intelligentsia."

This truth, its importance impossible to overestimate, is shown in the letters and petitions — on the trials, on miscarriages of justice, on civil rights — signed by people in all walks of life. Lidia Chukovskaia, a daughter of the well-known writer, Konei Chukovsky, wrote to Nobel prize winner Mikhail Sholokov, a consumate hard-liner, for instance, warning him that the Soviet people were in danger of being "robbed" of their "most precious achievements" of the past decade — "the persistent attempts to return to the rule of law." And it was none other than the former chairman of a Latvian kolhoz, I.A. Yakhimovich, who wrote to party ideologue Suslov urging "the observance of the Constitution, not its violation," and "the realization in practice of the Declaration of Human Rights, which Vishinsky signed in the name of our state."

In my own experience, the subject came up constantly among young people, and not only among dissidents. Reflecting a demand from honorable people that the Soviet Union come to *be* what it already claims it *is*, these desires were expressed to me from all directions and levels. In one day, I had two young men regale me with it.

The first, a Jewish boy who had never taken any part in politics or demonstrations, sat in a restaurant and with a nervous hand sketched several little boxes on a sheet of paper.

"Why should the defense attorney enter a case only here?" he demanded, pointing to the second box. "Why only after the interrogation? Why shouldn't he enter at the very beginning?"

The second, a physics student from Kharkov, sat in a park discussing calmly and unexcitely the general political situation. Then suddenly his voice rose.

"Why can't I leave the country if I want to?" he demanded. "It's written clearly in the constitution that I can leave if I want. The constitution says so."

"The Russians are much more willing to act today when people demand their rights, " commented a foreign legal expert who had carefully studied the situation. "In the '30s, they were much less determined to do this, whereas today if the subject is safe and non-political, the Russians will pursue it. The party has an interest in seeing that justice is carried out."

It is no more "little father" this and "little father" that — this being the term applied equally to the tsars and to their political descendant, Stalin. It is no more, "If only the tsar knew this," or, as even someone like Boris Pasternak could once say, in the '30s, "If only Stalin knew about the purges . . . " Today, more and more people want, not personal caprice, but the certainty of the law. Or, as one Sovietologist put it, "People want order. They've lived in a society with so much brutality, obsequiousness, disorder, fear and arbitrariness for so long, they desperately want a society where things are predictable, where there is a sense of order and justice."

There is even a kind of Ralph Naderism growing in the U.S.S.R. Writing in Pravda, two consumer advocates, staff members of the Institute of State and Law, the principal Soviet academic research institution in the legal field, in 1971 launched a campaign of official concern for consumer rights. The two, Alexander Y. Kabalkin and Vadim Khinchuk, specialists in contract law, wrote that "Suppose a tenant is late with his payment of rent. He becomes subject to a fine, and that is quite right. But suppose now that the light goes out in your apartment and an electrician is needed. You put in an emergency call, but he does not show up. The building management office takes the whole incident with exceeding calm. Isn't this evidence of a lack of legal equality between the tenant and the building office?"

What this means is that rights — and the assumption that man has legal rights — is beginning, just beginning, to filter down to the average man. Pleas for justice are widespread on these hammer-and-nails levels, but of course, pleas for justice on one

183

level soon spill over to the political level. So this area of "legalism" is the one on which the most malcontented and disillusioned about the society and the most idealistic can find themselves at one with one another.

In many ways, it is ironic that the law should play such an important role today, for immediately after the 1917 revolutions (Marx considered law an "ideology," Lenin thought it a "bourgeois anachronism"), czarist law was abolished and nothing new was created in its place. The juridical element was to disappear from human relations once the New Man was born. Decrees of the Supreme Soviet, were to be implemented locally by the People's Courts. But law was reestablished in 1922, and a new theory was developed to the effect that Soviet law — "socialist legalism" — was an expression of the worker's will. It is ironic that the present appeals should be made to the constitution of 1936, since that was the constitution written by Joseph Stalin at a time when constitutionalism and the law meant as little as it ever has or could. Still, even that constitution, which did do away with the class war and which did guarantee all citizens equal rights regardless of class origins, also assured Soviets of such elemental Western democratic rights as freedom of speech and freedom to demonstrate. So does the Universal Declaration of the Rights of Man, which the Soviets signed at the U.N. but which, like the constitution, has never been observed.

It was not until well after Stalin's death — not really until the trials of Sinyavsky and Daniel in 1966 — that the question of the law came to the fore. Then a new legal literature arose, particularly in such popular mass magazines as Literaturnaya Gazyeta or the Literary Gazette, examining every aspect and application of the law, and in letters and petitions to government officials, both dissidents and non-dissidents began questioning and demanding changes.

But in actuality, many things had changed already. Conviction by "analogy" was over. People could not be promiscuously picked up because someone in the Kremlin or the KGB considered them a "social danger;" in general, only crimes actually in the criminal code were enforceable. Class origins were no longer a reason for persecution and civilians could be tried by military courts only for espionage, while the once-notorious secret boards of the secret police were abolished. Actually, there were two principal tendencies extant: the elimination of extralegal terror and the liberalization, rationalization and humanization of both procedural and substantive laws within the legal system.

What's more, the concern over the law had taken on a new spirit. "Russia in the 19th century had a disdain for the 'dead letter of the law,' " says Dr. Edward Wasiolek, Sovietologist at the University of Chicago. "The Russian appeal was to truth. What they cared about was the 'soul of the law' — living, feeling, living trust.

"The dissidents today are appealing to the letter of the law. They say the constitution is not lived up to. This is something new."

What are the areas around which the "struggle for legalism" has centered?

First of all, dissidents have complained bitterly about the conduct of the political trials — such mechanical transgressions as the government's packing the courtrooms with jeering sympathizers, the obvious prejudice of the judges, the acceptance of false testimony and the forcing of the witnesses to leave the courtroom after testifying.

In order to show the world how these trials were conducted, in each political trial one of the defendant's friends compiled detailed "white books" on the trials. These were then sent abroad for publication and for rebroadcasting back to Russia and, as well, circulating in the literary underground.

Secondly, there are specific legal questions. Since 1958, Soviet legislation has provided for the presence of defense counsel from the time the preliminary investigation ends, but today there is considerable agitation to have the counsel enter the cases earlier.

In addition, under Soviet law, as in most European law, the defense lawyer is expected not so much to defend the defendant at all costs but to cooperate with the entire court in order to determine overall truth. In Europe, this can at best mean a real search for truth but in Russia what it often means is the predominance of ideology above objective truth.

This is the major question that concerns the scientists — and many others. Soviet law requires as a specific criterion that cases be decided "on the basis of law in conformity with socialist legal consciousness."

This, says Weiner, "in short requires the interpretation of Soviet laws in the light of their assumedly objective ideological underpinnings. It . . . directs the judge to look to party policy in determining the propriety of applying a particular statute to a particular fact situation. Thus, socialist legal consciousness provides the mechanism by which the political demands of the Party, clothed in ideological garb, can impinge on the conduct of a trial."

As to another question — that of what is constitutional — under Soviet law there is simply no way, up to now, of determining constitutionality.

Where do the scientists — and the law — stand now?

Men like Chalidze and Sakharov and many lesser scientific lights were first warned to stop their activities. Then Chalidze lost his job, and all his files on the committee were stolen by the KGB. Sakharov lost his top job as advisor to the Central Committee, but retained his investigative job. Finally, at the end of 1972, the Soviet government allowed Chalidze to leave the Soviet Union, with his wife Vera, and to lecture in the U.S. on the civil rights movement. To no one's surprise, once in New York, he was informed that he would not be permitted to return.

Yet, despite these setbacks, the work of the committee continued and even most dissidents felt there had been progress. The trials were a tremendous embarrassment to the Soviet government abroad, at a time when it was trying to give the impression of a peaceful respectable state and negotiate with Richard Nixon. It has seen fit to deny, for instance, that political dissidents are put in psychiatric hospitals — the very fact of their denial, which fools no one, illustrating a certain new-style response to external pressures and criticism. As far as everyday application of law, it is important that several Soviets who signed letters and petitions to the government and were summarily dismissed from their jobs, took their cases to court and were reinstated. "It is part of a modernizing trend that influences science and economy, as well," one diplomatic observer in Moscow, deeply engrossed in the subject of the law, said enthusiastically. "So far it is largely non-political but it is very important politically in the long run."

Still, the darkness of the mind is still there. One has only to look at the curious discussion recorded by the dissident Pavel Litvinov between KGB man Gostev and himself to see the flagrance of the system.

"It (the newspaper report) says that Bukovsky pleaded guilty," said Litvinov, as they discussed the trial of dissident Vladimir Bukovsky. "Yet I, who was interested in this case, know perfectly well that he did not plead guilty."

"What does it matter whether he pleaded guilty or not?" Gostev demanded. "The court found him guilty; so he is guilty."

✿ Chapter Fourteen
The Young Russian Woman — Beyond Emancipation?

"The time of womanhood, this tender womanhood, is past. Perhaps it is not so poetical today."

Mirdza Kempe, the national poetess of Latvia.

*T*HEY are beyond "emancipation" — beyond the sobriety of the fight for legal and professional equality with men and beyond such questionably enforceable rights as the "right to orgasm." They have education on such a par with men that they now comprise 58 percent of those with university-level educations. They have nursery schools for their children (and an ideological rationale about them that leaves them free from any guilt about leaving them there) and jobs wherever and whenever they can handle them.

They — the new Russian women — ought to be in feminist heaven.

Instead, by the time I got to Russia in the late '60s, I found a gnawing discontent among Russian women, particularly the young. They seemed to have gone as far as women could go; yet even there, on the far side of emancipation, they had come up against problems that indicate that, even if women's work may eventually get done, women's dilemma may well remain a lot longer.

By the time I started investigating the Soviet woman, all the old battles were over — fought and won. But were these largely quantitative answers — the ones the women in the U.S. and elsewhere in the world were fighting so hard for — really answering the questions? With their gut determination to be professionally equal, no matter the cost, they had gone exactly the opposite way of most American women — wasn't there something we could learn from them?

The first, most constant and most overwhelmingly expressed sentiment of Soviet women that I found was their love for and dedication to their work, almost to the point of fanaticism.

A typical response, not only from this generation of women but from the last as well, came one day in Volgograd, when I asked a young newspaper editor at the Komsomol's "Young Leninist," Galina Rezhabek, whether she would ever give up her work. "Oh no," she said, shaking her head firmly and looking at me as if I were wavering on the brink of madness. "No matter how well paid my husband was! Our women can't leave their work; they can't live without work. You probably will not understand this, but our women feel if they are not at work they are not persons."

Then she outlined how the magazine attempted to deal with and advise on the "problem" of the young wife in the family. "Should the young married women take part in community life in the same way as an unmarried one?" she asked, rhetorically. Then she answered, "There is the question of woman's pride in questions of love. How can she keep her individuality when she is completely in love and forgets herself as a person, when as a person she becomes completely dependent upon the one she loves? We are struggling for a woman who continues working and for a woman who continues to take part in community life. Of course, it is difficult, but we consider she should not be behind her husband."

This was not only the official position, this was also the passionately-held position of every single woman I met. As Alla Beljakova, the attractive young editor of "Smena" in Leningrad put it: "Yes, women have many problems. They are very busy, what with factory and family life, too. Some think they do not need education because married. But our children are so well-educated and so intelligent that if she wants her children to respect her, she must find time for education."

Beside her sat her assistant editor, a young man. She turned to him, as to a species. "We try to convince the men they have to help at home," she continued, fixing her gaze upon him, "and many do help. There's an example."

He looked a little sad, as he sat, exposed, under all this scrutiny.

"His wife is an engineer," Alla continued. "They had quite a bit of disagreement when he wanted her to stay home."

Did she win? I asked.

"Of course," Alla answered crisply, "Now woman has the right to be equal. We teach young men they should be self-sufficient."

But, self-sufficient: you know what *that* means?

Perhaps it was best illustrated in a novel, "A Week Like Any Other" by writer Natalya Baranskaya in "Novy Mir," which dealt with the typical middle-class *angst* of the Russian housewife. "Run here, run there," the author described her heroine. "A shopping bag in each hand, back and forth, streetcars, buses, subways. We have no stores where I live. After one year they still haven't been built." A reviewer, Ramara Rezvova, writing in Literaturnnya Gazyeta, decided that "Statistics show that this heroine's troubles are not unique, but common to people in all large cities," and she summed up that "The trouble with Olga is that her life lacks spiritual content. We have accumulated experience — political, military, economic. But now the new generation must gather a new kind of experience — that of the ethical meaning of daily life. The novel ends as it began, on a note of hopelessness. Apparently there is no way out."

Equal, yes! Self-sufficient, yes! But today this is clearly not enough. They have gone beyond that stage. Once the full bloom of equal education, equal pay and equal job opportunity began to wear off, women started looking around and they saw they were working, between getting and spending their salaries, getting and taking the children, getting and cooking the groceries, 16 hours a day — while their husbands, with no complaints about their "emancipated" wives, were working eight hours. They were expected to do not only their jobs, but everything. And the men didn't complain about their wives working — how enlightened!

Finally, belatedly, the women were realizing what was happening to them. "I came to our school one morning early last week," a teacher friend of mine in Kiev told me, "and another teacher was sitting there with her head in her hands sobbing and saying, "I wish I were back in tsarist days. At least then I'd just have one thing to do — be a woman at home and have men flatter me and do certain things for me. It's just too much." Irina looked thoughtful. "Yet we don't want to stay home. We consider that a kind of grave."

A beautiful blond Estonian artist, Valee Limber-Boatkina, whose whimsical and fanciful designs and paintings decorate many schools and public buildings in Tallinn, put it flatly, but without resolution. "Men should help more," she said, sitting in her workshop in the artists' union in Tallinn. "Instead they read and watch TV. But men are king of the house, and my husband is the same. There are some men who do everything in the kitchen." But now she frowned. "That's not good, either," she summed up.

What she really dreams of is a dishwasher — a banal dream, perhaps, but a realistic one. "I had a maid," Valee continued, sighing," but she didn't want to work in the house, she wanted to go to the factory. All women want to become cultured now, they want to make something of themselves."

She sat in her studio, holding a coffee cup, as, outside, snow drifted down over the beautiful medieval streets of Tallinn. "Women's life is difficult today, but interesting. We do not want to stay at home, we want interesting work. We want to develop ourselves. Some women still stay at home. You need a great love to do that. To be at home and prepare good food for one's husband . . ." She shrugged. "Women simply consider it too little."

In nearby Riga, the capital of Latvia, Mirdza Kempe, a dark-haired, somberly handsome women with sad eyes who is famed as the national poetess of Latvia, quite agreed. "Yes, everything has changed," she said, sitting in her simple apartment in a typical apartment block on the outskirts of the old city. "Women can do everything — pilot, seaman, whatever. Women are honored." She smiled. "But it is not so easy for a woman. She works at home, too. She is a little burdened. Spiritually? She is more independent spiritually, too, and she develops mentally stronger. Her personality has changed. I . . . I would not like to live at home, because I like working in my collective group, in a team. When you stay at home, you get depressed, even writing poetry, even looking at the moon."

These are the dilemmas in which Soviet women find themselves — and which are finally being expressed publicly in the more secure and more demanding younger generation. These girls, too, are dedicated to their professions, and women who are "only housewives" are shamefaced, even blushing, when they have to admit it. They are proud that four out of five Soviet women between the ages of 20 and 55 hold full-time jobs and, being intensely patriotic, they are cognizant and serenely acceptant of the fact that they are replacing the 15 million men killed in the war.

But at the same time, the undeniable thistle in the Garden of Eden is the fact that . . . . they have no household help. Before the revolution, 14 percent of the population of Leningrad worked in service occupations; today it is 1/10 of one percent. Nobody wants to do any kind of "service" occupation — it is looked upon as being beneath a Socialist person, and the famous actor-satirist, Arkady Reccin, is famous for scenes where the nurse comes for a job and ends up sending the mother out for a walk with the baby while she calls her girlfriend to come over and watch TV.

As a result, with household public services almost non-existent, except for the privileged few party leaders, and with the old "babushkas" or grandmas who have taken care of grand-children and many a daughter's household either dying or going back to work themselves, most women are frightfully overburdened. Surveys have shown that wives have half the amount of leisure their husbands and one hour less sleep a night. A Professor Kobalevsky, writing in Molodaya Gvardia or Young Guard, has tabulated that, in industrial districts, working women have three hours less free time on work days and 9 to 11 hours less free time on Sundays and holidays. In consequence, he determined, "the woman slowly neglects herself, loses her former attractiveness, and the one-time love dies out." Often the husband leaves the tired wife for a younger, eager activist, and then the whole process simply repeats itself.

Then there is the concomitant reality that women simply almost never reach the top. True, they outnumber men five to four and they provide 72 percent of the doctors, 30 percent of the engineers and scientists, 70 percent of the teachers, 40 percent of the lawyers, et al. True, they do not work largely for money — in a detailed study of the Russian family, H. Kent Geiger, professor of sociology at the University of Wisconsin, concluded that wives of Russian men with high-paying and high-status jobs were even more likely to work than wives of men who earned less. But in terms of political power, in 1970, only three of the powerful 195-"man" Central Committee of the party were women and only 21 percent of all party members were women. None were in the highest echelons of power. The last woman minister was Minister of Culture Yekaterina Furtseva, and, typically, it was always rumored that she was there because she was Krushchev's "friend."

"This is natural," said a Moscow woman lawyer, a trifle wearily. "Women get to a certain point in their careers, and then they simply have too many family responsibilities to be able to put in those extra hours a day that is what takes people to the top."

On the other hand, unlike in the West, women who are the wives of famous men gain little of the reflected prestige of their husbands. There is none of the appearing in public and none of the recognition that accrues to them in their roles of "first ladies." Indeed, many Russians do not even know whether Brezhnev or Kosygin have wives or anything about their family lives.

A third "problem" — which is the direct result of the first two problems and a problem more to the Soviet state than to the women itself — is the problem of babies. While there are, at the moment, 80,000 "heroine mothers" — mothers with ten children or more, who receive prizes — this is becoming more and more unusual. Emancipated women, if we are to believe the Russian example, prefer to make their money in other ways. They don't want many babies, preferring to use their new freedom and affluence to travel and buy the iceboxes and nylons they've waited for so long. And if you have to choose between another baby and an icebox, well . . .

The purely Russian birthrate of one child — that was, by the 1970s, the norm among the European Russians — is not enough to reproduce the population, which requires 2.2 children per family. Moreover, Asiatic Soviets are reproducing at such a high rate that within the next 50 years they will probably constitute a majority of the population — thus changing the country's entire racial makeup. That the Russians fear this and fear it strongly is clearly illustrated by the fact that this point about an imminent Asiatic majority is brought up in every article on demography.

"The working women have a terrible need for free time," Dr. Vladimir Kolobkov, noted sociologist at Kiev State University reports, "and children demand a lot of time. One child is enough to express the family's feelings. People want to travel more. They want a comfortable flat. Before the revolution, children were the 'savings account' for their parents. They would sustain parents when they could no longer work. Today people are not troubled about the future, so children have lost their role as a sustainer in the old years."

So not only the young women but the Soviet state is up against a substantial conflict as regards women, their rights and their reproductive capacitivies. Morally and ideologically, the state is committed to the equality of education and to work for women, and clearly the women want this. But there is also a terrific shortage of hands in the U.S.S.R., and, if the birth rate goes down any more, the state will be facing real setbacks to its industrial expansion.

Closely allied to all of this is the fact that young Russian women today want to be pretty, and that physical beauty is no longer looked down upon as a "bourgeoise hangover." Even fashion has come into its own, largely by way of a slim, attractive, soft-spoken young man named Vyacheslav Zaitsev, a designer the Russians like to compare to Yves Saint-Laurent.

There are many things unusual about the youthful Zaitsev, who was born in 1939, and one of them is that he is so agreeably nice. There are no high fashion affectations about him. He laughs a lot — he obviously is enchanted with that what is happening to him — and he is thoroughly charming. When I interviewed Zaitsev, he told me he wanted most of all for Russian women to "individualize" their fashions. "We want every woman to find her own individuality," he said, sitting in the small, unimposing office of the Dom Modelli (House of Fashions) with his sketches spread out on the floor in front of him, wearing a gray pin-stripe with belted back, maroon paisley tie and matching handkerchief.

Unlike the designers in the West, these Russian designers did not urge women to try to dress like or try to be something they were not. Dom Modelli's handsome art director, Ludmilla Turchanovsky, explained, "We always say to a woman, 'Ask yourself: Am I stout or not? Do I look like a sportswoman or a gentlewoman?' We tell them to consider all these things before choosing."

Since nearly all the designs are made and shown in open fashion shows so that women can buy the patterns and then make them themselves or else have them made at one of the many dressmakers in the country, the "industry" is still quite different than fashion in the West. Yet, by 1972, and even by 1967, it was difficult to find a young Russian woman in such major cities as Moscow, Leningrad or Kiev who did not look much like a young girl in the West — not, of course, the hippie young girl but the average, well-dressed young girl. Once, on a particularly remote part of the Trans-Siberian

Railroad between Nahodtka and Khabarovsk, I was witness to a tellingly amusing scene when a beautiful, dark-haired, particularly well-dressed Russian girl from a small local village had to keep insisting to a young Russian man that she was, indeed, Russian. "You're European," he kept saying, stubbornly, "You must be European. But where did you learn your Russian?"

The "beauty revolution" was bursting forth on all sides. By 1966, only ten years after the Komsomol was still shaving the heads of young people who wore outrageous hairdoes, the Komsomol sent a delegation of boys and girls to Italy to learn modern, chic hair-dressing. They opened a school on Kuznetsky boulevard to train others.

But to return to the central theme of Russian womanhood, why is there this passion on their part to work and to devote themselves so wholly to public life? Why are they so determined not to be "imprisoned" in the home?

One reason is simply because Russian women have always worked. They toiled in the fields and in the hardest type of manual labor and they fought in the wars alongside men. Actually, historians have traced three strands in Russian history: the subordination of women, equality in hardship, and also (the only really positive strain) creative equality. It was the last, which at that time existed only for the aristocratic classes of women, which is what most women aim at today — probably because it is a way to escape the brutality and degradation inflicted upon them by men throughout history.

Soviet women, 31 percent of whom worked before the revolution, received total equality under the law really only in 1917. Today, for example, divorce is routinely awarded if both parties agree; if one objects, the case goes before a people's court. Property acquired during the marriage is equally divided, both assume responsibility for raising their children, and alimony goes only to a partner who is incapable of working within a year after the divorce. Today men must help support illegitimate children — a sharp change from the Stalin days, when, because the state needed manpower, Stalin decreed that men need not admit paternity nor provide financial support for out-of-wedlock children.

One of the more stunning changes in the role of women has occurred in the peripheral areas, such as the Asian areas of

Uzbekistan and Azerbaijian. Before the revolution, in Uzbekistan, the houses had two parts: male and female. Women could enter the male section only when bringing food. They wore the paranja or veil from 9 years of age and never removed it. Here, and in Moslem areas such as Azerbaijian, the years after the revolution were years of sexual battle. Some fathers killed their daughters who tried to live in the modern way.

Today? Today the changes — not only in reality but in attitudes — have been stunning; so have the sometimes peculiar compromises with theory and reality.

In Uzbekistan one day, for instance, I was extremely surprised to see the extent to which even very simple peasants had changed in their ideas about women.

We had driven out to the countryside and stopped by an outdoor teahouse. The little pillowed platforms where Uzbek men go to lounge and drink tea and gossip here were extended like piers over a languid green river. Above were swaying willow trees, and an occasional oxcart trundled across an old bridge nearby.

Next to us on a nearby platform sat a group of seven Uzbek farmers from a nearby collective farm. In their traditional clothes, they could have been out of a world of 500 years ago, or even 50 years ago — when the Emir still kept mistresses and threw the one he liked best each day an apple as she bathed in the pool. Before 1917 these Asian women only went out completely veiled and if a woman removed her veil, her husband had the right to bury her alive.

Eventually, the man who was the natural leader of the group, a 53-year-old farmer named Dadsmotov Hosneden, invited us to join them for pilaf, which we all ate with our fingers.

"Do your wives work?" I asked him. "Of course," he said. "If they have small children at home, they don't. But otherwise — of course. They are equal to men."

When he asked me how old I was and I said 32, he exclaimed, "And you're not married yet?"

"I travel all the time," I answered. "Maybe in another year."

"But you should marry while you can enjoy your youth."

"I'm enjoying it now," I answered.

The striking thing was that all the men agreed that it was quite right and natural for a woman to travel around the world alone writing about it.

"Yes, It's true," Hosneden said. "When you're 80, you'll have things to tell your grandchildren about the whole world." Then he asked, "Do women have equal rights in America, too?"

Before we left, I asked him if they talked much about politics. "Not very much," Hosneden answered. "We work, we sleep (he put his hands to his head to gesture sleeping), we eat pilaf, we drink and we sing. We leave politics to others. It gives you a big head."

As to the peculiar compromises, there was the day in Tashkent in Soviet Central Asia when I visited the Barakhan Mosque, which houses the headquarters of the Moslem faith in Soviet Central Asia. Once the Moslem faith had been in total conflict with Bolshevism, but now there is so much public peace that the government tourist guides ask if visitors want to visit the mosque.

There, the scene was out of Arabian Nights. We were sitting at an exotic table loaded with bowls of fruit, exquisite blue and white dishes and flat moons of rye bread, drinking gentle Uzbek tea with one of the officials of the Mosque, Josip Khan Shakir.

When I suggested there might be a conflict between the fact that Islam allows a man four wives and the Soviet state only one wife, he shook his head vehemently. "But there is no conflict," he kept insisting. "Moslem law says a man can have four wives. But he is not obliged to have four wives. By Soviet law he can have only one wife. There is no conflict."

In a particularly poignant example of what-it-was-like, Balakishi Orydgev, a 148-year-old Azerbaijanian of one of the group of long-living tribesmen near the northern reaches of the Caspian sea, told me when I visited his home on a wind-swept plain, "My wife left the house and went to the adjacent village for the first time when she was 90." Why did he allow her to do *that?* I asked, tonque-firmly-in-cheek. He smiled a large, toothless smile. "I live on a mountain," he said, "I can see everything she does in the village."

Women in these areas, having known what is in reality an Asiatic male oppression, which is quite different from the historic type of Russian male oppression, seemed to be ecstatically happy with their new free lives. In particular the young ones were happy. But, among the purely Russian women, I often sensed, even today, the sulky harboring of something else: a deep disappointment with men, and a feeling that you could not depend upon them to take care of you.

"Somehow they never turn out quite right," an extremely pretty young divorcee, Anna Sholokhov, told me in Leningrad. "You feel you can't trust them. They're always drunk or unwilling to work. If you want a good job done, you have to call in a woman. Really, you're better off without them."

Or, in puzzlement, from a young woman lawyer: "A woman in the West is crazy to pin all her hopes on a man. If she loses him, she loses everything — her whole social standing, her place in society. She's nothing. Here a woman goes on just as before."

How many women, young and old, complained about the bane of Russian manhood — alcoholism! "They're always drunk, especially when you most need them." Even if they come to the apartment to do a job, in ten minutes they're dead drunk." And, indeed, consumption of alcoholic beverages keeps going up, with Soviet data published in Izvestia (1969) revealing that "more than 40 percent of all divorces are caused by the drunkenness of all of the spouses. In addition, there is an observable trend toward a certain increase in the percentage of divorces stemming from this cause."

Hearing girls like these speak, one thinks of the passionate, courageous Natasha in "War and Peace" or of the typically Turgeneven heroine of "On the Eve" who averred sorrowfully that "There are no men in Russia" and of the innumerable women of Russia literature — all stories where the heroines always seemed to be stronger and nobler than the heroes and where an inadequate man and a beautiful woman loved and parted in an ecstasy as exquisite as it was hopeless.

Laurens Van Der Post saw in the faces of Russian women a great resigned joylessness. To him, their "equality" was actually an inequality. He saw "the look of rejection which is implicit in the absence of special recognition by their men and their societies; this look I know so well in the primitive women of Africa."

Tellingly, within the families, too, it seems to be the mother who is the strongest and most-admired person. When Dr. Lisovsky asked 2,035 young people "Who, among your relatives or acquaintances, is an example for you?" 50.5 percent named mother, 27.6 percent father and 34.7 percent named their friends. A Wisconsin professor of sociology, writing in the United Nations publications, "Impact of Society on Society" on "The Embattled Human Male," noted that studies of parents in the Soviet Union indicated fathers did not play a crucial role in child-rearing because they were away from home so much because of wars and revolution. "In three societies that have flourished since the end of the second World War — Japan, the Soviet Union and the United States — the father model seems to be that a warm, permissive parent who provides affection and encouragement for his children but exercises very little absolute authority."

Other Russian women, however, see the freedom as leading to really good and beautiful marriages. "You see," said a teacher, Svetlana Melnick, "if you don't really love this man, there is no other reason why you should stay with him. You don't need him for support or prestige. So couples who live together truly live together because of love."

How do the men react to the "emancipated" woman? In my experience, they seemed to be perfectly happy to have women do all the work at home and bring home additional paychecks as well. Indeed, why not? Probably because of the peculiarly rough and brutal history, they seemed to have little need, as Western men do, for the witlessly "feminine" and for the artifices of contrived sexuality. I never heard a man complain about being emasculated or castrated by women — the possibility did not seem to enter their mind — although I did meet some young, very Westernized men who seemed to yearn for a Western-style woman. One said to me that he liked women who were "like cats who pad in and out, independent, going their own way, but delicious." He could not bear the "official woman" — in effect, the organized, perfected Soviet woman.

And now we are approaching the core of the problem of women in the Soviet Union in which, despite all, there has been little real revolution in attitudes and perceptions toward women on the part of men in the Soviet Union. It has been a real quantitative revolution and that is crucially important — to deny the importance of job opportunities, nursery schools and equality of education and before the law is to be foolish indeed — but the *qualitative* revolution is just beginning to come. Or, as Susan Jacoby, a perceptive young American journalist who lived for several years in Moscow, has observed: "The status of women in Soviet society suggests something else the Women's Lib has not taken into account: freedom from job discrimination, the end of old-fashioned, witless femininity, and even sexual emancipation do not necessarily change the traditional female role inside the home." Women have gained rights in Russia because they were needed to build the revolution — and because Marxist theory theoretically made them "equal." But they still are not truly equal because there has been no real revolution in human (male-female) relations.

To take just one indicator of what would mean equality, men have not started flocking to the kitchens to help their overburdened wives — nor will they soon.

One immediate answer here seems to be more public services — public cleaning bureaus that will clean apartments, nurses for sick children, laundries, and half-cooked foods readily available in the stores. These are only beginning, but they have high priority in future state plans.

Surveys show that most women themselves think it is most important to make life easier for them, rather than calling in their husbands to help them (perhaps they know the men aren't likely to do it). When the Institute of Applied Social Research asked them what they preferred, 50 percent answered "Shorten the work day;" about 70 percent said, "increase the output of household appliances and the places where they can be rented;" and about 30 percent said "increase the number of laundries, repair shops, tailor shops and other service facilities."

One sociologist, Zoya Yankova, stated categorically that household chores should be divided between wife and husband — by law. Another woman, Vera Bilshai, who has a master's degree in law, found this an oversimplified understanding of equality; she thought that what was important was not so much that men do the housework as that they respect women for their work in the home.

What it is slowly coming down to, therefore, is a kind of real women's liberation discussion — not just allowing women to work, for Russians have always "allowed" (or forced) women to work, but for a real qualitative revolution. And it is curious that the Russian women have forged ahead precisely in those areas where American women have been held back.

The Russian women already have built into their professional lives the idea of special compensations for bearing and raising children. Here, at least legally, there is the self-righteousness of men in the United States who say, "Very well, let her work, but then she has to do everything else, too." In the Soviet Union, the retirement age for women is the lowest in the world — 55. Women who have raised five or more children and raised them to the age of eight are entitled to a pension at 50, after having worked for 15 years.

They are just beginning a very basic discussion of "womanliness" and, in a recent survey, 90 percent answered the question, "What role do you think is most important for women — professional, sociopolitical or family-domestic?" with the answer, "All three." "Womanliness" they saw as gentleness, emotional sensitivity, solicitude and tact, plus elegance, attractiveness and charm. But 65 percent believed these qualities alone did not make for womanliness. They felt the concept also included independence, self-respect and self-confidence. Zoya Yankova, who took the survey, stressed that "the independent development of a woman's personality need not entail her taking on such 'masculine' traits as ruthlessness and overaggressiveness." She went on to define these, in either sex, as merely evidence of a poor cultural background and of inhumanity."

There is always the expressed need for a wholesale change in male attitudes — and for an even greater understanding that women are not only "equal," but that to be "equal," they must have some disequal privileges in order to make up for their disequal responsibilities. At least, the Russian women have Lenin behind them, and Lenin duly pointed out that housework can be "petty, mechanical and nerve-racking." Still, the Russian men do not really want to help with the housework. It has been truly revolutionary that, at Russian maternity centers today, young men have been taking part in "classes for fathers." When these classes were organized in 1970, fathers stayed away in droves, mostly because they were afraid their friends would laugh at them. Today, attendance is quite satisfactory.

In short, the kind of inward-turning, psychological revolution that is coming on all levels for Soviet young people is also coming, slowly, very slowly, in the area of male-female relations.

They are confused by the American women's liberation movement without quite understanding that they may be headed for somewhat the same thing. I discussed it one day at the Soviet Women's Committee, the group that deals with all contacts with women's groups abroad. What did they think of it?

"We understand that there are many types of 'women's lib,' " said Zoya Kurancheva, an official of the committee, "that there are many groups with many tactics.

"We sympathize with some, while others look ridiculous. They have not worked out formal goals and programs."

"We do not share the feminist approach," interjected Ludmila Balakhovskaya, general secretary of the committee. "We believe that women's problems are part of the whole society."

We understand the revolt against the image of woman as a toy," continued Miss Kurancheva, "and that you must create a new atmosphere and a new orientation."

"But we believe in the harmonious development of all talents," continued Ludmila Balakhovskaya, "and putting that knowledge at the service of society."

"We have to coexist, males and females," said Zoya.

"Of course, men and women should have equal pay," said Ludmila. "You can't use one group of workers against another."

The conversation drifted off — into confusion and indecision.

For what is just beginning to happen with this new generation in Russia today is that relations between the sexes — not the quantitative revolution of equal jobs, nursery schools and the right to dig ditches — are just beginning to be altered. Indeed, they are just *beginning* to talk about them. Or, as one woman sociologist, L. Kuznetsova, has written, there is a need for a "revolution in human relations" between the sexes.

If the Russian model — in many ways so much further advanced quantitatively than any other society — shows anything, it shows that the outcome of the struggle is not so easy or assured as it has been assumed to be; and that it must reach beneath the paperwork of university admissions and job applications and into the very soul and mind of woman and, even more, man.

ᕕ Chapter Fifteen
Sex in Russia
— Is Anyone Thirsty?

*"I regard sex like a glass of water,
from which I drink when I am thirsty."*

Madame Alexandra Kollontai, the early Bolshevik
exponent of "free love," to Lenin.

"But who wants to drink a glass of dirty water?"

Lenin

$\mathcal{T}$HE offices of Literaturnaya Gazyeta or Literary Gazette are
housed in a big old building with dark damp halls in downtown
Moscow. From them, every month, comes a magazine read by 1.3
million Soviets that, even by Western standards, is one of their most
effective literary efforts. Its powerful editor Alexander Chakovsky
looks upon his job as that of combating — and, of course, defeating
— his ideological enemies, who are everywhere. But his is no ham-
handed ideology. He does not hit the reader over the head with iron-
gloved colloquies. His aim, by calm sophisticated analyses, is to
convince his readers of the failures and multitudinous inanities of
Capitalism.

He is noted for his book, "The Meek are not Blessed," which is
aimed at young people. The title speaks for itself. Of course, sometimes even this modern polemicist's points and analogies run a little
wild as when, at the party congress in March of 1971, he placed
together as No. 1 enemies of the state "The Portugese racists, J.
Edgar Hoover, Right-wing Socialists, and Mobutu."

My interview at Literaturnaya Gazyeta was not, however, with
Chakovsky, who speaks only with the Central Committee, which

speaks only to the Politburo; it was with Ann Martinova, the crisp, dark-haired editor who wields her pen over American affairs. As we discussed various things, I was struck by the unusual rationality she displayed in discussing foreign affairs. She neither ranted nor insulted; she was obviously quite sure about her way, but she did not, like most Soviets in official places, try to destroy her interlocutor to make her every point.

The New Left? Yes, they had analyzed it and their conclusion — oh, as long as a year ago — was that it would not last long. "Love Story?" She got a little more excited. "Pure garbage. No social message at all."

Then, at the very end of our interview, for no particular reason, I asked her whether the magazine, which was largely aimed at young intellectuals, ever dealt with the "problem" of premarital sex relations.

All of her carefully built-up manner of insouciance and sophistication fell immediately into sullen bits. The blood rose in her pale white face, causing an untidy flush to reveal her feelings. Her lips became set in that pursed, unpleasant look that so often affects most official Soviets upon meeting any foreigner they are not trying to get something from.

"WE HAVE NO 'PROBLEM' OF PREMARITAL SEX RELATIONS," she snapped, throwing an angry look at me. "Our family life is very solid. This exists only in YOUR country."

At this point, my guide, Nellie Genina, shadow-boxed with her. "Every American teacher who comes here — that is the first thing she asks me," Nellie said, tossing her head back and with a haughty look that was unnatural to her. "We don't have this . . ."

And, of course, the society *looks* like it does not "have this." On the surface — publically — shows of affection between couples are almost non-existent. Men and women walk together as they dance together, foot lifted, foot put down, faces unsmiling, with as much sensuous grace as Charlie Chaplin. They use their bodies clumsily. The average Russian seems to have little rhythmic or rhapsodic sense, and anyone who tries even to do a modified little folk dance on a dance floor is likely to be told by some officious older "watchman" of society that that is "neculturnii" or uncultured. There is almost no flirtatiousness or grace in "real life" — as opposed to the sheer virtuosity of, for instance, the unreal life of the ballet.

Even some of the surveys, those massive magic purveyors of the modern mass will, support the idea that sexual freedom is neither permitted nor admired. In Leningrad, a survey of 2,035 young people voted that "sexual dissoluteness" was the "demerit" which gave them "the greatest disgust." And many, though they love his poetry, will tell you that they do not admire poet Yevgeny Yevtushenko because of his irresponsible multiple liaisons — because he "uses women."

All of this is, to put it in a colloquial Midwestern manner, bosh.

The experience with Ann Martinova — and many, many more like it — made it clear to me very quickly how impossible it is for the prudish older Russians to deal on any real or honest level with sexual habits and patterns among the young. Moreover, in *this* area, I believe they are not only parroting the official line, I believe many of them truly believe what they are saying. Apparently they honestly believe there is no such thing in Russia as premarital sex — a fact which illustrates more than anything I can think of the extraordinary dream world in which many Russians live.

For premarital sex among the young is so widespread, so common and so casual that one can only come to the conclusion, fifty years later, that they have actually come to take sex as the early Bolshevik Madame Kollontai put it, with as few concerns as a "drink of water." Sex among the young in Russia today has reached a point, with some exceptions of course, at which it is a totally amoral thing. Or, as Newsweek magazine put it once, "The Soviet Union is fast becoming one of the most sexually uninhibited societies among the industrialized nations of the world."

Why this tremendous break between the old and the young in ideas about sex? Partly it is because, outwardly, the older Russians are so inhibited — not only in sex but in everything. Those dark overcoats are more than utilitarian, they are symbolic of the inhibitions that take over the Russian character in all its dealings with other people. Contrasted and yet parallel to this — living alongside these inhibitions, among the older generation — is a very direct, and indeed, crude approach toward sex.

Russian men do not make "passes," (such a ginger, Western, British word, compared to what Russian men do), they have home runs, or try to, the first moment they decide they like a woman. They do not approach. They lunge. Their "attacks" are often so crude as to be unbelievable to Western women, who are either revolted or fascinated by the male barbarism of them.

Usually these lunges occur when a man has lost enough of his inhibitions through the most extraordinary bouts of drinking, and the only way for a woman to avoid him is to sidestep them or to physically fight them off; at this point, there is no talking one's way out. One European girl stopped to ask two young men what bus to take on a Moscow streetcorner; the one, who had been drinking, said only a few words before he slipped his arm around her and directly on to her breast. Another Western girl climbed in the front seat of a taxi, only to have the eager driver immediately put his hand on her knee while he told her how desirable she was. Every Western girl I ever talked to in Russia agreed, with some astonishment, that Russian men were the fastest, the most direct and, because of their often bear-like size, the biggest threat that they had met in any country. They have neither a sense of discretion nor a sense of place.

"Russian men are temperamental," Giselle Amalrik, wife of the dissident writer Andrei Amalrik, explained. "They are not gallant. Western women often think they're crude, and some of them like them because of that. They're intense, and they're jealous." She might have added that Russians are a strange combination of public puritanism and private, unabashed lustiness — Russian honeymoon couples leave their wedding party, for instance, go off and spend the night in whatever apartment is free, then rejoin the party for a couple more days of celebrating.

Nor are Russian women exactly coy. Simple and straightforward, they cultivate none of the feminine artifices of Western women and certainly none of the grace and gentility of Oriental women.

If they like a man, they show it. Quickly and unmistakably. One American diplomat who had traveled widely in Russia as a student and spoke good Russian once commented to me of his experiences: "I didn't mind in the restaurants in the evening when the girls asked me to dance, but when they walked me back to the table and pulled my chair out, I thought that was too much."

But, then, it must be remembered that Soviet archaeologists are claiming today that the Amazon women of Greek mythology were actually early Russians — the nomadic, warlike, hard-riding Sarmatians, who swept up and down the banks of the Urals more than 2,000 years ago. One attractive Russian blonde, asked how she would react if someone called her a descendant of the Amazons, she said, "I'd like it. I think of an Amazon as a strong, independent woman."

It should not be thought that Russian women are somehow unwomanly, however, for this is by no means the case. They are simply without any of the often foolish feminine artifices of other societies, both Western and Oriental. In their own way, they are deeply feminine and often very gentle. Typical was the case of a British correspondent who was doing a story on a young woman artist. He invited her with several friends to dinner one night and at one point in the evening he was astonished to find her in a corner convulsed in sobs.

"You only like me to work with," she said between sobs. "You are only using me for work."

"You can't mistake them," he said afterwards. "These women are very female females. They're not at all packaged like so many American women."

Or, as one Soviet woman friend of mine put it, "Whatever we do, we do all the way. When we love, we love all the way. If we turn to Communism, we turn all the way. We have tremendous passions but they are always beneath the surface."

Today, as in everything else, there is a generational break over sex. The old think the young's lack of inhibitions and sexual give-and-take is morally reprehensible. The young think the old's hypocrisy about sex is disgusting. But not only are the young freer in their ways, they are far less crude about sex. And, particularly among those with higher education, there is a new element coming into play regarding sex: the element of whimsy.

In Sochi, for instance, I was invited one day by King Neptune, who was none other than Sputnik Camp Leader, Lev Sergeevich, a husky, bronzed athlete who directed this camp for Russian and visiting foreign youth, to take part in their King Neptune party. I appeared at the camp's lovely stony beach on the Black Sea at 3 p.m., the appointed hour, and, frankly, I was curious. Having a "Neptune party" seemed to me to be about as Russian as their having a Fourth of July party in a stock exchange.

It was a beautiful sunny afternoon in October, and as far as you could see in every direction, stretched the grey, rocky, pebbly type of beach indigenous to the Black Sea. Behind us, across a stretch of prickly bush, was the camp: acres of attractive new buildings, dormitories, clubhouses and dining rooms. Already assembling on the beach were all the 18, 19- and 20-year-olds, mostly students, who had been given free trips to the camp as a reward for overfulfilling their quotas in their summer work groups. What a contrast they presented to the enormous walrus-like women on Sochi's regular beaches, in their regular underwear bras and their bathing suit "bottoms" made from scarves tied around their ample middles!

From anything they could, these nubile young girls had assembled comical costumes. Many were dressed in bikinis decorated with palms, painted sweatshirts, and lipstick remarks scrawled on bits of flesh. On one male leg was written: "I need a woman." A girl decorated her thigh with the succulent, "Love . . . boys . . . sin." As King Neptune suddenly appeared on the horizon on water skis and skied right up into the shallow water, the group broke out into a wild orgy of twists and danced jitterbugs to the tune of recordings. Then King Neptune, having discarded his skis, stalked with comic solemnity up onto the beach and mounted a "throne" — a decorated chair which the youngsters had provided.

"Now I'm going to see who has been good and who has been bad this year," Lev Sergeevich began, much in the manner of a summer-time Santa Claus. "Neptune will reward those who have been good," he said, as the crowd roared, "and the sinful will be thrown into the sea." Another, greater roar, and more impromptu dancing. "Neptune," he said, louder now, "warns everyone to live in accordance with law and order." An even greater, more imprudent roar. Then he turned to a pretty blond, tantalizingly dressed in a sarong, with provocative phrases about sex and love painted on her body. "Do you have any sins?" he said, looking at her as if she certainly must.

When she admitted "I have so many sins I can't remember them all," the boys picked her up and threw her wiggling form in the sea.

A dark-haired girl named Tamara, who told me later she was a geologist, was rewarded with a seat by the king's side for her goodness. "She's the only girl the boys haven't slept with," he noted, in an aside, matter of factly. This evoked a huge collective cheer, plus an undercurrent of good-natured booing.

Another girl was brought up and was sentenced to be kissed on the ankle by a boy, who soon was kissing her on the knee and if King Neptune himself had not intervened . . .

Before they could name Miss Black Sea, Miss Charleston, Miss Water Ski, Miss Sputnik and Miss Rock and Roll, I, too, was dragged up and asked, in true Russian fashion, how much my trip had cost. "Too much," I said. "How much do you earn?" King Neptune wanted to know. Finally, unwillingly, I answered, considerably understating it but still throwing a momentary gloom over the party. But when I was asked what I most wanted and I replied, "To kiss King Neptune," the shouts of glee went up again and my salary, outrageous to Russian thinking, was forgotten.

It was the same that night, when I came back to the camp. First we sat in one of the dormitory rooms, drinking wine and eating plum cakes. Somehow politics and ideology never came up. Then couples began to kiss . . . and kiss . . . and kiss. "The girls were often the aggressors. "Isn't he beautiful," one girl kept saying, as she passionately affixed her gaze upon the boy she liked. "Isn't he beautiful?" Then she would throw her arms around him and kiss him long and passionately. "And she's the camp's Minister of Culture," the boy next to me told me, drily. At the end of the evening, couples finally coupled up, drifting off to the beach and into the less hostile — and scratchy — areas of the brush.

This was the way it seemed to be everywhere there was a chance for it to be this way. The young people were not immoral — that expletive did not even seem to enter into it — they were spontaneously amoral. They were simply doing what seemed normal, harmless and guiltless to them. And when I asked the young people about sex, they answered in just exactly the opposite ways from their elders and from the official answerers like Ann Martinova.

"It's just a normal healthy response," a young teacher named Inara in Riga told me, "We have no puritan questions. If you want to, you want to. Nobody minds if you make love if you love each other and certainly not if you intend to spend your lives together. But you can change partners, too." A male student at Moscow University, considered one of the superior hotbeds, said simply, "Some girls won't sleep with a man at their first meeting, but they're in the minority." And a young Ukrainian, Yuri, trying to get a visiting American girl to go to bed with him, was unmoved by her protestations of love for someone else. "What," he demanded, "does that have to do with it?"

It seems to have nothing to do with it at all. "Sex among the students is not looked upon as a moral thing," commented a foreign diplomat with long experience in Moscow, including a student year of his own. "There are some with strong family or religious ties, and their behavior is quite different. But they are atypical."

A prominent Egyptian psychiatrist, Dr. Mustafa Fahny, came to Moscow one summer to visit his son, a student there, and was stunned by the sexual freedom in the universities. "The Arab boys come from a very conservative and restricted society," he confided in me one day. "The Arab girls are like flowers — buds that never bloom. Here there is complete freedom. The boys are fascinated by the sensuousness of the society, and I have warned my son to question whether this is good. I wonder if a man will be a good father, having lived under these conditions. They are all together in the dorms, and when they close the doors, nobody asks questions."

The students do indeed have an advantage over others in their society; they have a *place* to make love that is more or less private, they have doors to close behind them. In the universities, dormitories are mixed, with men and women in the same buildings and often even on the same floors. Though there are usually several to a room, it is common for a men to invite a girl to his room, bring out the sausage, the bread and the vodka, and simply lock the door. The roommates are very understanding, for the time will surely come when they, too . . .

Some couples are lucky enough, through influence or chance, to get a "khata" — a Ukrainian word which means "hut" or, in slang, an empty room where a boy and girl can live together or make love — of their own. One couple in Kiev, who shared a bath and kitchen in a communal apartment with seven other people had an interesting Khata: a Playboy centerfold on one wall faced an icon of an old Russian madonna on the other, while love beads hung on the window above one chair, a double bed and a 400-ruble radio-phonograph.

"There was lots of screaming in both our families," Katya, the young woman said, describing how they decided to live together.

"Most young people in the Soviet Union would not do what we did. But our parents could not stop us. I still see my family. They don't approve, but they put up with it." She and her love, Misha, who were interviewed by the Washington Post's Anthony Astrachan, called themselves the generation with "eyes open" and estimated that about 20 percent of their colleagues also had their eyes opened.

They also told Astrachan that marijuana or hashish cost between 30 and 50 rubles for 11 grams or about three and a half ounces and that they were called "plan" — a special joke in the country of the five-year plan, which referred to the concept of yielding its own high.

Others, however, are not that lucky; some must even resort to what I have come to term the ambulance answer. I heard about ambulancism in love first from a young German businessman, single and seeking adventure, who came to Moscow in the summer of 1971 for a medical convention. Soon he met a pretty, black-eyed Russian interpreter and the two (more or less) fell in love. At least, they wanted badly to *make* love.

But what to do? His room was probably bugged — bad for her. She shared an apartment with her mother and brother — bad for him. There are no motels.

But being a typically innovative modern Russian girl, she soon solved the problem. She got a friend, an ambulance driver off duty, to drive them around the outskirts of Moscow with the curtains closed for a couple of hours each night. They made love in the ambulance.

The same unassimilable duality that is present in adult-youth ideas about sex is also present in ideas about how one should fall in love. The Soviet state's attitude has always been to try to persuade young people to lead moral lives by defining "good love" and by discouraging too much "water drinking."

And what is "good love?"

"The choice of a girl should depend not only on a man's private attitude or his private virtues, but on his attitudes in community life and his contribution to society," Tatyana Melnukova, an editor of "Young Leninist" in Volgograd explained. "She should make her judgment not only on him alone but on him as a representative of the collective he works in."

But this idea — that a man or a woman should pick a mate on

the basis of whether he meets his factory quote or not — is mocked by most young Russians today.

On this level of the average young person, sex still tends to be a wholesome, straightforward thing, acted out with few guilt pangs and staged with little emotional or theatrical roccoco. On the "bohemian" level, however, when you start to deal with the upper intelligentsia of writers, artists, musicians and actors, there is a good deal of substantive orgiastic drama that reminds one of nothing so much as the great orgies of Dostoevsky in the 19th century.

One of the very few foreigners to be taken into this society, a young and very intelligent Western diplomat, described these parties to me. "It's typical, for instance, that a man will take four girls to bed before 15 people," he said, as though he were describing a military maneuver. "Usually the husbands and wives retire to different rooms when they go with other people, however, and the spouse will send someone else in to get the husband or wife. But they usually go home with each other.

"Many of these parties are real brawls. What do they do? Oh, for instance, they drink a lot and they vomit all over the floor, then people fall in it. You or your wife will be talking to someone and suddenly he or she will reach for your private parts. They can't understand why neither I nor my wife take part in these parties all the way; we're always making excuses. The girls turn right on; I still haven't figured out whether they're just being honest or what."

This society, even today, and even despite or because of Communism, is probably the closest to a truly "bohemian" society that exists anywhere in the world and some of the "arrangements" would seem peculiar even to the most individualistic artists and writers. Bella Akhmadulina, the leading young poetess and former wife of Yevtushenko, is a baby-faced, almond-eyed Tatar who is now married to prose writer Yuri Negibin. Their living arrangements in their luxurious Moscow apartment seem to suit everyone; his dominating mother oversees the household, his first wife is their official housekeeper, and for special occasions Bella wears the clothes that Yevtushenko bought her in New York.

In this society, homosexuality is accepted as an ordinary thing, even though officially it is outlawed and punishable by three to eight years in prison. As far as homosexuals are concerned, this is no sexually permissive society at all. "With all the tricks at their disposal," G.G. Gromzdov wrote in a book on sex education for the Ministry of Defense in 1964, "homosexuals seek out and win the confidence of youngsters. Then they proceed to act. Don't under any circumstances allow them to touch you. Such people should be immediately reported to the administrative organs so they can be removed from society." How much homosexuality there is in the rest of society — among the pitied "masses" — I could not tell, for no one would talk about it.

But, among the bohemia, I heard a good deal of talk about incest, particularly among sisters and brothers. Some intellectuals seemed absolutely fascinated by it, regaling me with stories of their friends who had suddenly fallen in love with brothers and sisters, some who went on to live together openly, etc. "Is there anything like this in America?" one pressed me with eager anticipation.

For the Russian who wants sex outside of marriage or outside of affection — in effect, on a commercial basis — there are also "ways" even though Soviet officials, of course, deny this. Prostitutes for the poor people are usually to be found at the railroad stations, which for this and various related reasons turn out to be some of the liveliest spots in the Soviet Union. Girls with higher sights, like foreigners, work their way into the foreign currency bars of the Intourist hotels that cater to foreigners. These girls cater to them, too, and, in the process, often earned up to 100 rubles a night. One night in the Leningrad foreign currency bar, I was sitting talking to a young Russian, while a buxon, rather tired-looking blond Russian girl whom he knew was being unusually nice to some very drunk Finns. "I hate to see our women like this," the Russian spat out. "But you can buy anything here for dollars, including our women."

This sentiment seemed to be illustrated in Moscow's Hotel National in 1966, when it was raided for its bargirl-prostitutes. The girls explained to foreign correspondents that "we didn't do it for pleasure, we did it for dollars," before they were sent away for seven years.

Many of these girls, of course, are sent to foreigners for special reasons. They operate on different levels, usually according to how they look and, one supposes, other talents. I know well they exist because I was personally treated to an interesting sampling of how this particular "service" — which sometimes is designed strictly to give pleasure and succour to the tired visitor and sometimes is designed to provide information and blackmailing possibilities to the incumbent KGB — works.

I was having dinner at the Ukraine Hotel in Moscow with an Arab friend whom I had known well a year earlier in Cairo. His name was Muin Besieso and he was an enormously talented poet and playwright — so talented he had been brought to Moscow for a Pushkin festival and to talk to the Taganka Theater's impressive director Lybimov about having his plays produced there. I had not been expected at the Ukraine by his guide — nor did the powers-that-be have any reason to believe I, or anyone else, would appear, for he had called me completely on his own. At any rate, as we sat there talking above the unholy din that is the Ukraine's dining room, this apparition — that is the only thing to call her — appeared. She was a young, nubile girl with long black hair parted in the middle and hanging down both sides. She was wearing a green sweater so tight her torso somewhat resembled a green hillcock covered with grass just mowed.

Her white pants were tighter still. I won't describe them.

Now, no "good Soviet girl" would ever be allowed, dressed in this "disgusting," "subversive," "hyenaish," "bourgeoise" manner (to cite just a few *weak* Soviet terms of reprobation for this kind of dress) in *any* Soviet dining room, much less a tourist high spot like the Ukraine. Yet despite the fact that the dining room was filled, she was ushered up to the table next to ours, where it was clear she knew no one, and another place was set for her. (Subtlety is not a Russian trait.) She immediately began to preen, to stretch her arms, and thus her breasts, and to flirt in the most obvious manner with Muin. From time to time, she got up, and walked around, always managing to walk by him and brush against his shoulder as she looked yearningly at him.

"I feel as if I know the girl," he remarked drily during dinner. "Twice today she pulled up behind me in a car and got out when I did — once in a Renault, once in a Rolls Royce."

I don't know if he got to know the girl much better or not, but I do know this kind of "comfort" is often provided by the state for visiting dignitaries . . . particularly if they are married at home and the state may one day wish, oh, for one . . . reason or another, to find cause to remind him of the contraband passions of his "Moscow nights."

But if there are these curious, arranged affairs of state, there are also patterns — routes that the Russians themselves follow — for finding casual romance. Just as the American woman goes to Mexico for a vacation and just as the Swedish girl heads to Italy or Greece, the northern Soviet women, newly divorced or just bored with her marriage, goes to Georgia or Armenia. This seems to be particularly true for women from the Baltic republics, probably because they are more advanced in their thinking and independent in their actions.

"When a woman from the Baltics comes here," one Georgian told me, knowingly, "we all know why." And, of course, the dark, handsome, cordially available Georgian men are so happy to oblige. Within hours, indeed within minutes, adventure will raise its smiling head. Light-haired women merely sit down at a table in Tbilisi and they are showered by notes from men at surrounding tables, dutifully delivered by the experienced waiters.

Another way of "arranging" things, in a country where there is simply no free space for love-making and where families live wall-to-wall in their small apartments is for young people to buy round trip tickets on the Leningrad night train. It's actually quite a neat compromise. They leave Friday or Saturday night, sleep with their lovers all night on the train in a compartment for two persons, spend the day in Leningrad, then return Saturday or Sunday night. The cars are excellent, the tea is hot, the tracks are smooth, and, so, apparently, is the love.

Indeed, many elements revolving around sex are "arranged" in the Soviet Union, despite the fact that sexual choice — eros — was supposed to be freed by the revolution. Some people marry because the other person has an apartment in a desirable city which they cannot remain in otherwise. Diplomats sometimes marry because, in order to go abroad, they need wives. There is a tacit acceptance of many things that would be considered totally unthinkable in the West. Often, for instance, couples are separated for a year or for years by their work. One Bratsk teacher had spent two years in Leningrad getting advanced training and leaving her husband and son behind.

"First I was joking when I said I was going," she said. "Then he said, 'yes,' and I thought he was joking." She stopped for a moment. "Maybe he thought it would be convenient," she added drily.

Actually, the new permissiveness in sex today represents a turn almost back to the early "free love" days of the beginnings of Bolshevism. At that time, the town fathers of Vladimir, the ancient capital of Russia, proclaimed that "Any girl reaching the age of 18 and remining unmarried is liable to be penalized for failing to register at the Bureau of Free Love." "Winged Eros" was aflight, and nothing would stop it soaring. It was then assumed by many of the early idealists that marriage would become a thing of the past; only love would bind man and woman together.

Behind this basically emotional view of the world was the theoretical Marxist thesis that marriage was just a bourgeois institution whose sole function was to insure the orderly transfer of property from father to son. If you believed this, it was easy to cancel the existing laws regulating it. At this point in history, couples needed only to appear before the district party chief in order to declare themselves married; it was much the same for divorce.

It was Stalin's "Asiatic" prudishness toward sex and his concentration on production rather than reproduction in the 1920s and '30' that reintroduced sexual continence . . . with a vengeance. Suddenly kissing was forbidden in movies; the nude form, in art. The family was emphasized again, and free love was frigidly frowned upon.

Actually, Stalin's attitudes toward sex were very much in tune with the ideas of old Russian folk medicine, which claimed that sexual activity was not only normal, but a very important regulating function of the human body. The folk practitioners recommended moderation, but never abstinence, and they recommended continuing sexual relations as far into old age as possible.

Even today, these recommendations seem to bear fruit, if we may express it in that manner. In Abkhasia, a Caucasian land where the people live well up into their 100s, the Abkhasians attribute their astonishing longevity to the fact they postpone beginning sexual relations until they are 30 (sometimes even abstaining on their wedding nights) and they continue them well into their mid-100s.

There is no danger of young Russians today postponing such satisfaction for so long — although they certainly may continue that long.

Part of the change in sexual manners doubtless is due to World War II, when the U.S.S.R. lost upwards of 20 millions of the country's most virile young people, mostly men, leaving, even a generation after the close of the war, 19 million more females than males in the country. Probably at least in part, it is the presence of these many unattached women — plus the more free-thinking ways of the post-war generation — which has led to the new "swinging."

But what every foreigner, after having made his observations and calculations, begins to wonder if this: if there is so much sexual freedom among the young, why is the birth rate so low that it is deeply concerning the powers that be about future reproduction of the Soviet state? What do the women do?

The answer was and is singular and simple: abortion. It, too, may be as easy as taking a drink of water but it is surely not so pleasurable.

On his tour, Dr. Fahny was taken in Tashkent to visit a famous abortion hospital. He shook his head in disbelief as he recalled it. "I looked at the faces of the girls and they were all blond. That means they came from elsewhere. They just came in and filled out the form and waited. I took a picture of them standing in line. One would go in and five minutes later she'd come out. There's no morality at all connected with it here; it's like eating a meal."

Most girls don't even feel this moral compunction to go somewhere away from home, like Tashkent. They just go to their friendly corner hospital. I met girls at Moscow University who had had anywhere from three to eight abortions before age 25, and it didn't seem to disturb them as much as it does women in the West.

Galina Mamayeva, a very proper young Soviet woman from Khabarovsk in the Far East near the Chinese border, told me simply, when I asked her about contraception, "If you get pregnant, you just go to a doctor and you can have an operation." When I told her that at that time abortions were illegal in the United States, she asked in astonishment, "But what if you already have five children and don't want another? Or if you're too sick to have one? It's only right to do something."

There was a curious dichotomy, however. She was unusual in that she had very puritannical thoughts about discussing sex with men, for instance, and also about premarital sex. "If anyone knew a couple was having relations . . . we certainly would not speak to them." This did not apply to men, however. "You know, men develop earlier," she said in a worldly way. She thought they should "learn" by having affairs with "older women."

Galina's ideas probably arose from the fact that she lived in a very, very provincial town (there is hardly any place in the world more provincial than Khabarovsk) and came from a tight-knit family. They mirrored her Alice-in-Wonderland innocence on contraception. "If you've had relations," she said, very school-teacherish and very serious, "you just sit in a hot bath right away." Then she mentioned a magazine particularly for women in the countryside which showed you how to make a diaphragm from a lemon peel and a string.

The inter-uterine device? The pill? Almost no one uses these. There is a deep-seated fear of the pill, and only some of the women of the elite use it, for it is only available on the black market in the big cities. The inter-uterine devices are used only on an experimental basis, and the efficacy of cheap (2 cents) Russian condums can be judged by their favorite and expressive nickname — galoshes.

Despite talk like Galina's, however, and despite the low cost of $5.50 for an abortion, I did not find that *all* young Russian women were that enthusiastic about abortions. Many felt it was a shameful thing — that is why many would go as far as Tashkent, where they knew no one. What's more, the conditions in the clinics are dismal. In the supermarket atmosphere of the quick fix-all, where first-timer young girls of 17 find themselves next to callous middle-aged women who have had six abortions, no anesthesia is used and screams fill the waiting rooms as well as the operating rooms, where three or four such operations are performed in the same room.

Moreover, despite the Soviets' unquenchable penchant for programming and teaching everything in their society, they have provided no sex education at all in the schools. This, as much as anything, shows their extreme prudishness on the subject, and one survey showed that 65 percent of children gained information on sex from each other, only 6 percent from their parents, 6 percent from the school, and the remainder from reading, movies or hearsay.

This is a direct result of the peasant prudishness about sex that has always permeated Russian society and that caused even the famous pedagogue Anton Makarenko to write, "No talks with children about the 'sex' problem can add anything to the knowledge that will come of itself in good time."

But it may be that in the future both the need for better contraceptive devices, for sex education and for a more honest look at sex and its exigencies will be met with some action. In 1970, for instance, the U.S.S.R. produced its first sociological study on sexual habits and styles since the revolution. Surveying 620 young men and women in Leningrad, two social scientists, A.G. Kharchev and S.I. Golod (Communist Kinseys?), found that among students 53% of the males and 38% of the females said they condoned premarital sex. Among young graduates earning their own living, 81% of the women felt that premarital relations were all right if the woman was in love.

(It is interesting — and instructive — that this survey of *actual behavior* conflicts to the extent it does with the earlier survey cited in Leningrad on *ideas about sexual behavior*. But from our own experience in the United States, we should be aware that the survey on actual behavior is most probably much more true than is the one on abstract ideas, in which a person often modifies his real feelings to fit into ideas imposed upon himself by some model of society.)

In reality, more than half the women reported having had premarital relations before they were 21, as did nearly half the men between the ages of 16 and 18. What's more, the men who had not "sinned," said they *had not* only for "lack of occasion" — the bleak imperatives of the cramped housing situation. "Where, oh where?" could well be the name of a Russian love song.

The two socioligists, moreover, severely criticized the "double standard" and particularly singled out for criticism a then-popular Soviet film which showed a man beating his fiance because she had told him she wasn't a virgin. "Women should have the right to have premarital and extramarital sex life," they insisted.

They even went so far to put much of the blame on the burgeoning divorce rate on Soviet educators who still refuse to recognize that there is a need for sex education in the schools. "This is a difficult and sophisticated matter," they wrote, "which demands, in a number of cases, education and re-education of educators themselves. To put this matter off or to ignore it would be to jeopardize too much, because socialism and Communism are first 'people,' and people originate in marriage and family."

One wonders why Ann Ivanovna never read that booklet. Or, worse, if she did, why she could not bear to talk about it.

❧ Part III
The State Forms,
The State Reacts

✿ Chapter Sixteen
The Formation of Socialist Man

"Our family is not a closed-in collective body, like the bourgeois family. It is an organic part of Soviet society, and every attempt it makes to build up its own experience independently of the moral demands of society is bound to result in a disproportion, discordant as an alarm bell."

Anton S. Marenko, Soviet child care specialist.

*O*NE of the most surprising things about the Soviet Union is to find, in one place and one place only in this mass society, a genuine atmosphere of charm and whimsy. Everything else from the Soviet period is drab and standardized. For reasons beyond most observers, the same Soviets who stand doggedly and without expression in grey lines at the Hermitage and Tretykov gallery for hours to spend a few minutes looking at masterpieces never think of putting up a painting in their own flats. Until the end of the 1960s, officialdom never thought of decorating a public building. There was no such thing as intimacy, a quiet corner or fanciful design — only fluorescent lights, heavy, standardized figures of socialism, and too-great, too-open, too-symbolic squares.

Yet in one place there is charm, whimsy and color, and that place is in the nursery schools and in the kindergartens of the Soviet Union. In these schools, there are charming pictures of bears and birds on the walls. In contrast to the dull, imagination-less dress of the parents, the children go to school warmly dressed in red woolen bonnets, embroidered sweaters and bright booties. All of adult imagination seems focused on their babies. More than anywhere else in the world, there is a deep and abiding conception of the children as the Soviet state of the future; they are nurtured, loved, disciplined, and, above all, they are formed — so formed that a four-year-old, given a western ballpoint pen on the Leningrad train to Novorod, asked immediately: "Which pen is better, yours or ours?"

Nothing, but nothing, is left to chance. In stark contrast to the laissez faire system of child-raising of most modern Americans, the Soviets believe, firmly and finally, that a child is a small human being . . . to be molded, loved and intimidated, usually by his own collective group, into the type of human being the state desires: Soviet man. This has been the idea of the Soviet state since the very beginning, since 1917, and this is the idea of the Soviet state today.

As M.A. Prokoviev, Minister of Education, once put it, "It is necessary to guide school children scientifically during all the 24 hours of the day, instead of only five or six hours when in school." The role of parents is not downgraded — far from it, despite what many Westerners mistakenly feel. The truth is that most parents concur with the state in its style of upbringing. "Children have to learn they exist only because of society, that they are nothing in themselves but only a part of society," is the way one mother described the relationship. Moreover, the parents' is not only or even the major authority.

As the famous pedagogue Anton Makarenko wrote: "In our country, the duty of a father toward his children is a particular form of his duty toward society. It is as if our society says to parents: 'You have joined together in good will and love; rejoice in your children and expect to go on rejoicing in them. That is your own personal affair and concerns your own personal happiness. But in this happy process you have given birth to a new people. A time will come when these people will cease to be only a joy to you and become independent members of society. It is not at all a matter of indifference to society what kind of people they will be. In handing over to you a certain measure of social authority, the Soviet state demands from you correct upbringing of future citizens. Particularly, it relies on a certain circumstance arising naturally out of your union — on your parental love. If you wish to give birth to a citizen and do so without parental love, then be so kind as to warn society that you wish to play such an underhanded trick. People brought up without parental love are often deformed people . . . ."

The story of how this "Soviet upbringing" is accomplished is a fascinating one . . .

Galina Petrovna, the blond and robust director of a large Volgograd kindergarten, sat behind her desk in a small office decorated with funny pictures of dancing brown bears and yellow chickens carrying baskets of eggs. Self-assured and cordial, she was a nice woman by any standards. And, in contrast to the many tormented, confused and threatened American teachers of the last few years, she was highly confident about what she was doing.

"Children who stay with us from six months on are stronger," she said, with assurance. "They are more steeled. They don't catch cold so much. It's been proved in practice that those children who go to school and kindergarten are better developed than those who stay home."

There was not the slightest question in her mind that children were better off on all counts being in school from infancy. And certainly the sturdy, happy little children in Galina Petrovna's kindergarten and nursery school were a good advertisement for her — and, thus, the state's — ideas. In the cheerful nursery, the infants were obviously well cared-for by nurse-teachers (salary 80 rubles a month) who obviously enjoyed their little charges, all the occasional screaming and the constant wetness notwithstanding.

The price the parents pay for this care depends upon their income, but it is minimal, the highest charge being 12 rubles a month. Moreover, they can bring the children early and pick them up at evening or arrange whatever schedule is best for them. Nursing mothers are permitted to leave their work to nurse the babies. The children's characters are formed in the nursery from the day they arrive. In other rooms, the older children sat around little tables drawing and making molds of clay and, in the afternoons, sleeping in rooms with the windows open. Soviet pedagogues are convinced that mothers are too protective in not giving children enough air.

Since I was a visitor, I was treated to a pleasing little performance. I was ceremoniously seated in the kindergarten while all the little 3- to 5-year-olds marched in neat line, arms unevenly wagging, singing "Let There Be Sunshine," the favorite song of Russian schoolchildren.

I must admit I was impressed, not only here but elsewhere, with the way the children were being raised. Never did I see any of the surly boredom of the slick smart-aleckness or the egocentric self-centeredness of many American children. Never did I witness the embarrassing spectacle of adults being bullied by being afraid of children. Never did I see the hostility so prevalent in many American schools between teachers and children — indeed, the relationships between them were warm, respectful, and, often, argumentative. Much the same relationship as in a good family.

As far as I could see, almost everyone, including mothers, agreed that even tiny babies were better off in school. The Soviets believe that mothers tend to spoil children, make them selfish and egotistical and lack the abilities to give them the systematic training and benefits they can get at school with other children and under supervised training. They say the routine is better for them, and so is the sharing they have to do within their own collective.

The collective rules a child's life to an extent undreamed-of in the West. In the parks, for instance, if a child wanders away or if a mother is not properly supervising her child, other adults will immediately step in. Children are taught to respect public property or face ostracism from the group (the worst punishment) and so the cities are immaculate. In the schools, collectives compete with each other, but individuals don't — so they do learn competitiveness. Within the collective, children care for each other, support each other and discipline each other. If one child in a nursery is bad, flowers will be withheld from his entire table — a highly effective prophylactic measure.

A typical example occurred in a Russian classroom where two American teenagers — the girl speaking good Russian and the boy understanding only minimally — were enrolled. When the teacher wrongly blamed a Russian boy for something the American boy had done, the American girl, stung by the injustice, cried out "It was not the Russian . . . . it was the other way around."

After class the teacher told the girl, "You have done a terrible thing. You were disloyal to your group."

This illustrated only one of many differences between the American and the Russian system. For the collective has its good points and its bad. On one hand, it cements loyalty to others close around you and prevents excessive egocentrism; on the other hand, like so many things in the Soviet system, it stifles honesty. Dr. Urie Bronfenbrenner of Cornell University, the American specialist on Soviet education, has also noted that Soviet schools always clearly stress right and wrong and black and white in tests — in contrast to the complexity and ambiguity of American tests. He also stresses how different is the Soviet collective from the American-style peer group; while the collective is closely tied to and supervised by adult society, the peer group is "relatively autonomous and cut off from the adult world." As to discipline, both in class and at home, the principle form of discipline is "temporary withdrawal of affection," as the manuals call it. Corporal punishment is considered very low class and "neculturnii," or uncultured. Character formation, moreover, is considered at least, if not more, important than simple academic training, and Soviet children are graded weekly on cooperation, conduct and willingness to share common tasks.

When the Soviets say to Americans, as they often do, "We are better formed than you," what do they mean? They mean that they are formed in a more systematic way. They talk about going to the theater, visiting museums and reading books — they tick off these cultural watermarks like the apocryphal airline stewardess ticks off, "Coffee, tea or me" — as if the most important thing were not the substance but the *fact* of going to the theater and the *fact* of reading a book. It is highly mechanistic and highly involved in having the correct attitude and the accoutrements of culture. Or, as "Rules for Schoolchildren," the highly authoritarian "program for the cultivation . . . . of habits of disciplined and cultured behavior," puts it: "Self-discipline was desired because with it conformity and obedience would become more perfect." Even in literature, there is constant reminder that you are helping someone by expecting him to do something for society — that a lack of this can kill character, and it can even kill love.

Through training like this, at the earliest possible age, the Soviets hoped to create a new generation of "Marxist men" who would share and share alike, and they are still working at it avidly. At the Pedagogical Institutes for Pre-School Children throughout the country, for instance, research is constantly being conducted on how best to form the child. They stress that the school is "another family," and they believe that abilities are largely "created" in a child, that they are not primarily inherent. So they *create* a school that is rich in pictures, colors and rhythm. They say, "If you give me a child with limited potential, I can make him, through providing him a rich environment, a normal human being. If you have one with high potential and don't put him in the best possible environment, he will stay dull forever."

"We don't say that a child is born with abilities," said Anna Mihailovna Leuchina, a professor at the Pedagogical Institute for the Pre-School Child in Leningrad. "We dismiss that. We say a child is born with the beginning stages of abilities which have to be developed."

Professor Leuchina, a charming white-haired woman with a delicate face, a lace collar, and the manner of all those devoted teachers throughout history who have loved children, was more than just a classroom teacher. She had developed many of the special, most advanced programs for pre-school children, particularly in mathematics.

"We believe you can start to work on developing the mathematical ability of children very early, she said in her gentle but firm voice, as she sat at a table in the institute. "Even very early they can see different things around them and they can count them in some way. A child can't count from 1 to 5, but he can say to himself, I have one candy and you have one, and he can make the comparison. After the age of one year, he can compare and see whether things are equal or not equal. What we are doing in nursery schools is teaching them by comparison — whether something is more or less. We put one thing on top of another, and the teacher asks, Is this equal? He answers by putting more in the line that has less. That kind of comparison means counting. After he is taught equal and non-equal, he can be taught numbers."

In another program, designed to develop sensory perception as well as the arts, the child listens to music that "sounds" like animals. "First it is gay," the professor explained, "and the teacher says, 'Hear how gay it is. It sounds like the rabbits.' Then comes the heavy music . . . the bear and then the fox. Nobody tells them what kind of music, but they remember. Then they themselves act like the animals. Then they play the music again and the children draw what they hear. It makes them extremely sharp."

This kind of pedagogical experimentation is going on constantly on all levels of Soviet education; once accepted by the Ministry of Education in Moscow, programs such as these then become "law for teachers throughout the country." It has advantages — a necessary amount of standardization for a huge country, a certain rationality that permeates the entire system — and it has disadvantages. Yet the disadvantages that could be expected — too much stereotyping, for instance — have not necessarily come to pass. The generation to come out of this system, while unquestionably more disciplined, less probing and less rambunctious than its counterpart in the West, is certainly very seeking and far more questioning than the pedagogues envisioned or perhaps would wish.

But it is not only on the school level that the child is formed in Soviet society. It must be remembered that — not unlike the old initiation into the "American way of life," where the Boy Scouts, the voluntary associations, the public parades and displays and many more formulative elements supplemented and supported the basic axioms of society that were mainly taught in the schools, the homes and the churches — everything in Soviet society served to back up the ideal of Marxist education.

From the time a child is in grade school, he or she is in the Pioneers, the single organization of youth that predates entry into the omnipresent Komsomol. They sing, march, train and have meetings, usually in Pioneer "palaces" that were the former homes of the wealthy. I could not help but feel in these palaces that the "Lenin rooms" or "Lenin corners" — rooms filled with Leninabilia, such as pictures, flags and statues — resembled nothing so much as some American rooms filled with Lincoln or Washington memorabilia.

At the same time, parallel and concomitant to the "extracurricular" character training, runs a tightly-organized program. Education is now compulsory from the first grade, which children enter at age 7, to the 10th grade; the children then have the option to continue either in the academic high school or to switch to vocational schools. Education is a passion with the Russians, and they have reason to be proud that, whereas in 1915 they had an illiteracy rate of 75 percent, today the country is almost wholly literate.

The curriculum is standardized, with a heavy emphasis on rote learning. In elementary school, children have 24 periods a week and 30 to 34 periods in secondary school. Mathematics is studied for 19 years, physics and a foreign language for five years, chemistry for four. In addition, there is a heavy load of Russian language and literature, history, geography, biology, astronomy, mechanical drawing, fine arts, music, physical education and a variety of mechanical classes. Most neglected in teaching is the written word — composition — and most neglected in spirit is a thrust toward innovation and independence of thought and inquiry.

When a child graduates from secondary school, he must take the exams for the university or for one of the many specialized institutes which form a vast secondary level of higher education. At the Volgograd Pedagogical Institute, the assistant pro-rector, Boris Sergeevich Kubantsev, explained how it is done. "How do we choose our 6,000 students?" he asked. "The first entrance exam serves as the main criterion. We also take into account recommendations from school and their grades there. Those who have been working at the school (such as a Pioneer leader) and those with excellent marks are admitted first. All exams for all institutes of higher education are given at the same time, so they can't try for more than one institute in one year, but they can try again next year or take evening courses. What happens after graduation? They work. After graduation, students have guaranteed work and they are given the possibility to choose where they want to be. But mostly they go to the rural areas because there is no demand for teachers in the cities. If a person gets married, he or she has a right to find his own job and he goes to the area or city educational commission to find work."

Since all education is free — students in institutes of higher education are given stipends, usually about $30 a month — they are expected to take jobs offered them after education, no matter where or what. "They can turn the first job down," one educator said, "but to turn down two or three would not be accepted."

Wherever he goes, the collective will follow him, and so will the entire system of collective formation — in his work, in his housing block, in the magazines he reads. Even, should any of this trouble him, in psychotherapy.

In his housing, when he needs something he will apply to the local deputy elected by the housing collective, and the deputy will forward any request to the larger city collective. In his work, should something go wrong, the matter will be dealt with, not in an individual manner as in the United States, but in a communal manner.

In Odessa, I asked a journalist from a nautical newspaper, The Sailor, what he would do if he, as a journalist, found out, for instance, that there was corruption on one of the ships. Would he simply print it and let the chips fall where they may? "We work under the Minister of Shipping," he began, solemnly, "and if we found something wrong on the ship, we'd try to talk to the person involved. If that didn't work, we'd print it and then send it to the captain. If he didn't do something about it, we'd send it to the Ministry." In effect, it was all done "within the family." When I tried to explain our system of journalistic ethics, by which a journalist conceived of himself as a person who "stood outside" society, he was horrified. "Nobody is outside society, he shouted, "nobody." When I tried to explain that this was, of course, a relative expression, he got even more angry. And when I mentioned that there young reporters on our paper who had started their own publication criticizing the paper, he was even more horrified. "Why," he demanded flatly, "don't they fire them?"

Much the same is true on the proliferous youth magazines (Yunost, Molodaya Gvardia, Komsomolskaya Pravda, Salskaya Molodozh and many more) that advise and form youth. "We believe our main task is to help bring up a new generation which is spiritually beautiful and physically healthy," Igor Zaharoskho, an editor of "Molodaya Gvardia" or "Young Guard" told me. "The moral education of the younger generation is the main task which we try to fulfill through the education we call Communist education. We believe that this bringing up incorporates all the best features of mankind."

And much the same is true in psychotherapy. Psychiatry is not widely practiced in the Soviet Union, and psychoanalysis even less, but there are now a number of hospitals with in-patient and out-patient care for troubled people. The prominent American psychiatrist Isidore Ziferstein lived more than a year in Russia studying their methods of therapy and made some particularly cogent observations on the differences in methodry between the two countries. He found that the Soviet method, to a far greater extent than the American method, involved "guidance, reeducation, advice, reassurance, support." The Soviet psychotherapists actively guided the direction and content of each session. The therapy was carried on predominantly in a "climate of positive relationship, toward which the therapist strove." Here, as in the classroom, Dr. Ziferstein found the atmosphere of "one big family" — the collective reasserting its many-headed nature again. The Soviet psychotherapist directly advised the patient and even called upon the Komsomol, the community and the patient's place of work to help in the therapy. "These factors," Dr. Ziferstein concluded, "are intimately related to a basic characteristic of Soviet society: it is what I would call a 'parental-collectivist' society in which everyone is, or at least is expected to be, his brother's keeper."

But, very well, how has this extraordinary organized system of educational formation worked? Has it turned out the perfectly-modulated young "New Men" of Socialism? Has it, where Christianity failed, made man his brother's keeper? Has it done away with class differences and class conflicts?

First, it is necessary to admit to and admire the formidable victories of Soviet education — the turning out of massive numbers of well-educated young people, the obliteration of illiteracy, the creation of a scientific (if not in other respects a cultural) elite which has come to challenge the scientific community of the West. They have created a system of education and indoctrination that is unquestionably superior, *in terms of what it wants to accomplish,* to the one in the United States. They have not lost track of the core of education — character training — and they have imbued their youth with a sense of serving society and a sense of brotherhood, however imperfect.

However, one does not have to negate these truly astonishing and admirable accomplishments to see that, largely because they *are* an advanced and developed country, they are now passing on to many of the new problems that afflict all developed and post-developed countries.

Already the pressures for success are so high that Soviet doctors and educators have produced evidence of a near epidemic in ailments ranging from nervous rashes to heart trouble among children barely to their teens. "It is no secret that between 20 and 25 percent of students must repeat one of their grades because of ill health," the Komsomol newspaper "Komsomolskaya Pravda" wrote in 1971. Doctors particularly pointed out the special mathematics and English language schools, where pressures are especially high, as leading to such problems as crooked spines, high blood pressure, neuroses and allergies and heart trouble.

Moreover, as the average level of education grows higher and higher, there is more and more pressure, on all levels, for more independence of action and study. Because of this, beginning in 1966 high school juniors and seniors were allowed to choose four hours of electives, and the number has been increasing ever since until, in some universities, independent work and has become the norm for selected experimental groups.

Nor has a total classlessness been one of the outcomes of the Soviet educational system. On the contrary, since higher education is such a coveted privilege, which is awarded to far fewer than in the United States, and since it is not a "right" which accrues to anyone, regardless of a place for him to perform his profession in the working world, the privilege of higher education has created a distinct elite. For many secondary school graduates, there is simply no hope of ever going on.

"I believe we have what the Americans call a syndrome of rising expectations," one social scientist commented. "Intellectually, I know we are going to have a great many unhappy young people on our hands. Realistically, I know the number of university places is not going to be significantly increased in this Five-Year Plan or the next or maybe even the next. How can our government spend money to train students for jobs that don't yet exist in our economy? And yet we encourage our young people to dream that they can become anything, do anything they want. I don't see any answer right now, only fiercer competition to get into the universities during the next ten or fifteen years."

In his era, Khrushchev tried to attack these problems of limited access to higher education, particularly on the part of rural youth, and elitism through a number of "reforms." In a kind of Moscow-style "cultural revolution," high school students had to go out and work in the factories or on the farms for two years before they could enter the universities; 80 percent of the university places were saved for them. Then, after 1964, the system was totally reversed because, as the Minister of Education said in March, 1965,

"We had been compelled to reject qualified high school graduates and admit poorly prepared production workers." With this change, the Soviet Union voted clearly for the training of an elite, privileged by brainpower, and not for the Chinese system of "permanent revolution" in education.

This did not, of course, solve the vexing problem of the rural youth, for the system unquestionably culls out the children of the worker and, even more, the peasant long before he reaches the level of higher education. A famous survey undertaken in 1963 in Novosibirsk showed that children of the intelligentsia were twice as likely as lower-class children to continue their education after high school; actually, 70 percent of the former as against 35 percent of the latter went beyond the 10th grade. Of those working class children who did go on, most of them enrolled in technical schools rather than universities. In still another step on the way to elite-forming, workers' children dropped out of high school much more frequently than children of the intelligentsia, and peasants' children as high school graduates very nearly did not exist.

There is clearly a nouveau riche in the Soviet Union — a nouveau riche in educational privileges. As Dr. Jeremy Azrael, Sovietologist at the University of Chicago, has written, this was accomplished by "a growth of 'class consciousness' which the schools seemed powerless to prevent and often subtly encouraged, e.g., by stressing that the fate of academic failures was to become common workers."

In the beginning, the Soviet pedagogues looked upon their vast and complex nation as one big control group. They believed that the minds and thoughts of children could be held constant while they worked out their experiments. Only this was not being done on rats and rabbits, it was being done on people.

To a great extent, it worked; they *have* created a far more educated far more cultured, far more aware young person. But they are now at the point that they have succeeded so well on that minimal level that they are reaching the level where the person — and the person's desires — are affecting the state. Whether with men or women, whether with a state or an individual, whether with the wealthy or the poor, maniuplation has never proceeded only from one direction.

✿ Chapter Seventeen
How They're Dealing
With Their Problems

"Youth has learned to reason. But why reason?
The order is given — obey.
Thinking has no place here."

A Russian woman judge at the trial of a soldier
who had been redrafted and unsuccessfully sued for
his rights in court.

*I*VAN Tikhonovich Komov is typical of those stern unblinking
men, Soviet apparatchiki all, who seem to walk through life with
their lips curled. Never a smile, never a kind word for anyone
outside the tight little island of those who stand firmly on Soviet
belief. Always on the watch, for there are enemies without and
within, waiting every minute for the felicitous moment to spring.

Thirty and twenty and even fifteen years ago, the Ivan
Tikhonoviches' lives were relatively simple. They reacted to any
threat to their Maginot line of ideological belief with the mailed fist
— the slightest sign of disbelief or the wrong family name and the
recalcitrant man or woman or 15 month-old child was sent to
Siberia or executed. That did away with a lot of problems, and with
a lot of people, and with a lot of honesty and creativity, all at the
same blow. Many of the Ivan Tikhonoviches wish life were that
simple today.

But the awful thing for them is that they see the world changing
around them, and, even in that bulwark, the Komsomol, where he
is a member of the Central Committee, the answers to problems are
seen in various lights by various people. For them, with their routed
minds, it is a bleak time.

First, they are facing a substantial rise in juvenile delinquency and in hooliganism. This became so intense in 1966 that Moscow created the Ministry for the Protection of Public Order to deal sternly with drunks, hooligans and thieves. Parents with offending children aged 14 to 16 were themselves fined 10 to 30 rubles for minor criminal offenses.

By 1972, there existed even the startling fact that the Soviets were admitting the existence of juvenile crime. In February, Izvestia published a long article about a gang of teen-agers who began with petty thefts and ended with murder, getting their kicks out of violence and mayhem. "My life was in a fog — I was bored with everything," Vladimir Suckhov, one of the teen-agers explained, when captured. "I didn't need anything special. We had everything at home. When I committed my first thefts, I found it interesting. A mystery entered my life. I wanted to commit crimes for the sake of the crimes themselves."

Tellingly, several other articles proposed greater use of sociology and social psychology in coping with teen-age crime rather than the strictly punitive measures of the party or the Komsomol. Alexander Yakovlov, author of "Criminality and Social Psychology" and deputy director of a research institute on Soviet law, described such teen-age gangs as an "informal community" in effect the equivalent of a subculture in the nomenclature of the West, living within its own tightly-knit community and with its own harsh codes of conduct. They gave the boys a feeling of belonging that they did not get elsewhere, he said.

But in many ways, crime is the least of the problem because it still affects only a small percentage of the young. Far worse to the Soviet ideologists is the more wide-spread indifference to the system, as shown by dropouts and dissidents and a much larger group who is loyal but simply finds ideology uninteresting. To be passive observers, to watch from the sidelines, or to simply observe is not permissible; remedies have to be found for these "crimes."

One reaction to the sins of the present generation is certainly the spasmodic hard line. But it is nothing compared to the days of Stalin; 5 to 12 million innocent lives deliberately snuffed out is not to be compared to a few hundred 3- or 5- or even 1-year prison sentences for demonstrating or for published criticism, as bad as that is. But when pushed, the Kremlin men are perfectly capable of giving out prison sentences or exiling a malcontent to Siberia or, as they did early in 1972, warning art and literary critics who have shown a "conciliatory attitude toward artistic and ideological trash" and have been lax "in exposing the reactionary essence of bourgeois 'mass culture' and decadent trends."

Indeed, there has also been an increasingly hard line on ideology since the Czech invasion of 1968. It is not widely known that late in 1967 the Politburo set up a task force under ideologue Mikhail Suslov to investigate the possible effects of a liberalization — they were really considering some form of loosening up. But the "Czech spring" convinced them, as they had only feared before, that any liberalization would lead to a return to bourgeois life or to dissolution. And so ideology, which was always under the jurisdiction of a special commission of the Central Committee, was soon being dealt with more harshly by the new Ministry for the Protection of Public Order and by the armed forces.

The difference today is that this is not *all* of the reaction. More and more, the men in leadership positions are seeing that, in place of the whip, they need to try to *inspire* the new generation of Russians. And so they wage ideological campaigns, employ sociology as a tool, try to spark "patriotism" with new programs, and gradually give in to a limited individualism in education and to a limited, Sovietized version of some of the cultural attractions of the West.

The day I visited Komov in his office in the Komsomol, he immediately launched into an exposition of the new way. "Perhaps this is not interesting to you," he started, "but we have a new program. We are trying to bring up a new generation in the experience of the former generation."

Knowing how monstrously thankless a job this is, I asked him, "Why?"

"We have now a new generation that has not experienced war and not suffered the hardships of revolution," he said. "On the other hand, ideological subversion has increased. Some Western ideologists — they are actually propagandists — are trying to take youth away from the class struggle and from speaking of patriotism so they will not defend the country as they used to. Different sociologists of the West speak about the 'no-class society', of societies divided only into good and bad. There is also the theory that Capitalism and Socialism are coming closer. That's why, in order to fight these ideas, we are trying to educate our young people in the spirit of Proletarian Internationalism."

He paused, then went on, seeming in his person as stern and one-dimensional as his stern, simple office, which was empty of any decoration, much less any frivolity:

"Why is it so important for us that young people know the value of what they have and how it was achieved? Take, for example, the idea of free education — they take it for granted. They do not know how it was achieved at the cost of how many lives and how much labor. The younger generation must know these things. Among the young, there is very often the idea that all the exploits are over. In peacetime, what can they do? Our task is to bring up in young people the idea that there is still heroism."

Many of the same sentiments and frustrations were expressed — but in a different way — from another one of the regime's main ideologues, Alexander Chakovsky, editor-in-chief of Literaturnaya Gazyeta in a speech in January, 1968, at a congress of Russian "workers of culture." "In the first years of Soviet power, we lived in hardship and poverty," he said that day. "At that time, it seemed to some of us that, with the growth of material well-being . . . culture would spread automatically and that . . . bad customs inherited from czardom would disappear. Today we can say: such a theory of automatic development is false. For neither the fact that man has moved from collective living quarters to a private apartment, nor the growth of real income, nor other factors of rising living standards lead to a flowering of culture."

He dismissed the idea of a Maoist style "cultural revolution" (the cultural revolution was, that year, just at its height in China) to reinvigorate a listless population but he offered no real panacea except a more bold creative approach for "our youth, which did not go through the political struggle and accounts for a large percentage of our population . . . "

Correspondent Paul Wohl of the Christian Science Monitor, interpreted Chakovsky's ideas of the new generation as "politically undereducated people of the '60s for whom everything is reduced to the formula: 'I dare, I am bold.' "Actually," he wrote, "Mr. Chakovsky is much more concerned with the boldness of the regime's critics than with finding a radical solution to today's spiritual malaise of the Soviet people. His and the regime's problem children are 'the people who have come up in the '60s.' For many of them, 'even the great fatherland's war is merely a childhood memory.' "

To "raise a new generation in the experience of the former" — I thought about that. And everywhere I traveled in the Soviet Union, I observed them trying to do just that. Because of the constantly displayed lack of passionate gratitude on the part of the younger generation, the Komsomol had put all of its energies in the last few years behind programs of patriotic education designed to conjure up the glories of the past. It had young people out "following the paths of the heroes" of the revolution and of World War II, meeting with elderly battle veterans, seeking out lost documents and studying the history of famous battles.

Despite constant avowals of hatred of war and war propaganda, the Soviets have other programs, such as the DOSAAF or Volunteers for Support of the Military, a paramilitary training organization for all ages. DOSAAF even has very young people driving tanks, shooting, jumping rivers with gas masks and digging around old battlefields for mines and bodies. The newspaper pictures and stories about these "youthful adventures" are often very grim and frightening, especially for a country which continuously boasts of its lack of "war propaganda."

From Leningradskaya Pravda or "Leningrad Truth", Jan. 10, 1971, on the "Winter Lightning Expedition" which, in all the country, involved some 15 million schoolchildren:

"A freezing January morning. The paths and byroads of the Nizny park of Petrodvoretz are blanketed with whitish smoke. And suddenly from behind the snow-covered bushes shoots a white signal rocket. Automatic arms fire is heard, and the explosion of grenades — from the shore of the bay to the highway a naval landing forces through: it's breaking through ('in combat' to meet tanks come from Leningrad to the 'Oranienbaum Five Corners!')

"But this is not an episode of the time of the Great Fatherland War. It happened a few days ago. More than 500 children — children of Leningrad textile workers and agricultural workers of our oblast — are vacationing in the Pioneers' winter sports camp. During the vacation days here they decided to carry out the winter military game in the same places where in the battle for the city of Lenin occurred the famous landing of the brave Baltic fleet sailors . . . After a short time, the red flags fly from the heights."

But the attempts to mold "this generation in the experience of the former," was not only taking the form of an intensified patriotic training, it was also taking these other forms:

— A new and increased ideological campaign on all levels aimed at digging in against Western "subversion" and "bourgeoise influences."

Ideologues like Komov, intelligent men despite their blinkered ardor, fully realized there was a flagging zeal on the part of the young. At the same time, under the banner of peaceful coexistence, they were opening their formerly shuttered land to the West on the technological front in an avid attempt to import the technology it had not or could not create for themselves. The idea was to bring Western technology in but keep Western ideas out: a tormenting task, but not one to discourage the determined men in the Kremlin.

This new ideological campaign included a rise in the volume of antireligious propaganda in the press, a growing emphasis on indoctrination in the factories and schools, and the founding of a new U.S.S.R. Philosophical Society. As Mihail A. Suslov, the party's ideological spokesman expressed it at a conference of social scientists: "The ideological battle between Capitalism and Communism is sharpening and is embracing all spheres of social life." Social scientists, he said, must be in the forefront of ideological work to improve the Marxist-Leninist 'tempering' of Soviet students, and the party must play a larger role in supervising the work of higher schools and scientific institutes.

These admonitions came right on the heels of the 24th party congress in March, 1971, when an exchange of party cards was called for as a means of purifying the party, i.e. getting rid of old party hacks and trying to up the quality of party members.

What the party was only half beginning to understand was that these campaigns could backfire very easily if they were not imposed delicately on a population that was increasingly sophisticated. As one artist told me, "Among our group, maybe Solzhenitsyn wouldn't have been so popular if they hadn't made so much of him. Now he stands as a hero. Bulgakov is popular, too, because he wrote about the White Guard as human beings. They were the White Guard, but they were also Russians, they just saw things in a different way."

In their half-understanding, as part of the new ideological campaign, they were not only permitting the reading of more of the old pre-Revolutionary Russian philosophers, they were also permitting the showing of, for instance, more American films. The idea was to fight something by knowing it, but it was clearly a dangerous risk because, as most Westerners have found out the hard way, to know something is not necessarily to hate it.

— A program of projecting the emotions aroused and satisfied by old ceremonies to new Marxist ones.

In Volgograd, for instance, the Komsomol changed its form of strongarm atheistic education, after finding it way off base.

"We understand now that in some cases the reason for belief in God lies not with the priest but in ideology and in one's own consciousness," Genadie Yaskovic, a tall, witty young man who was secretary of the city Komsomol, told me. "So to the religious morals, we now try to oppose a social moral. Our methods of atheistic education are to persuade and explain, and we do this at meetings and individually."

They found, Yaskovic went on, that the reasons many young people gave for going to church was that "It's beautifu" or "It's solemn." So, instead of force, instead of mocking elderly worshippers and attacking young ones, the Komsomol started "folk holidays" to vie in beauty and solemnity with the religious holidays. Easter is the spring "Festival of the Birch Tree"; Christmas is the "Festival of the Russian winter"; the holidays are complete with beauty queens riding in open cars, flowers, pancakes (blini) and dancing.

Whereas once the Soviets assumed that man could live without ceremony to mark the high moments of his life, his loves, his procreation and his dying, today the government admits that man does not live by austerity alone.

At the Birch Tree festival, for instance, they choose the prettiest girl in the village and make her queen. "As spring appears in the world, the most beautiful girl appears in its center," he explained, smiling almost beautifically. "We like spring very much, we like greenery. We give the Russian girl bread, as if we were giving it to the spring. We play, dance, sing and eat pancakes. The festival opens the new period of life for the rural collective body. Spring is not only the guest, she is also the hostess of the day."

This kind of holiday is observed in different parts of the country under different names, but even more important is the change in the wedding ceremony. In the earliest days of Bolshevism, marriage was a simple registering at the marriage bureau (if one wanted to observe the bourgeois custom at all). Later, marriages were observed but in a starkly simple manner, until youth rebelled against such a lack of sentimentality.

Today, while marriages tend to stack up unromantically in the "wedding palaces," which in the older cities are now the former palaces of the wealthy, in ceremony they are not at all that different from weddings in the West. I watched Galina and Nikolai Purtob get married one day in Novosibirsk. Both were nicely dressed — she in white, he in a dark blue suit. She was carrying white gladiolas. The "alter" was of blond wood with a silver hammer and sickle emblem on the wall behind it. There were attractive Uzbek rugs on the floor.

"Is your decision to be married sincere?" the director, a pleasant, stocky woman named Ludmilla Alexandrovna Kosova asked.

"Have you thought deeply about your decision?"

He murmured "Yes," and she murmured "Yes." Not "I do," just "yes." They were man and wife — and now they could go on to several days of revelry with friends in which the most common wedding custom was for the friends to shout "Bitter, bitter, bitter" and for the wedding couple to kiss because "Kisses are sweet."

All of this is simply another emanation of man's apparently universal and unquenchable need to observe and ponder his life at marked intervals and not simply to march through it.

— The preempting of jazz as a Komsomol entertainment.

For years, jazz was seen as "revisionist," "bourgeois," "cosmopolitan" and a number of highly uncomplimentary other names. Young Soviets are forced to listen to it over the foreign radio stations and, if they were caught, the Komsomol, in its gentle way, got its "shock troops" to take care of things.

But since about 1960, all of this has changed. Jazz bands

flourished all over the Soviet Union, particularly in many of the "out" spots like Lithuania or Minsk, and Radio Moscow soon had a jazz expert, Alexander Batyshov, a big, handsome, bearded jazz enthusiast. As Valerie Genichev, the suave young chief of the Komsomol Central committee's ideological department in Moscow said, "If youth is going to be interested in jazz and pop music, it's best to do it through Komsomol." What better example of how the taste of the young is changing officialdom instead of officialdom changing the youth?

Ironically, by 1971, despite great successes like Duke Ellington's tour that year, jazz was already dying out — and rock music was taking its place. "The great peak of jazz here was in 1966-'67," Batashyov told me in Moscow, with a scowl of disappointment. "Since then, the jazz curve has been winding down and down. Now jazz is free to play and jazzmen earn good money, making arrangements or working as song writers." He thought for a moment, "Possibly jazz can't be played by 'fat people'," he said. Which was one of the most perceptive remarks I ever heard in Russia.

Moreover, when, as in some places still occurs, there is some old hard-liner stopping modern music, the young soon counter attack. When, Pravda Ukrainy or "Ukrainian Truth," the official Communist party organ of the Ukraine denounced Western music as "howling," a group of Ukrainian young people, wrote a letter angrily denouncing the article and asking, "Why, in Poland, Czechoslovakia and Yugoslavia and other non-Western countries no one reproaches young people for singing modern songs and dancing to pop music? Is it possible that for Soviet young people there exists a special kind of Eastern style? Is it possible that the author of the article wants to build an artificial wall separating us from our friends and from everything modern?"

This was a very clever retort, for the suggestion of an "Eastern style" was a devastating hint at the "Asiatic" that every Russian fears lies hibernating in some dark place within him. And if you just substitute "Western" for "modern," you soon see which way the young want to face.

Of course, there *is* a counter counter-attack, too. In the case of Pravda Ukrainy the editors got a soloist for the Kiev Philharmonic, V. Goncharenko to write a reply to the youths. If they wanted light music, he said, why not turn to revolutionary hits of several decades ago? Why not "Our Locomotives Run Fast, Our Stop is in the Commune?"

— Changes in schooling, in particular the new individual work permitted in higher education.

In 1967, during my first trip to Russia, like most Americans, I still thought — not without reason, of course — of a monolithic Soviet educational system in which conformity was stressed at all costs. So it was tremendously exciting, as well as surprising, to sit in school after school across the country and hear educators talk of a new individualism.

In Leningrad: "We want students to do individual work," G.I Shatkov, vice-rector of the University of Leningrad, told me cordially, as we sat in his office. "All of our experiments aim at the same thing — to provide more time for individual studies and individual bents. Our first aim is to teach man how to work as an individual, how to do creative work, not only to provide him with the knowledge and to train him to do research." Like everyone working in this area, he denied heartily that this emphasis on individual work was incompatible with Soviet collectivism. "In our opinion, the collective spirit does not refute individuality but helps individual development," he said emphatically. "Somehow we do not draw a line between collective and individual development."

In 1967, the school had just created new faculties of psychology and of "complex social studies" (the first such sociological institute in Russia) to "use methods of the humanities and science to study individual personality in society." Scholars were dealing with problems of psychological incompatibility among workers and within families — problems that would have been recognized a few years back as stemming only from society's imbalances. They were experimenting with shortening lecture hours in order to give students more time for individual study.

Carrying the new experiments even further, in 1966 the university admitted one group for only half the traditional work load and found it did just as well as the one with the traditional program. In scientific societies in the university, students were doing special research projects, such as studying how decisions were made in the local soviets and recommending changes — something equivalent to American graduate students studying the progress of bills in Senate committees.

While experiments such as these certainly are far from common within the Soviet System, they are beginning to blossom out in many of the finest schools — almost always in advanced schools where the new elite is being trained. Also exemplifying this opening up of Soviet education are the so-called "faculties of social professions" in Irkutsk, Novosibirsk, Tomsk and other Urals universities.

Under this curious program, so akin to the early American approach, students began in the early '60s to do research under expert professors on lecturing, choir, orchestra, chreography, and other "social professions." They were then expected to go out and give lectures to others and to "deepen the knowledge of the people." It was the creation of the well-rounded man — something the United States pioneered in, often to an absurd extent — carried to its ultimate degree.

While all of these changes are far from common, they do most certainly represent a measureable trend. Even the Soviet Minister of Education, Prof. Mikhail A. Prokoviev has said that "the number of school hours devoted to compulsory subjects is too great and our curriculum is too rigid. There is no scope for reasonable initiative."

All this may simply be, as the Russians now claim, a normal development of Communism. But is it difficult to see how they can stress individualistic aims in education and train a young man who can think for himself in the sciences without training at the same time a man who will think for himself about his political environment, his intellectual milieu and the world around him. And it is difficult to see how they can maintain revolutionary fervor at fever pitch in a post-revolutionary generation where the original change-the-world passion has dimmed.

The reasons behind all these changes in the ways of forming and changing the young, come down, in the end, to fear of a lack of patriotism. But is there such a lack? Are these young men less passionately devoted to the "motherland" than their fathers and mothers? What do they think about such things as military service and how do they conceive of patriotism as a concept? Is there an anti-war or anti-military movement anywhere near commensurate to the ones in the 'States? Have the government's prophylactic measures had an effect?

It is only fair to say that many children are just as totally imbued with old style patriotism as their parents and just as passionate in their feelings, for while many of the incessant monuments to the war are maudlin and overdone, others are tremendously moving. Some cities are, in themselves, monuments to the horrors and courageous grandeur of the war, and they move youth, as well as visitors from other countries.

Volgograd, nee Stalingrad, is one of these, and it seems to exist today only to serve the memory of the war. I remember thinking, when I saw that perfectly laid-out modern city with its long, look-alike apartment buildings standing in silent rows like gravestones, its single charred remaining ruin from the old city and its monuments and vigorously-burning flames for the fallen on each corner, that "The battle of Stalingrad ended 25 years ago, but the battle is not over." There was a hush about the city, as if several hundred thousand people even today were moving about in a shrine. From my hotel window, no matter what time the day or night, I could hear the sorrowing music from the monument to the fallen on our corner and I could see the little girls and boys — usually 9 years old — guarding the monument until their time was up and they solemnly marched out while others solemnly marched in.

"It is a big honor for Pioneers to be on guard here," Nadezhda Ivanovna Dyvroneva, one of the Pioneer leaders, told me. "Only those who are worthy and win the competitions for discipline and grades are permitted to be on guard. We want to imbue feelings of respect and responsibility among children. Children from other cities write to ask to have the honor of being on guard and one can't read those lines without excitement. It touches one's feelings deeply."

The handsome, stoutly-built woman reached into a drawer and brought out a letter. "This boy," she said, adjusting her glasses, wrote, " 'I was standing on guard Nov. 1. That day I was admitted to the Komsomol organization. I wanted to sing, but I couldn't do that because I was on guard. I understand I was given a great honor, and I fulfilled the task given me with pride.' "

No one can fairly doubt the truth of these profound feelings for homeland, and they have always flowed in rivers deep in the Russian soul. But, at the same time, as children get older and, particularly, when they grow more educated and sophisticated, their patriotism takes a different form. Many of them, while perfectly patriotic in any normal way of looking at things, become sick to death with the constant reminders of their parents' wars, while the older generation seemed chained to a blackboard where it must keep writing out the horrors and the glories of the past in a chalk that will not fade.

It is this generation's real but undemonstrative patriotism that has led to the accusations on the part of the more hand-line older generation that this generation is, even, pacifist. In a short story, "What is it You want?" by the super-conservative writer Vsevolod Kochetov in the magazine "Oktyabr" or "October" in 1969, the father tells his son that "you people are carefree; you believe too much in the peace-loving sirens — both the ones abroad and ours here at home. Your emblem has become the Biblical dove with the olive branch in its beak. Whoever slipped it to you in place of the hammer and sickle?" This novel, one of the most conservative in many years, became an even greater topic of conversation among the intelligentsia than Solzhenitsyn's expulsion that year from the Writers' Union — it was so conservative it advocated not only the isolation of Soviet youth (and, indeed, the whole of Russia) from the bourgeois world but also from the rest of the Communist world!

Actually, since the Soviet Military insists that war always be shown only in its most primitive and heroic moments, there is not a real pacifist movement, although such keen observers as Colette Shulman say there is a "great hunger" for one. There *are* anti-war and anti-military songs, always underground, such as the famous Bulat Akudzava's ballads:

"And if something is as it shouldn't be — we don't worry!
As the saying goes, 'The fatherland has ordered it!' How
nice it is not to be blamed for anything, To be an ordinary
soldier, an ordinary soldier."

Much of the dissatisfaction that could arise is skimmed off the top by the fact that young people who are accepted to study in the institutes or the university do not have to fulfill military service, although they do study military subjects in a Department of the Military. This, of course, causes a further escalation of anti-elitist feeling on the part of the poor boys who are conscripted and go, for instance, at a base pay of six rubles per month into the Navy for three dull years.

The State Forms, The State Reacts

There have been some cases reported in the press where young men have taken draft dodger cases to court, but they are few. The closest we in the West have heard about any real questioning on the part of Soviet soldiers was during the 1968 invasion of Czechoslovakia. Correspondents and diplomats who covered that tragic time noted, with fascination, that many Soviet soldiers were openly embarrassed by the role they had to play — especially with Czechs taunting them as "savages" on the street. Reportedly, the divisions sent to Czechoslovakia were then sent to remote areas of Siberia rather than back to Moscow or the big cities, where they could spread the word of their disquieting experience.

This is about as close as Russia has got to the anti-war anti-nationalist phenomenon in the United States in the wake of the Vietnam war. They are only beginning to approach the stage where they will extend themselves beyond a self-righteous nationalism, although the youth are, as has been pointed out, certainly becoming more sophisticated in their ideas of patriotism. Moreover, since the withdrawal from third world "adventures" such as the Congo after Khrushchev's fall, they have artfully avoided the kind of obvious intervention that could have hypoed this kind of reaction.

In the end, what men like Komov worry about in the dark of night is not the fact that this generation will be consciously disloyal — they won't — but that they will be relativists; that they will judge people and countries simply on whether they are good or bad and not on whether they are Marxist or Capitalist. The real fear behind the talk of ideological subversion is that they might become too tolerant toward the systems of the rest of the world.

And in this the Komovs are right. It is the first Russian generation in this century to have the confidence to reach outside of itself, to extend itself beyond the traditional Russian self-centerdness and to demonstrate the beginnings of a national generosity — to stop nursing its own wounds and to see and understand and empathize with the fact that other peoples suffer too.

Ironically, the older Bolsheviks were the consciously, self-proclaimed internationalists, but they were internationalists only in terms of hegemony over other countries. This generation is *truly* internationalist, in that it wants to *know* other countries and cultures, not dominate them — much in the same way as American youth does.

This, of course, makes the young tremendously suspect.

Something clearly must be done about them.

But, despite everything the elders do, the young are not going back to the unitary passions of 1917. And eventually the Soviet Union will have to catch up with *them.*

✌ Chapter Eighteen
Why They're Listening to the Surveys

"The program of the Communist Party of the Soviet Union indicates that the social sciences are the scientific bases for the direction of social life."

P.N. Fedoseev and Y.P. Frantsev,
two prominent Soviet sociologists

A PERCEPTIVE young Western diplomat sat in a "Stolovaya" or lunchroom in Moscow, observing the throngs of Russians rushing by outside. "You see," he said, "they have found they can build things and industrialize. They've got their ideology. Now they wonder what for, how to live inside it. That is where sociology and psychology come in."

Just a few weeks earlier I had sat in the main Komsomol office in Volgograd, talking to Oleg Besedin, the tall, thin secretary of the Komsomol city committee, which had its own team of youth sociologists working for it. Throwing his arms up with a touch of drama, Besedin proclaimed grandly, "Sociology — we are no exception. We are also ill with the disease. It's like Gallup. We can't work with youth without knowing it."

And just a week before that, I had visited the Chair of Scientific Communism at Kiev State University and talked with its chairman, Vladimir Kolobkov, a devoted Marxist who firmly believes that the "new Marxist man" of Marxist thought is about to arrive, oh, any day now. How will he be brought to bloom fastest? Through the application of sociology. Dr. Kolovkov had five young sociologists working for him, investigating everything from work habits and youth's ideals and interests to why more city than rural youth go on to higher education to the uses of free time.

"We are all working together in the institute to form the personality of the new man," Dr. Kolobkov said, as we walked down one of Kiev's beautiful streets, the trees then golden in autumn. "One is trying to find better ways to study, to inculcate ideas. Another is working on another aspect. I do not say we will have the Marxist man by 1980, as some have claimed, but maybe in several decades." He smiled broadly, for he is a cheerful man and an optimist.

"More and more Soviets are becoming involved in personality and psychology," he went on. "This interest is connected with the personal mind. We are all working together in the institutes to form the personality of the new man." Golden leaves showered down around us, like falling sun beams. "The formation of interests is not accidental," he continued. "We must consider the strivings of youth, but also of society as a whole. But if our planning does not coincide with the striving of youth, there is the danger it will be of a formal character. Or if it is not planned enough, there is the danger that the forming of the spiritual life will be of an accidental character. We are trying to find a golden middle between (state) planning and the (personal) strivings of the young."

These three men all illustrate one of the most important developments in the Soviet Union today and one of those with greatest consequences for youth: the blooming, the flowering, the *passion* for sociology and psychology. As one Soviet magazine remarked, "Sociology was a Cinderella, now she is a queen."

Soviet sociology is still an infant "science," if, in Western terms, it can be called even that. Compared with the West, its methods are painfully simplistic and, because of the basic duplicity of the system, what it tests are often not the questions truly relevant to youth. It has to step carefully. It does not want to find out more than the government really wants to know about a system which believes that the emotions are based in the physiological and the psychology in the social.

Still, the fact that today the government — which until the '50s was using only unalloyed terror as its single instrument of "persuasion" over its people — is concerned enought to find out what its people want and think represents a real internal revolution in methodry.

Everywhere I went, I was enormously surprised by the enthusiastic air of sociological and psychological inquiry that was prying into everything in Soviet life. Sociological institutes were springing up like weeds — there were almost none in 1960 and between 80 and 90 by the end of the decade. The young sociologist, a highly fashionable figure among youth, was wearing out his shoes polling everybody on everything — from the University of Leningrad to the Volgograd Komsomol to the Lithuanian institutes.

There was a great deal of cross-fertilization, and it was no accident that there were several lines of research being pursued in nearly all the institutes — lines that revealed a great deal about what was troubling the Soviets today. One was research on work — why groups of workers could not get along, how workers should use their free time, how the state can make being a worker a satisfaction in a state where every upward-striving young person despises workers and wants to be an intellectual. Another line dealt with extensive testing on how and why young people chose careers, why they dropped out of school and how they developed good or bad work habits. Still another area — perhaps the most important — dealt with research being conducted on the ideals and interests of youth.

A typical questionnaire, this one conducted by Yunost magazine, asked "Who is your favorite hero?" "What merit do you value most in people?" "What is your idea of happiness?" "What virtues do you like most in your contemporaries?" and "What is your opinion of work?

Along with such basically superficial surveying by the sociologists, a new interest in psychology was growing that, in addition to many other things, included a mini-revival of Freud. "We think that the method of Freud is interesting," Dr. Vladimir Lisovsky of Leningrad University told me, "but we disapprove of explaining social problems completely through the instincts."

To the young, sociology clearly represented a new way out. Sociologists like Lisovsky and Kolobkov were men who, at least in person, spoke the least ideological nonsense in the Soviet Union; they came closest to the truth because they could say in social science jargon what you could not say elsewhere. As young William Taubman observed during his year in Moscow University, "The student critics spoke of sociology as the most objective way to study society, as the opposite of propaganda."

Lisovsky, for instance, will say, his clear, forthright eyes filled with honesty, that "Instead of saying youth is good or youth is bad, we should study youth. Do you know," he asked, as we talked in his office in a big, aristocratic old house near Leningrad's riverfront, "that 70 percent of Leningrad was born since the revolution and that half is under 26?"

A medium-sized, brown-haired man who could easily be taken for an American and a man with an ardent curiosity, Lisovsky is the closest person I met to the man who "tells it like it is." Perhaps that unusual trait is due partly to the fact that his parents were "Old Believers," those fundamentalist Orthodox who were so similar to American fundamentalists in their lack of cant and in their direct approach to God and truth. He will tell you, for instance, that "After the 20th party congress, social life became more free. We gave more range to the individual inclinations of the masses." Or that "Youth overestimates its own experience — it only values the experience of the generation itself."

In 1969, Dr. Lisovsky, along with a fellow sociologist, Svetlana Ikonnikova, did a fascinating study on youth called "Youth in Our Time," which, if you can read between the lines of unquestioned propaganda and barely proven premises, tells a great deal about the personalistic strivings of Russian youth today. After beginning by warning that "authority" alone is no longer to be relied upon, the authors state that:

"While, formerly, socialization of the youth was mainly done by borrowing values and knowledge from a very narrow section of people, young people today find themselves exposed to the action of various, often sharply differing sources of information. As a result, young people will not accept any single set of values or rules of behavior. Persuasion comes to the fore in this new educational situation.

"It is not enough for a young man to know that the occupation to which he will devote his life is socially useful, he also wants it to correspond, at least basically, to his personal ideals and aspirations and to help him display to the full his intellectual endowments."

Then the authors go back to studies and surveys done in 1927 and 1929, when they noted the "increasing importance of collectivism as an ethical principle of human relations." They quoted the authors of *those* surveys as writing that "Collectivist habits are strenghtening, and a new type of man is emerging, who knows no conflict between the personal and the social, who has organically and consciously linked his fate and life with the fate and life of his class." At that time, Lisovsky and Ikonnikova point out, young people wanted simply the basics of life: a good meal, parents, a minimal education.

When they start to investigate today's youth, however, they find them wanting much — very much — more.

Very often in the booklet, I was stunned at the astonishingly broad conclusions the authors would draw from very limited questions. Asked, for instance, their opinions of their contemporaries, 86.4 percent gave a positive response (1,758 answers), 12.5 gave a negative response (255 answers) and 1.1 percent gave no reply. From this, they gathered grandiloquently that "Thus 86 people out of one hundred are proud of being part of the Soviet youth of the '60s, they admire the deeds they perform, have no bitterness, regret, skepticism or disillusionment. This shows that the general tone of the youth is quite high and means that young people share their aims and ideals with their coequals, value their qualities and believe in their staunchness and civic uprightness."

More interestingly, they found that the more critical judgments of their contemporaries came from the groups with the lowest and the highest education. Most interesting, when asked what traits they valued most, 64 percent named honesty; 54 percent, patriotism; 42 percent, cordiality, kindness, and sympathy; 37.9 percent, modesty; 35.3 percent, the ability to work well; 28 percent, singleness of purpose; 18.6 percent, collectivism; 17.5 percent, intolerance of shortcomings; and 15.5 percent, optimism.

Here, I would pick out as highly telling the fact that "honesty" — a trait relatively unknown among or spoken of among the older generation of Russians — is named No. 1 in importance and that collectivism is rated very low, as is optimism. Both of these latter are traits the older generation is downright fanatic about.

"What repels a young man," the authors write, quite honestly, "is everything dishonest — trickery, deceit, hypocrisy, theft and treachery." How curious that these should be precisely the words any normally decent person could best apply to the Stalin era!

The authors sum up with several pages destined to prove to "Western ideologists" (they do so inadequately, for me) that youth is not "apolitical" today. (The reason I found it unconvincing was they they asked them "Are you interested in politics?" — something most people would naturally answer "Yes" to — rather than asking them any probing questions about ideology or its interpretations.)

In the summation, they write: "To sum up the foregoing, we may say that the sympathies of the modern Soviet younger generation are with people of high professional qualification who are devoted to their work and seek to be of maximum use to society; they hold dear the interests of their country, are principled, capable and active, and also generous, attentive and friendly."

A trifle overstated, perhaps, for what they had to base it upon!

From these investigations into youth, the sociologists often next proceed to the concept that hangs over everything else — the concept of the "New Man" or the "New Marxist Man" or the "New Soviet Man."

Khrushchev, always the optimist, was convinced that the New Man, and thus Communism (in place of present socialism) would flower by 1980. Men like Lisovsky and Kolobkov and their colleagues are not this sanguine, "We take the point of view of Marx that each epoch creates a concrete man," said Kolobkov. "According to this, this social epoch has created a new man. We feel it every day. He has new features not observed in Russians before the revolution and not observed in many countries. The main feature of the present generation is its idealistic convictions. We can assert they are there, and they can be proved by things like the Great Patriotic War. We saw a real outburst of patriotism. And we can prove it by the fact that nowadays overwhelming numbers are working conscientiously — we have many examples of labor patriotism. Also 'new' is the collectivism. I've been abroad and seen other societies and we are more developed."

Others, while still believing in him, are less precise about New Man's specific characteristics. "We do not speak of New Soviet Man so much now but New Man," Valerie Melko, the psychologist-physicist at Kiev State University said. "He is still conditional. We speak of new features in a man. The problem is just in its beginning. It is very difficult to say how far shall we go and reach in this way."

Most important, the sociologists, though generally optimistic, *will* point out (as Soviet officials and as most Soviet citizens will not) areas of weakness. Sitting in Dr. Lisovsky's office in Leningrad one day, three of his assistants and I were chatting under his friendly and approving gaze about recent studies they had done, when one of the young women began talking about individual initiative and leadership qualities. "We've studied students' ability to organize themselves and also others," she said, "and we found out that their esteem for organization was not high. It is not very hopeful. When we asked them what interferred with their work or what made it ineffective, they said lack of ability to organize themselves for work. They do not have the orientation to organize. We have come to the conclusion that for practical work we must first pay more attention to self-organization and later to the organization of others."

The unusual frankness of this observation is notable, but so is the contradiction in Soviet thinking. For, other surveys, which I have quoted in earlier chapters, have been praised by Soviet officials because they showed that young Soviets do not seek leadership positions — and, thus, power. Actually, the basic observation is the same in both cases; it is the contradiction in the interpretation.— the first saying it is good, the second one saying it is bad — that tells a great deal about Russian thinking.

In the beginning, the early Bolsheviks thought they could form men like you molded a piece of clay — condition a man to Communism the way Pavlov conditioned his dogs to salivate when he rang the bell. As Pokrovski, the historian of early Soviet Russia wrote, in one of the more apt interpretations of Lenin's thought: "We Marxists do not see personality as the maker of history, for to us, personality is only the instrument with which history works. Perhaps a time will come when this instrument will be artifically constructed, as today we make our electrical accumulators. But we have not yet progressed that far."

In the '20s, it was assumed that the psychology of the new generation would be so completely remolded that there would arise not simply a better-educated, less-threatened man but a very new breed of man, a man perfected, working not for himself but for society, now that the corruption and greed of private enterprise was crushed. At the 22nd party congress in 1961, he was described as "harmoniously combining spiritual wealth, moral purity and a perfect physique." His moral code: "the principle of collectivism and comradely mutual assistance."

It has become increasingly evident that they have not "progressed that far" today, either. Implicit in all of the sociologists' work — and the abundant recommendations they make to the Soviet state — is the realization that man (in effect, his personality) has proven much too obstreperous, much too singularly unmalleable, to form that easily.

So the ground rules had to be changed a bit. The Marxist maxim that "environment determines consciousness," while still lip-service, has in reality given way to the empirical knowledge that consciousness must be carefully investigated (thus sociology). The very fact of investigation proved the basic independence of consciousness. The concomitant maxim that once the need for such intensive manual labor dropped to a reasonable level, the New Man would devote himself to ennobling leisure pursuits has also been lost — on the contrary, the New Man often seemed to be most interested in drinking himself into a Russian stupor.

So what has happened is that changes that never were imagined in those early, halcyon days now have been happily and sometimes not-so-happily ensconced, — because they exist and nothing can be done about them, — into the bedrock of modern, revised Communist theory. "Personality" and "the individual", once thought to be tentative and wholly dependent upon environment, have now shown themselves to be creatures with their own will and independent energy. And modern texts on "Scientific Communism" state clearly that the march of Communism has always been the march toward the development of the "individual personality."

This is why it is least important in many ways to look for changes in Russian youth on the level of political change, where it is so much more difficult for external changes to occur. Actually, they are coming much more quickly — and they are far more measureable — on the level of psychology and sociology. It is these changes that eventually will lead to political change, but from within and probably non-violently.

Sociology is not new in Russia, of course — it thrived during the Slavophile-Westerner debate of the 19th century — but all non-Marxist sociology was soon prohibited by the new Soviet regime in

1922. Under Stalin, "sociology" was simply political propaganda and it was not reborn in any realistic way until Stalin's death and the de-Stalinization that began in 1956.

What happened was simply that the growing to adulthood of the new generation coincided, not only with "the thaw" but with the turning to the "scientific management of Communist society." As the society became a mature, industrialized society, the idea grew that society must be efficient. And an efficient society had to be based on initiative, not on terror, which the Soviets were learning was as crippling to the GNP as to the human spirit. New ways had to be found to work out — peacefully — how to make man want to work, how to place young people in the right professions and how to make men loyal in a post-terror and post-ideology stage of development.

In the vacuum that followed the end of Stalinization, the social scientists came forward, saying, "We have the answers." Soon they were entering into a highly sophisticated discussion with their society as to how best to persuade, cajole and form man to more or less accept Communism of his own free will — painlessly. The drive was to make Communism fit — scientifically — the new body of young Russia. The renaissance of the social sciences was the sign that Soviet society was one that was beginning to talk to itself.

Even then, Russian sociology was totally different from American and European sociology, its spirit being described by American sociologists Robert Merton and Henry Rieken as "most like market-research in the United States: on a low level of abstraction and largely confined to ferreting out facts that can be taken into account in making practical decisions."

Still, it advanced. In 1958, the Soviet Sociological Association was formed. In 1963, the Presidium of the U.S.S.R. Academy of Sciences directed all its scientific bodies to examine the methodological problems of the natural and social sciences. It was no exaggeration that Fedoseev and Frantsev that year announced that "In fact, a new stage has arrived in the century-long development of the Marxist science of society."

It had.

It was different, far different, of course, from the sociology of the West; but soon Soviet sociologists were to reveal a surprisingly broad knowledge of Western scholarship (another opening in the curtain separating academic disciplines, as well as everything else). Moreover, Soviet sociologists have of late continued arguing for more reliable data, arguing that basic social problems cannot be solved unless one is able to investigate them fully.

And this is why sociology is so attractive to the youth — it is the one place where, through the instrumental eye of cold statistics, one can at least begin to approach truth.

While Western sociologists try not to exaggerate possibilities for the future, such experienced sociologists as Alex Simirenko have predicted that, within ten to twenty years, Soviet sociologists will show far more "ideological tolerance" and they will be involved in "comparative empirical research on an international scale."

Another philosopher, the brilliant Lewis Feuer, after months of lecturing and studying in Russia, came to the conclusion that "The younger sociologists have as quietly as possible discarded the dialectical methodology." According to Marx, he has written, "there were no universal laws of social science; each social system had its specific sociological laws, but a law common to diverse social systems was out of the question. The Soviet sociologists, under pressure of their actual researches, have found themselves obliged to drop this dialectical outlook."

He cited the case of Professor Kharchev, the Leningrad sociologist who specializes in marriage and the family, who told him that one-fourth of the married couples might be living under "abnormal housing conditions," but that this was a situation common to all industrial countries. When Feuer observed that he was engaged in a "revisionist enterprise," because according to the dialectical standpoint there should be a Capitalist law of population and a Socialist one, but not one common to all industrial societies, Socialist or Capitalist, the Soviet denied it was revisionism; it was not revisionism, he said, to ascertain a general law by means of concrete researches.

In general, Feuer found "an emerging diversity among Soviet philosophers," who were all supposed to be strict dialectical materialists but simply used that Marxianism as a protective house to hold three major trends: scientific realism, existentialism and pragmatism. The scientific realists simply believe in the reality of the physical world; he placed them with American philosophical questions of 35 years ago. The existentialist he found concerned with the concept of alienation and with "problems of freedom and ethics which were banished from the conscience in the Stalinist era," "more concerned with the quality of individual life than with the tactics of ideological class struggle. The last group, he wrote, was drawn to American pragmatism and concerned itself with "such ambiguous concepts" as "practice."

Feuer goes so far as to predict that "the next era in Soviet intellectual history will be one of a contest between social science and ideology." He foresees an end to the philosophical "technism" bred in the Bolshevik period out of the economic requirements of the time and predicts a far greater dedication to the historical sciences and the humanities in the future. He also sees clearly that what is still feared in terms of the works and ideas of Freud is not his philosophy but the possibilities, within the psychoanalytical method, of "bringing into consciousness the strange manifold contents of the Soviet unconscious."

It was Feuer, too, who, after four and a half months in the Soviet Union and after being asked to give a last talk on his impressions of Soviet sociology and philosophy, reluctantly agreed. What he said no doubt shocked them, because it dealt, first, with how they ignored studying Stalinism and anti-Semitism and, second, how they ignored the conflict of generations. "I had, in the course of my travels found ample evidence of such a conflict," he wrote. "At Leningrad University, at an open meeting of the Communist organization of the Philological faculty, students had challenged and ridiculed the apology which the editor of Neva tried to present for the new party line against abstract art. No Soviet sociologist, however, had shown any readiness to study the phenomena of conflict."

Another keen observer, sociologist George Fischer, while he fully appreciates the extraordinary ties between the state and its servant, sociology, has noted "something of a generational difference between 'pure' social and political philosophers in the Soviet Union and the philosophers presently immersing themselves in empirical social research." The "pure" are in their 50s and 60s; the philosopher-sociologists are between 20 and 40. The older continue to march about in the domain of Marxist ideology, while the younger, no less convinced of doctrinal truth, nevertheless have become involved in field studies and new research methods.

The big difference here is that the young are far more interested in using scientific methods, such as cybernetics and modeling, to find out what man is; the old are simply trying to prove with more doctrine that he is what their doctrine says he already is.

This is a *big* difference.

And all of it points to something else — what Sovietologist Tibor Szamuely, writing in London's "Spectator" magazine, calls a "truly historic change." This is the emergence, "for the first time since the 1920s, possibly even since the revolution, of a genuine, independent public opinion." This public opinion is making itself heard and felt for the first time through these initial, oversimplified, childlike, but in the end, uniquely honest, sociological surveys.

Moments of insight, moments of truth! They come so seldom in the Soviet Union, but when they come, they dazzle the long-time seeker with much the same blinding glare that the oasis enthralls the man long lost on the desert.

"There was a conference of sociologists in Bulgaria," Dr. Lisovsky told me in Leningrad in 1971, "and Russians, Americans and Bulgarians got together." He smiled, a small, friendly smile, for he is a good man. "One American gave a paper on the idea that youth no longer is, as it was earlier, a 'white paper on which anything can be written.' "

Did the Russians agree?

He smiled.

"Yes," he said.

❧ Chapter Nineteen
America and Russa: Which System Has Done Better at Socializing Its Young?

"It is not at all a matter of indifference to society what kind of people your children will be."

Anton Makarenko, great pedagogue of the Soviet period whose works laid the basis for Soviet education today

*O*NE bright summer morning in the summer of 1972, Dr. John Howard, president of Rockford College in Rockford, Illinois, far from the Kremlin towers of Moscow, sat in his warm, book-lined office on the ultra-modern campus and spoke eloquently of a concern about modern American youth that has afflicted many conscientious adults. "We have had a default of adult leadership," said this tall, spare man with the piercing eyes, leaning back in his chair. "Higher education has lost its way in this country.

"As I study history, I see that every society, primitive or advanced, that evolved a system of higher education perceived two basic essentials of the process: to transmit knowledge and skills and to create a process which can create people who can live affirmatively within that society. For reasons I cannot totally say, much of our society today has abandoned this second aim — and has made a virtue of it. In a survey of 10,000 university professors, for instance, on the objectives of the university, the number one concern of almost all was 'to protect academic freedom.' " He shook his head.

"As a result, the student becomes simply a disembodied mind. There is total indifference to his state of mind, his attitudes, his well being. If education does not concern itself seriously and effectively with character education, then Americans should not be surprised if they see an erosion of character and citizenship.

"We have a generation of students who have been cheated. They have grown up without a frame of reference. The churches used to say 'Thou shalt' and 'Thou shalt not.' The young grew up with the idea that there were limits. This generation is blessed with a very strong streak of altruism. It is a genuine altruistic impulse, but one that finds very few legitimate channels through which to direct itself against the relativism that overwhelms our society. It has eliminated for the intelligent and sensitive and intellectual portion of the young the possibility of standing strongly on behalf of something.

"We've debunked the heroes. Now even the leading churchmen say it is a matter of your own conscience. Anyone standing for something is ridiculed, so young people choose for their heroes those who attack. I am convinced that by far the greatest impetus for the young to use drugs is their desire to ease the pain of the purposelessness and cynicism and the loss of confidence in the institutions of society, which create a kind of cosmic forlornness."

In his job as a member of the President's Commission on Drug Abuse and in his university post, Dr. Howard has been in a prime position to observe the forces hammering within the souls of American youth. But his observations have also been made, in different ways, by many other critics of the "socialization" of American youth.

Dr. Morris Janowitz, the prominent sociologist at the University of Chicago, made much the same point to me one day. "The extent to which young people can identify with the nation today is questionable," this intense, fast-talking, fast-thinking man of ideas began. "Somehow the American high schools will have to undergo a change. They need to be organized more along the lines of an instrument of socialization, as they were in the beginning. There is something of this appeal in the commune movement. We are one of the few societies without a national youth movement. In short, we need things to link youth to the nation."

But perhaps the critic who is hardest on the United States, with its mid-century affluent rootlessness and purposelessness, is Cornell University's Urie Bronfenbrenner, who has specialized in studying Soviet education and socialization processes and in comparing them to their American counterparts. Repeatedly, he has warned that the Soviet system has been far more successful and efficient than the American one *in producing the kind of younger generation it desired.* Indeed, if current trends in American education persist, he has written, "we can anticipate increased alienation, indifference, antagonism and violence in all segments of our society." What he would like to see is American parents reinvolving themselves in their children's lives, schools again playing the role of training children for social responsibility and classes generating "organized patterns of mutual help."

In effect, all these — and many other — critics are saying that the fabric of American life has been seriously rent at mid-century, partly by a loss of faith in the institutions and values of the republic and partly by an adult generation that, for various reasons, did not pass down to its children a cohesive structure of beliefs and values that would permit them to live with a sense of certainty and an assurance of purpose.

But does this mean, then, that the United States has been less successful than the Soviet Union — its great competitor in the 20th century — in preparing a new generation? If it did, it could tell us a great deal about the way the next 50 years would be lived, for the question of which of the two societies which have typified the two political, social and economic poles of development in the modern world has done the best job of socializing its young is no moot question. It could tell us which people is going to have faith in and fight for its system. It could show us which system is going to survive and dominate the future of the world.

It is a particularly important question today because, despite the gratifying alleviation of Cold War hostilities and the lessening of the martial competition that era engendered, there remains a healthy competition of ideas; the competition today does today and doubtless will in the future revolve about whether democracy can "do it" as well or better than socialism, all the while keeping her soul intact. At the very core of this question is the innermost question of what kind of new generation Russian youth will form — and what kind of future American the young Americans today will form.

So, despite many qualifications, if I am to ask myself the key question, *Which society has done the best job of socializing its youth?* I would make many of the same criticisms of Howard, Janowitz and Bronfenbrenner and answer, "The Russians."

This does not mean that the Russian youngsters are necessarily smarter, more creative, more intelligent or more decent human beings; it does not mean they are more pleasant people. It does not even mean the older generation of Soviets is pleased with them; indeed, the elders often feel they have created a generation of ungenerous vipers, children of victory who are too spoiled and narcissistic to celebrate the sacrifices of their parents, careless offspring of affluence. No, it is meant to be an objective observation, and one based strictly on the question of successful socialization.

It means that the Soviet state has structured its ideological formation throughout society, and particularly in the schools, in such a manner that this generation, while in many, many ways dissatisfied, has fallen less far from the ideological tree than the '60s generation in the 'States.

To review, and capsulate: this generation of young Russians frightens its parents by wanting much more freedom — to think, to speak, to write, to read — but few are totally alienated from the Marxist system. They simply want to perfect it — and probably a majority has not lost faith that it is perfectible. Like their elders, they drink to mawkish and maudlin excess, but they are not poisoned by drugs. While they bitterly criticize the enforced emphasis on the sugary, simplistic sweetness-and-light optimism in the popular arts, most young people seem happy there is no pornography and that their cities are not being degraded by an "anything goes" commercialism. They find the emphasis on violence and morbidity in the West totally unacceptable, and such Western excesses as Vietnam have shaken their faith that democracy really offers them an attractive alternative.

While there is deep criticism of the older generation, particularly for its silent complicity in the crimes of Stalin, there is, as yet, no massive crisis of authority within the Soviet Union. Authority is respected or at least feared so much that it is obeyed. A traditional respect for parents remains that seems to carry with it more elements of real love than elements of fear.

In sharp contrast to the situation described by Howard, Janowitz and Bronfenbrenner, Soviet schools have not, like American schools, lost their function as the formers of the character of the new generation; indeed, character formation is considered to be their *major* function, and they perform it often with a too-pedantic passion. And although there is some disagreement over how to do it, there are few nagging doubts in the minds of most Soviet parents, officials and educators about what kind of "new man" they want to form. There is no idea, as in the West, that youth is somehow a value in itself — peer groups are stressed in Soviet schools, but only to reinforce societal values, never to exist apart from adult society.

What makes it difficult for many young people, even those who cannot bear the political totalitarian aspects of Soviet society, really to rebel is the fact that they believe that many of their society's values are good ones — even the dissidents respect these and do not want them changed. There is a high official respect for "culture". Children are taught (even though these values are not always respected in real life) that man, not money, is the most important thing: that man's work is the arbiter of his worth; and that Communist society, in which every man has his respected place, is the ultimate stage in the development of mankind.

Where both dissidents from and enthusiasts for Soviet society come together, moreover, is on the plane of effectivenss — they believe that history is going to judge each system on what it eventually turns out, not on the functional means used. And, in my experience at this midpoint in Soviet history, as the Soviets slide into their third generation since the revolution, more young Soviets feel that their system, despite its brutalities (which they hope and believe are now a thing of the past) has "delivered" for the average person, while the United States has not. Despite their criticisms and their demands for change, a majority seems to have faith in the future, citing the lack of unemployment, the systematic economic development, free education, pensions, health care and other social welfare aspects of the Soviet state.

There are a number of reasons why this should be so:

— At this moment, despite all their failings, the Russians have created values that are far more congenial for a mass society than has the United States. Often by brutal means, they have prohibited the rise of the kind of sick violence infecting the Western world. Their people have, at least, an ideological rationale for living together in a crowded earth, and there is little of the proligacy of the West in terms of material goods, if only because there are so few consumer goods.

In short, the U.S.S.R. has myths for a 20th century mass society defined and developed, while Americans are still living — often at screaming point — within the old individualistic myths of the frontier, which are notably inappropriate to a mass modern society. Some forward-looking Americans, of course, have attempted to define new democratic communitarian technocratic myths for modern society, but at this point the country is suspended between the past and the future, as unwilling to accept new ways as it knows them to be necessary.

— The Russians have dealt more realistically with personal competition, the drive and need for fame and ideas of responsibility in work (and I say this largely about their announced ideals, not about their practice). I did not find Russian young people so compulsive about fame and fortune, although they were adamantly demanding about having what we would consider to be basic material goods. Although it is slipping in real life, there remains as a prime concept of society the idea that manual work is a positive good.

— The Russians have created a society that is much more modern and realistic about women's needs in the modern world. While the U.S. is still fighting with itself over such unthinkables as nursery schools, raising children in communal ways and women working, the Soviets have largely solved these problems. Americans look at nursery schools as a means of shunting off an unwanted child; the Russians, as a responsible move for a stronger and more controlled family. They have allowed and forced women into the labor force to solve real problems, while American women play at public involvement with such things as volunteer work.

Every person is formed — culturally, politically, psychologically — and then linked to others in a manner on many levels in which there is more trust (giving your tiny baby to a nursery school to care for is certainly an important indicator of trust, in addition to other things) than in the U.S.

But despite these basic differences, there is something very curious happening: despite the fact they arise from quite different ends of the spectrum and despite the fact that the methods of socialization are radically different, there are some uncanny similarities between Russian and American youth.

When I first started looking at Russian youth, I was most impressed with the differences between Soviet and American young people. The Americans were filled with a freedom they often stretched to anarchy; the Russians, despite their distinct stirrings, were still caught tight in the straight jacket of authority. The Americans revelled in personal liberties; the Russians, while trying hard to overcome the fear of personal freedom of the Russian past, were still relatively collectivist compared to the U.S. While Russian youth was reacting to too much formation within its society, American youth was seeking out new formative structures — new political formations, communes, group marriages, innovative child-raising schemes.

But after I got deeply into the study of Soviet youth — and particularly after the summer of 1972, when I did an in-depth study in Illinois of 300 typical young Americans between the ages of 18 and 24 — I began to realize that there were indeed some striking similarities bred of the fact that, despite all the differences in ideology, we have here two highly-industrialized, developed countries whose very development has brought about a convergence of tendencies, just as it will doubtless lead to the same convergence with other countries when they reach this level. The fact is an important one, then, if we can say, as I believe we can, that the characteristics we find here might well be found later in other youths.

What are these similarities?

Both are generations whose basic formation and view of life and their nations have come out of one chaotic, traumatic event which influenced all their perceptions and very nearly destroyed their faith in their countries: the demythologizing of Stalin and the Vietnam war. The American mission came out of Vietnam just as sullied as the Russian mission came out of Stalinism.

("My whole generation is disenchanted, and I don't really know why," Charles Schmadeke, a college student from Galena, Illinois told me. "A lot of it was Vietnam, but people give too much credit to Vietnam for this disenchantment. It's much more than that. We don't know what's legitimate any more." Then this young Nixon supporter, pure Midwestern gothic with a rakish moustache and smile, hit upon a way to typify the phenomenon he was trying to describe. "For me, the disenchantment started with the scandal over the $64,000 Question program on TV when we found it was all rigged. I compared that to America today. It's like Horatio Alger —

the idea that you can make it if you work hard enough. Then you find everything's rigged." He paused and added with a note of sadness, "I find America like that."

("After the death of Stalin, I was terribly upset," Natasha Orlova, a pretty blond teacher with a wispy smile, told me in Kiev, as she poured out her heart. "It was a great disillusionment for me to hear about how crimes — I can't tell you how deep, I couldn't even go to the institute to study for two years. I lost all interest in everything. It wasn't until my marriage and my husband began to explain things to me that I began to feel again." She was crying now very gently. "Now . . . I don't want to know things.")

One of the results of these two traumatic events has been the emergence of a new kind of patriotism in both countries. This has become such a subject for concern among the rulers of both the U.S. and the U.S.S.R. that they have even expressed the fear that the young would not fight for their countries. Actually, the new style of patriotism is remarkably similar in both countries. In both, there is little faith in the state per se as an untouchable symbol of patriotism; instead, the new patriotism answers more to the people, to the vast physical beauty of the countries, and to the human qualities which transcend borders and such ephemera. (Both of these generations dislikes borders.) Their patriotism responds, not to exclusive flag and symbol, but to the broader, inclusive world about them. In their way, they are true internationalists. But their internationalism is enormously different from, say, the internationalism of the '30s. It is not ideological, not political, not adherent to groups; it is infinitely personal and human — one to one, man to man, woman to woman, child to child, human to human, dog to dog.

("A person who speaks up in what he feels to be the best interest of fellow human beings anywhere is being truly patriotic," David Blasco, a brilliant student at Northwestern University. "Our first responsibility is to Earth and the people on it. All of us breathe the same air, participate in the same water cycle. Someone who burns a piece of paper to make change is being entirely more patriotic than someone who burns soft coal to make money. Patriotism seems irrelevant. I grew to consciousness at a time when you couldn't be proud of your country. I hope the time can come when I could be satisfied with it."

("We have more in common with intellectuals in other countries than with peasants here, and yet we are told not to associate with them. It is absurd — men are going to the moon, and we cannot talk to other human beings." An artist's wife in Russia.)

Both American and Soviet young people are also reacting, with every fiber of their being, to the reality and pressures of advanced industrial society. In both societies, many young people have simply "dropped out" into inward-turning lives. Outside of politics, incorruptible, privatistic, they can live lives of pristine purity far from the thundering herd.

In Russia, the searching for something beyond the nuts-and-bolts stage of early building Bolshevism has led to the passion for the spiritual life of man in art, in personal relations and even in Communist organization — not to speak of the quest in the past, where human and not technological values predominated. In the U.S., this same search has carried many young Americans into every kind of social and religious experiment with communes, Eastern mysticism, spiritualism and even magic.

("Even if you know how to do things, the problems of 'What for?' remain," Valerie Melko, a brilliant young physicist-psychologist at Kiev State University, told me. "Why do we use modern technical things? What do they give to man on a spiritual level? If there is one thing typical of this generation, it is its tendency to analyze everything and to understand everything independently of past judgments. Youth does not share the opinion that technical progress will solve social problems automatically. Fascism showed that. The tendency today can be compared with the tendency of the Renaissance: to put man in the main spot, to make man the most precious thing in the world."

("I was raised very religious," said Anita Lanz, a Chicago girl. "When I was confirmed, I wanted to be a missionary. Then I said, 'Fuck it to the whole thing.' Later I saw that God is in the people, he's in the grass, the rain, the thunder, the lightning and the snow. It's that type of thing: people concerned with other people. Religion is caring about yourself, each other, the world. It's a religion between you and yourself, between you and your concept of life.")

And, in both countries, among the young there is a deep concern for independence of thought and a concern for truth, wherever it may lead you. There are also similarly changed attitudes toward work. In both countries, the young have all but lost the Puritan Ethic which has come so bountifully into play in both societies. Among all of them, work no longer is looked upon as a value in itself; it is a value when something of value comes from it — and it is important to the individual human being when and only when it means doing something "interesting," something that grips his passions and broadens his personal horizons.

("Experiences are much more important than material things," said Casey Tomala, a Bensenville, Ill., furniture store clerk. "Young people are beginning to see that getting the college education, the house in the suburbs and the two-car garage is not the way. They are beginning to see that education really isn't that important. Success in the traditional sense isn't that important. It is much more important to have lived.")

("Who will be the worker in the original sense? Graduates today dream of individual creative work or independent research. They think it is more romantic than being a shop steward. It's not a question of money — workers get the same money as intellectuals. It's not a question of social equality. It's just a question of the diploma and prestige." Alla Beljakova, editor of the Leningrad youth newspaper, Smena.)

In both societies, adults worry about their offspring being soft — soft on Capitalism, soft on Communism, unpatriotic or unresponsive to the old symbols, unwilling to work hard or simply too spoiled by affluence and permissiveness. Yet, they are not really any of these terms; the terms are not even relative, and other words should be used to describe them. These are generations arisen out of consumer societies. They are young people who are united in the absence in both of them of a tragic sense of life; concern over pots and pans does not lead to a tragic sense.

In both countries, this generation is the "generation inbetween," — a generation not so passionate and angry as the Russian generation of the early '60s nor the American generation of the mid- and late- '60s. These are the generations absorbent, in which the rebelliousness, the new values which grew out of it and the changes of a momentous time in both countries are being absorbed into the new body politic as natural and inevitable things.

Interestingly enough, even many Soviet social scientists are willing to admit that there are many similarities between Soviet and

American youth. Dr. Lisovsky at Leningrad, for instance, surveyed a group of visiting American students on the "components of happiness" and compared their answers to the answers of his Russian subjects. "The Soviet answers were: interesting work, love and respect from others," he told me. "Mainly, the American answers were the same, although in general our young were more socially inclined. American youngsters had a deeper interest in private lives." That was in 1967, however, and by the time I returned in 1971 he was convinced that American youth had become much more "socially aware."

Another survey done by Estonian students at the University of Tartu in Estonia by Dr. Mikk Tetma, who was in charge of the laboratory in the sociology of education, was then compared with a comparative survey done by American sociologists F. Herzberg, B. Mausner and P. Goodman. Tetma found that there was a "striking difference" between the two, particularly in that American students rated "security" high as a consideration in career choice, and also "leadership" as a reward. He summed up saying that "the replies of our Estonian college students testify to the fact that they have freedom to choose their professions, since they are not preoccupied with security, success or power. They are motivated by values of a higher order."

But when one studied the percentages, there was actually an astonishing correlation that he apparently chose not to see. When asked to rate the importance "of being creative and original" in one's profession, 48 percent of Americans rated it a "very important requirement" to 38.3 of the Estonians and 13 percent on each side rated it an "unimportant requirement." When it came to rating the importance "of being useful to others," the Estonian and American percentages were within a few percentage points of each other, as they were when it came to the importance "of making a good living." Americans rated "achieving position and status in society" higher than Estonians, as they did the possibility "of exercising leadership" (32 percent of Americans rated it very important compared to 9 percent of Estonians). Certainly, one wonders why Dr. Tetma should be so pleased with young Estonians for not wanting to exercise leadership — an informed Western guess would be they want nothing to do with the hackneyed type of leadership their republic has had since it was taken over by the Soviets.

My own proportional observations also came out similar between the two countries. I would estimate the Russian young people at about these percentages: extreme and active enthusiasts for the regime, 10 percent; somewhat dissatisfied and wanting changes within the regime, 50 percent; highly dissatisfied and increasingly vocal or else turning increasingly to themselves in privatistic withdrawal, 30 percent; and extreme dissidents, 10 percent. My observations of our Illinois youth came out at about the same percentages.

And while the reasons for the similarities between the two groups are many and far too complex to deal with fully in a small space like this, there are some reasons that can at least be suggested. One is the sheer force and fact of advanced industrialization — there is every reason to believe that it will cause many of the same human responses in every country in which it occurs, and, indeed, it already has. But another factor is what many see — and what I believe fully to be the case — as a real "convergence" in the ideas, development and values of the United States and Soviet Russia.

Russia is changing from being a rigidly cohesive society to a *relatively* relaxed society. The United States is searching for more cohesiveness. They are becoming less politicized, we are becoming more so. Strangely enough, the Soviets have made individualists and loners of many of *their* youth, while the Americans have made experimental communalists out of many of theirs. The U.S.S.R. is a country whose social problems are largely momentarily solved, while its technological and political problems are not solved; the U.S. is a country where technology has been developed to its utmost, while its social problems and, less, its political problems are not solved.

The American system has had a basic unidealistic view of man (his impulses must be controlled by limiting his power) that enabled most Americans to live an uncommonly decent life, while the Soviet system has had an unnaturally idealistic view of man (he can be perfected, and will be forced to perfection whether he likes it or not) that has left most Russians leading a very dishonest life.

But in terms of changes occurring today, each seems headed slowly but steadily toward the other. The U.S. appears to be changing from a character type in which values were internalized by parental, church, and school training to a type in which values are externalized; the Soviet Union appears to be going the other way — from collectivism to a greater individualism. We need mass goals for a mass technological society, instead of a 19th century individualist one, and the Soviets need tempered individual goals for a new generation that feels its uniqueness. The two countries could learn from each other, if they would.

Certainly there are differences. The Americans sing paens to personal freedom and to individualism, while even today the Soviet Union officially deeply distrusts these values and idolizes the collective spirit. Russians even drink individually — to get away from the collectivity and finally lose themselves in the self, while Americans drink to join the collectivity, to be a good fellow among fellows. In many ways, the two countries are contorted mirror images of each other.

And yet, despite this, as de Tocqueville saw in 1830 in "Democracy in America" there is something that links the development and even the missions of the two countries together in the history of the world. This is the fact that the United States and Russia, in different centuries and in different ways — one through evolution, one through revolution, one through democratic concepts that evolved from ancient Greece, one through Marxist concepts that evolved from the Germanic philosophers, one emphasizing freedom, one emphasizing security, one individual-istic, one collectivist — have created the first two mass societies in the world.

Sometimes in Russia, despite the great differences, I had the strange feeling that I was in quintessential America. In the factories, for instance, there were signs all over. "Director, be sure and use all safety devices!" "The Moral Code: one for all and all for one; He who does not work does not eat; Be considerate to your fellow man. Fight shortcomings." In "Lenin rooms," those patriotic corners in the schools and in the Pioneer palaces where Lenin memorabilia are displayed in effusion, I had the feeling that this was no more than the kinds of patriotic display of Lincolnabilia or Washingtonabilia in schools in the United States. There are feelings about human equality, ideas of emulation of moral behavior, concepts of the enrollment of people in their own destiny, exhortations to work, plus a certain functional view of man and a certain mechanistic view of the world that are common to both societies. In each, there is a secular religious fervor that has gone through its period of feeling able and wanting to save the world. In the United States, it was "Americanism;" in the Soviet Union, "revolutionary socialism." Each gave the world a post-religion secular religion for the masses.

But all of this may seem rather optimistic on the Russian side and rather pessimistic on the American side. Is this really fair? How does this jibe with my observations about how dissatisfied Soviet youth is with the absurdities and brutalities of the Soviet system? Am I saying now that Soviet youth is *not* dissatisfied — or that their parents' generation is not dissatisfied with *them*? Am I suggesting that the Soviet young, with all their covert anxieties, their subtle changes of values and their often errant anger, will not change Soviet society?

I am suggesting none of this. To say that Russia has done a better job to socializing its youth *to Soviet values* does not mean that this generation is intrinsically better than the American generation of the same age. On the contrary — I find American young people far more likeable, intelligent and idealistic. I am only suggesting that Soviet society probably has structured itself in the way it is going to be — a Marxist economic system and a Communist party political system — while the U.S. has some serious rearranging to do. But it is also clear to me as to many observers of the Soviet scene, that their structure is in trouble, too, and that the new generation, for all it's socialization, will have a sharp and prophetic influence on the future formation and structuring of the Soviet state and, thus, on the world.

ᕝ Chapter Twenty
The Shadows in the Wings
— But will Russian Youth
Affect the Future?

"To have a feeling for the liberty
enjoyed in the other European countries,
one must have sojourned in that solitude without repose,
in that prison without leisure, that is called Russia."

The Marquis de Custine in 1839.

*W*ILL the younger generation in the Soviet Union, with its new thoughts and ideas about life and its relative lack of fear, eventually change Soviet society? Or is the Communist system so all-powerful — so heavily, overwhelmingly oppressive — that it will silently form youth into its image as easily as the master sculptor forms his clay? Those, of course, are the questions.

It is only fair to acknowledge at the start that many Russian specialists — men and women who have spent their lives studying Soviet life — are pessimistic. They see the frustrated young individuals of today inexorably being turned into the little wooden soldiers of Communism of tomorrow.

"I would warn against being too optimistic," Dr. Barry Farrell, Sovietologist at Northwestern University, told me. "You see kids at 20 who are radical or who have ideals — but what will they be doing 15 years from now? Many Russian kids today are less humanistic than the former generation." He pointed to the traumatic liberalization of Czechoslovakia in 1968 which, brought on a Soviet invasion that almost sent that country back to Stalinism. And he was unusually competent to speak on the subject for he had specialized in Czechoslovak affairs and had many contacts there.

"The Czechs thought things had changed," he said, pensively. "A friend in Prague told me, 'You'll see, the Russians have changed. They wouldn't invade a Socialist country again.'" But then he thought a second time. "On the other hand, maybe what happened was that the Czechs didn't see that, though things were changing underneath in the U.S.S.R., the old leadership was still in power — those changes still hadn't reached the surface."

I reminded him, too, that, just before the 1968 invasion, in the highest levels of the party in Russia there was a highly significant move, apparently on the brink of success, to liberalize the party's ideological stand — particularly in the areas of granting more freedom to read, know and travel. The fear instilled in Russian party leaders by the liberalization in Czechoslovakia, in particular by what they saw as a Westernization in the press, killed this move for the time being; but it is highly unlikely these impulses would not arise again when the moment was propitious, for they are impulses always pounding from inside against the forehead of the Communist state.

Then Dr. Farrell added: "If you believe things will not stay the same, you have to set up the hypothesis that they *will* stay the same, and then tear it down."

All right, then: here is the negative hypothesis:

The Soviet Union remains an oppressive totalitarian state. Dissidents are still sent off to insane asylums because officials think that anybody who seriously questions anything is "insane." Freedom of speech still barely exists. Young people start out, like young people everywhere, idealistic and hopeful of change. Above all, they want freedom . . . . to think, to feel, to travel, to learn. But soon the system overwhelms. If you don't conform, you don't get ahead. If you don't fit in, you may no longer be sent to Siberia, but you'll certainly be confined to the dregs of Soviet society, where ambition is meaningless, where there is no future and no appeal and no escape except the psychological suicide of total introversion or the physical suicide of political mutiny.

"I take two positions," Dr. Edward Keenan, Russian history professor at Harvard University, mused one day as we talked on the Cambridge campus about this hypothesis. "There seems to me to be a lot of evidence that it can't go on like this. But as a historian, I have to accept the fact that it *can* go on. It's done it for fifty years.

I've seen too many people in Russia worn down, not exactly settling into suburban acquiescence, but drinking too much . . . . self-destructive things. This remains a very stable, very conservative society. The system not only picks the people who play the game, but it drives intellectual people into other, less sensitive areas — this is real control."

So in 15 years — say, by age 35 — the young idealists have become mature cynics, say these men. They don't ever totally conform, at least not in the dark of night, but they soon learn to see the system as omnipotent, and eventually they passively give up and give in.

That is the "hypothesis" which men like Farrell and Keenan and many others whom hard experience has taught to be cautious and unsanguine about Soviet affairs put forward.

The other major group of trained observers, many of these journalists, go quite to the other extreme in their predictions (prophets abhor a middle ground!). Men like American correspondent Anatole Shub, son of the famous Sovietologist, early Russian Social Democrat and friend of Lenin's David Shub, are convinced that Russia is heading, not toward anything like peaceful stagnation but toward a "devastating explosion," as a nation of peasants becomes imperfectly urbanized. The prominent LeMonde writer, Michel Tatu, who served a long time in Russia, insists that the country has entered a "pre-revolutionary phase of development," and Shub agrees, "primarily because none of the current Soviet leaders or ruling institutions have shown any sign of movement toward a guided evolution (in the Yugoslav, Czech or some other indigenous manner). Quite the contrary."

Other fine writers like the Yugoslav, Mihajlo Mihajlov, have predicted a merging of Marxism and Christianity in the new Soviet state — as a result of the present spiritual searching. He has written: "It is clear that a new generation is being born — a direct product of socialist 'scientific spirit' — which will send Hegel, Marx, science, technology and socialism, in the forms in which they now exist, to the devil. This generation is being born in the East, not in the West." And to complete the circle of the contradictions, we might look to Soviet dissident writer Andre Amalrik, who is convinced that the state cannot survive until 1984, modern time's symbolic year of infamy, because a class war will pit the "destructive movement of the lower classes" against the "constructive movement" of the new "middle class".

Both of these ends of the spectrum, alternating between the idea that Stalinism will last forever (despite the fact no such thing as Stalinism even begins to exist in Russia today) and the idea that upheaval is imminent (despite the real stability of the Soviet state), seem equally unreal to me. Many other Russian specialists — and many diplomats and many correspondents, such as I — see the situation quite differently. I suppose we are middle-of-the-roadish. We see the new generation as a force in itself, a force partly active and partly passive that will not be forever cowed and molded into old forms and that will gradually but certainly evince new reactions on the part of the government.

This intermediate position is taken to a degree by Colette Shulman, the Russian specialist at Columbia University. "Many of the young Russians think things will not change," Mrs. Shulman commented to me one morning over coffee in her lovely Riverside Drive apartment, filled with Russian paintings. "They say the next generation of leadership will be the same old thing. In a fundamental sense, they are probably right. The next generation of leaders will most likely govern with more efficient and sophisticated techniques, but this is not of itself an improvement, since efficiency can also be used to strengthen political controls over people. But while the leadership prospects are not encouraging, I do think that future leaders, who ever they may be, will have to reckon with a new generation of young people whose life experience has been quite different from that of their elders."

Another Soviet specialist who is even more optimistic about change is a young Western diplomat who has served in Moscow, studied and is considered an expert on Russian youth. Since he is still in the diplomatic service, he cannot be quoted by name. "Of course, youth will make a difference," he told me, vehemently, "because it means the difference between the educated middle class and the leadership is diminishing. The leaders' own children are more sophisticated. *Their* children will be even more subtle. Look at Kosygin. Look at his daughter. She's very sophisticated, very Westernized. This is bound to have an effect. Russians expect a certain cultural level in their leadership today. It's a very sensitive issue to say someone is 'Asiatic,' or in effect backward. It means they want to become European, as they always have.

"I can't see any radical change in this society for a long time, but it will simply gradually become more Western. In 50 years, if the West remains reasonable, it will have lost its restrictiveness. Ultimately, I think the future of their country is in good hands. Of course," he warned, "these changes will not necessarily make them more reasonable . . . and it will make them better opponents."

Still another of the "optimists" is Averell Harriman, a man who has known and negotiated with Soviet leaders from Stalin in the 1920s on and can hardly be accused of looking at them from a viewpoint of naivete or innocence. "The trend toward greater freedom of expression, although still extremely limited, will, I believe, continue," he says. "There will be setbacks, as we have seen in the stern sentences meted out to Soviet authors Daniel and Sinyavsky, who went beyond the limits of 'propriety.' Yet, with expanded education, further decentralization of administration and the growing complexities of Soviet life, it will become more and more difficult to control thought and expression in that vast country. The Soviet system has shown flexibility through convenient reinterpretation of Marxism-Leninism to adjust itself to changed circumstances. I believe that we will see that process continue."

These are very close to the conclusions I reached after five months of working intensively inside Russia and four years of researching Russian youth from outside.

For this generation of Russian youth — raised in peacetime, vastly better educated than its parents' generation, much less afraid of the past or of the outside, unused to endless sacrifice, skeptical about given "truths" and preferring to corroborate everything with its own empirical truth — is far more individualistic, free-thinking and relativistic than its fathers. In place of the insecure, inferiority-ridden arrogance of their elders, who insisted everything Russian was superior, these young people ask foreigners, "Tell us what you don't like about us." Instead of Marxist cliches being repeated by rote every minute of the day, they will say things like, "Our ideology is best in theory, but yours is best in practice."

To the older generation, economic security was more important than anything — more important than opportunity, more important than love, more important than truth — because it had known such misery in impoverishment. But to this generation, that experience comes second-hand. Before, the state defined man simply as a producing, consuming creature with no mystery or spontaneity about him; thoughts of principle or ethics in our sense of the words were simply inconceivable. Now, man is beginning to be thought of in Soviet Russia as a value in himself, and, as the brilliant sociologist Lewis Feuer has put it, today's Russia is witnessing the very gradual reassertion of "the values of individualism, of questioning, of the religious spirit, of the ethical personality, of human relations transcending party comradeship."

There is nothing mysterious about all this. It would, indeed, be something startling in history if this new generation, formed by a different experience than its parents, did not form its own new sphere of existence. And it must be remembered that passion and activism are not the only forces for change; passivity and disinterest can be powerful forces for transformation, as the Soviet leaders are seeing.

The Russians *have* created a New Man, just as the Americans created a New Man, the American; just as any developing society creates a *modern* man with modern perceptions and modern outlooks and a modern mentality. It is just not the New Man they expected. Objective conditions can play tricks on all of us.

But how will these new attitudes and outlooks *change* society?

Perhaps the best way to show just how deeply they have operated to change Soviet society is to take the changes wholly or in part instigated by the dissenters; being the most sensitive and difficult area, this area most vividly illustrated that things can be done and are being done.

"Even in the last five years, I have noticed a change," Pyotr Yakir told me, and, with his past and present experiences, he can hardly be accused of being a pollyanna. "Five years ago, Sinyavsky and Daniel published abroad and they were jumped upon, tried and sentenced. Now, many publish abroad, and they are not arrested. Before, they would arrest you for standing outside a trial. Now, even TASS is forced to provide information on some of the trials. Even the fact that Kronika has lasted for 40 months is a big change. The reason the government is being more cautious and prudent in the case of Kronika is that it is trying to acquire respectability among the nations of the world. They do not want to damage the facade."

Valerie Chalidze, head of the scientific group of dissidents, also "hopes for the better. Things are a lot better than they could be. The protests have helped. It's hard to talk about separate forms of protest, but in general it is good when people express their opinions. I do think the authorities pay attention.

"If one person does something and is sent away, that's just one case. But if a hundred do it, and then a thousand, and they're sent, too, the authorities can't pretend they don't exist."

"A lot of foreigners raised in different traditions and with different educations can't realize the significance of five people demonstrating in Red Square," Yakir went on. "In 1936, under Stalin, not one person in a million would even have thought of it. Foreigners think, 'so five people demonstrated and got three years — what's that?' But to us, it's extraordinary."

"I think Yakir's basically right," Dr. Reddaway continued. "Many taboos, such as publishing abroad and all, have come down, and they won't come again. They won't go back to the old terror — they can't do it again. But I think the regime doesn't care so much about what people think as that it fears that what foreigners think will get back to the man in the street. It might undermine the government's own position vis-a-vis its own people.

"If one starts from the basis that Soviet leaders are basically worried about their own standing in the eyes of their own people, one sees that if their image deteriorates, they fear the people may organize against them."

It is not, of course, that the government could not easily destroy these budding movements if it wanted to. Indeed, within a year after my talks with Yakir and Chalidze, it was trying to do just that. Yakir was finally arrested, and Chalidze, permitted to leave with his wife and travel to the United States to give lectures on human rights, was then informed he could not return. Yet even these dark developments probably did not greatly alter Yakir's observation; he knew he would be arrested eventually. He saw quite clearly that the Soviet state would for some time to come pirouette back and forth with frustrated intensity between taking the hard line and giving a little more freedom where political matters were concerned; and he saw that this very indecision was what was new and was precisely what illustrated the change.

And at the same time, the Soviet state was allowing 14,000 Jews to emigrate to Israel in one year (more than in the previous ten years put together). For the truth is that the country today is faced with various paradoxes — paradoxes which arise out of the various contradictions between what the country was in the past and what it must be if it is in the future to continue developing in a growingly complex world (Concentration camps, no; computers, si).

But the dissenters admittedly are a tiny, untypical group. What about the real shadows in the wings? What about the masses of non-dissenting, loyal but critical and searching youth? Will they have an influence? I am convinced they will, because there are too many objective factors for change, most of them caused by the sheer pressures of a new and different generation and a new and different time, that are creating a new future:

— One of the greatest pressures for change is the bad working habits of the Russian worker, who is far beneath his Western or Japanese counterpart in productivity, despite the work ethic preached by the party. It is no accident and no whim that Party Chief Brezhnev stressed over and over in 1971 in his speech to the 24th party congress ("Ten days that didn't shake the world," the pundits called it) that the state needed to create more consumer goods, in effect, because otherwise people would not work. What they are trying to do, belatedly, is to strengthen the Russian Calvinist ethic that never quite enamoured the workers through a modern consumer come-on.

His announcement that for the first time consumer investment would grow faster than capital investment was a direct attempt to put products in the stores to keep people working for something and keep the money moving (savings accounts, for instance, grew from 20 billion rubles in 1965 to 50 billion in 1970, but the money was "dead" money because there was so little to use it for).

Here you have a first major break in the heavy industrial armor of the Soviet state — a giant step away from pouring all its wealth and energies into heavy industry and a new concern, motivated by whatever, for the individual. Here you have a reaction of the government to the desires and demands of the people and particularly of the youth — a reaction that, in its typically perverse Russian way, might even be thought of as a reaction to public opinion.

This new emphasis on consumer goods, of course, is coming about, not to pamper or please youth but to control them in a new way. Still, as we should know from Russian 5-year plans, Russian plans do not always work out as they plan.

As one highly-placed American diplomat put it: "You can't get a modern industrial society to operate on fear. It has to develop on incentives and on faith. The Puritan Ethic is held in Russia by the party but not by the mass. They have to build a modern society with people who just do not like to work too hard, and therefore they have to give them more and more what they want. And if Japan becomes the second industrial power in the world? Then they'll have to answer to why all this sacrifice only to be number three. It's the problem of how the individual in a modern system can work within a totally centralized political system."

— Closely related to the reaction of the Soviet state to problems of work productivity is the problem of how to organize the Soviet economic system to meet the new competitions of the outside world and economic sluggishness inside the Soviet world.

Here, too, the state is involved in a great crisis of ideas. Young economists, far less ideological than their elders, want to run the economy with mathematical models, not on rigid theory. Many of them want to use some variety of market mechanism. Already the reforms of 1965, which introduced in a limited manner the nasty idea of profit, judged a plant on how much it earned and used part of the profit as bonuses for the workers to encourage them to work more, are in effect in some 40,000 enterprises. But they are reforms that have gone only halfway. The managers have not been given the free hand they needed to make them work, as Moscow continued to set their prices and decide what they were to produce and how much. The party officials in the factories would not let the managers fire unneeded workers.

Now, economists in Moscow, Kiev and in the famous Academic City near Novosibirsk are saying that the Soviet Union must embrace modern economic management — everything from computers to export programming to better-trained managers — if it is to thrive economically. Even if all this were done, it would not mean the Soviet Union was going to go Capitalist — that is absurd; the socialist form of the country is set. But it would certainly mean much more individual initiative in management and eventually in consumer choice — and it would thus certainly answer many of the yearnings of this generation.

— As the Soviet system groaningly adjusts, as it becomes a more complex society with many more forces at work and demanding to be heard, there are innumerable new examples of the manner in which individuals on all levels are creating an internal, spontaneous criticism of society. So long as this criticism does not enter the realm of the political in ways that could be construed as threatening to Westernize the system, the state has reacted with sympathetic attention.

To cite just one example, and one that shows dramatically how concern for the consumer is coming to the fore, in 1971 two Soviet Ralph Naders appeared suddenly, writing in Pravda that the consumer was virtually helpless under the law. They demanded a review of everything from rent contracts to laundry establishments, which, they pointed out, were guaranteed against losses while the consumer had no protection at all. The two writers, Alexander Kabalkin and Vadim Khinchuk, were specialists in contract law.

This kind of stewing in Soviet society is proceeding on all levels. The Kremlin chiefs are finding it far more necessary than in previous years, for instance, to fan out throughout the country, wooing support from "voters" for their policies. (It boggles the mind to imagin Stalin or any of his men doing this!) There is a definite campaign to attempt to get lower party members and local party councils to operate more independently and thus more effectively. (Can you see Lavrenti Beria encouraging local "self-government?") It has been suggested that, with the glut on the market of such items as unpopular old models of iceboxes, door-to-door salesmen take on recalcitrant housewives.

I would also foresee more and more voluntary criticism arising from within the bowels of Soviet society in the areas of women's rights, problems of pollution control, and concerns of the 50,000 local councils or soviets.

— The Kremlin hierarchy is obsessed with "ideological subversion" and, to combat it (i.e. Western ideas), the leaders have embarked upon a new campaign of persuasion and remembrance of the past. This includes, however, not only fighting Western liberalism, but permission to read the old, formerly-banned pre-revolution philosophers, as well as some Western writers.

It must be remembered that the government is doing this in part because it has greater faith in the people today; the government is less fearful, if only because it is so strong. But it must also be remembered that this "loosening up" is in response to a search going on among youth . . . . and a search can take you anywhere.

The impossible balancing act on a seesaw whose springs are none too certain is to allow — no, to capture and seize and drag howling into the Soviet Union — Western technology, while at the same time vaccinating the people against Western ideas.

The extent to which the Soviets may be prepared to go even to buy off the West's lorelei attraction — and the extent of the barterability of elements today — was shown early in 1972 when Literary Gazette's cunning editor, Alexander Chakovsy, suggested to American Congressman James Scheuer that Moscow would relax its persecution of political dissidents if Western radio stations beamed at Russia would cease "anti-Soviet propaganda."

— There is an inexorable dialectic at play in Soviet society — not the dialectic that the early Marxists worshipped, but a new dialectic. It says that as a country becomes more worldly and sophisticated world power, as it reaches out for respectability in the world, it must inevitably open itself to the ideas of the rest of the world.

It is very simple: you cannot have fun and trade and technology with President Nixon while at the same time protecting your people from foreign "infection." You can't open a country and close it at the same time.

As this occurs, as more Russians travel abroad, as more foreigners visit Russia (2,000,000 a year now), new ideas are bound to infiltrate Soviet society. This by no means points to any end to Marxism, but it will certainly mean a dilution of the rigid, know-nothing Marxism of the older generaion. Ultimately, the Soviet Union is going to have its Pentagon papers — and they will make ours look like the revelations of a Sunday School class picnic.

For despite its isolated power and might, the Soviet Union is gradually being penetrated by the rest of the world. Young Russians do not even have to go to the West nowadays to see what is outside, they can see it right in Eastern Europe — they can see it in the Soviet-hating young Czechs, in the independent, belligerent Yugoslavs, in the demonstrating Poles, Rumanians, Hungarians and Bulgarians, who have many more refrigerators than they.

There is something else that is highly possible, if we are to believe such Soviet specialists as Columbia University's Zigniew

Brzezinski; this is his assertion that the Soviets, like all developing peoples, will have to go through the advanced technetronic" age (technology plus electronics) which the U.S. is now going through. Then they will have many of our problems and they will increasingly be forced to deal with them in new and modern ways.

What has happened, then, is not that the state is suddenly and willingly giving up its brutal obsession with capital formation at the expense of every basic human and spiritual need of its citizens. The Soviet state has not suddenly become humane, pliable and citizen-serving. Rather, it has developed to a point where the human demands of its citizens are making themselves felt, where men are spontaneously and eagerly crawling out from under the dark shroud of Stalinism and the inhuman crush of the Communist machine of forced capitalism and collectivitization that has dominated this society so darkly for so long.

The system could manipulate the person before precisely because he was so isolated, so uneducated and so afraid. Today, with this generation, this person is disappearing. And so the state wavers back and forth, between the carrot and the stick.

What it can do to kill spontaneity and desires for freedom in the short run is considerable. But what it can do against an entire generation in the long run is open to question. It is like trying to hold back the sea, as every wave breaks one of the old shibboleths on the beach.

But, even if it were agreed that this generation will create quite a new and more liberal Soviet state, what would this really mean to the United States?

One argument contends that a liberalized Russia would be less of an aggravation for the West, because it would be more like us: more rational, less ideological, more reasonable, more agreeable. Our systems would grow together — converge — in a kind of ideological give-and-take, with theirs leaving more room for individualism and democracy and ours becoming more socialistic.

The counter-argument is that, yes, we might well get along with them better personally, but what does that have to do with it? We'd still be basically involved in an ideological struggle, only now we would no longer have the enormous advantage of the fact that so many Russians who went abroad were so personally obnoxious to most of the other peoples of the world that they destroyed whatever they were trying to build. Marxism itself would suddenly become more attractive to many peoples in the world for whom, before, it was anathema.

No less a hawk than Georgi Arbatov, head of Moscow's U.S.A. Institute, asserted, on a trip to California's Center for the study of Democratic Institutions in 1971 that, even if there were such a thing as ideological "convergence", (a concept that all official Soviets deny and despise), that would not mean the two countries would get closer. "We have a number of examples in history where it was precisely the similar societies that had the worst relations," he said. "The first World War began among similar countries, not those that had basic differences. Take the Christians. In their relations with Buddhists and pagans, they simply tried to convert them. Sometimes ruthlessly, of course. But when there was controversy within the Christian world, it led to the most terrible of wars."

Despite the real kernels of truth contained in this type of reasoning, I do not see this as the probable outcome of the scenario of the new generation. I do see the next generation of Russians as being more worthy adversaries in the world — but I also see the adversary relationship between the U.S. and Russia as being vastly deintensified. It seems probable that the competition between the two countries will be a peaceful one and that, given no wars and given a continuation of democratic ideals in the West (without whose competition and constant reminders of freedom I do not foresee any continued liberalization in Russia), that the changes now occuring will continue. A return to the terror of the Stalinist mode is impossible today, not for moral reasons but because the new-style Russian leaders know it would destroy, not only the initiative of workers and scientists which is needed so sorely to take Russia on the last steps to becoming a truly developed country, but because it would devour the perpetrators of the new terror just as it devoured the perpetrators of the old terror.

The trends toward the use of persuasion, toward surveying, toward public opinion as an operative factor in Soviet life, toward legalism as an arbitrating force, toward greater freedom to reach out and know other peoples are too deeply embedding themselves now as realistic responses to the demands of the new Russians.

In the long run, too, the best argument for the efficacy of Russian youth as a force for change is the fact that no nation can continue ultimately in policies that run contrary to the mind, mentality and makeup of its people. And this political law has never exempted dictatorships or totalitarian governments in modern times. Whether Hitler's Germany, Stalin's Russia or Stroessner's Paraguay, totalitarian regimes exist for any period of time only because they have the political, psychological and spiritual devotion or acquiescence of the majority of the people. It is an equally incontrovertible rule of revolution that once the reigns are loosened in any authoritarian body, they can never really be wholly tightened again.

Moreover, Russia throughout its history, has never been *only* tyranny, *only* ingrown nationalistic arrogance, *only* that peculiar oppression of the spirit that seems to inhabit the Russian steppes like a wraith of inevitability. Russia has also known democratic strivings and human justice and the joys of the spirit, and within her today she still holds these like a small, jewel-like present she is preserving to give someday to a loved one yet to appear. She has alternated between them, in a momentous struggle with herself, and she is alternating between them now.

The younger generation is hanging heavily on one side of this struggle. It is tired of the past, tired of hearing its parents say, "Don't you care how we suffered? Don't you remember the war, the American threat?" Much like American youth when up against this kind of fruitless interlocution, they are reacting with a blank, uninterested stare. And this is good and natural.

In the bad memory of a new and different generation, the world gains new possibilities of living together in peace and decency.

❧ Bibliography

The Battle for Stalingrad, Marshal Vasili Ivanovich Chuikov, Ballantine Books, N.Y., 1964.

Bratsk Station and other new Poems, Yevgeny Yevtushenko, Anchor Books, N.Y., 1967.

Colleagues, Vasily Aksyonov, Foreign Languages Publishing House, Moscow.

The Collective Family: A Handbook for Russian Parents, A.S. Makarenko, Anchor Books, N.Y., 1967.

The Conflict of Generations, Lewis S. Feuer, Basic Books, Inc., 1969.

The Demonstration in Pushkin Square, Pavel Litvinov, Gambit, Inco., Boston, 1969.

Fathers and Sons, Ivan Turgenev, Collier Books, N.Y., 1962.

A Hero of Our Time, Mihail Lermontov, Collier Books, N.Y., 1964.

A History of Russia, George Vernadsky, Bantam Books, 1967.

How the Steel Was Tempered, Nikolai Ostrovsky, Foreign Language Publishing House, Moscow.

In Quest of Justice, Protest & Dissent in The Soviet Union Today, edited by Abraham Brumberg, Praeger Publishers, N.Y., 1970.

Issues of Problems of Communism, edited by Abraham Brumberg, U.S. Information Agency, Washington, D.C., 1966 through 1975.

Issues of Soviet Life, published by Moscow Editorial Board, Moscow, 1966 through 1975.

Krushchev Remembers, Little, Brown & Co., N.Y., 1970.

The Kremlin's Human Dilemma, Maurice Hindus, Doubleday & Co., Publishers, 1967.

Lenin, by David Shub, A Mentor Book, N.Y., 1948.

Lenin's Last Struggle, Moshe Lewin, Pantheon Books, N.Y., 1968.

The Life of Mayakovsky, Wintor Woroszylski, The Orion Press, N.Y., 1970.

Man, His Ideals and Reality, Eduard Rosenthal, Novosti Press Agency.

The Marquis de Custine and His Russia in 1839, George F. Kennan, Princeton University Press, N.J., 1971.

The Master & Margarita, by Mikhail Bulgakov, Grove Press, Inc., N.Y., 1967.

Memoirs of a Revolutionist, Peter Kropotkin, Horizon Press, N.Y., 1968.

Message From Moscow, An Observer, Alfred A. Knopf, 1969, N.Y.,

The Mind of Modern Russia, edited by Hans Kohn, Harper & Row Publishers, N.Y., 1955.

The New Russian Tragedy, Anatole Shub, W.W. Norton & Co., Inc., 1969.

The Nihilists, Ronald Hingley, Delacorte Press, N.Y., 1967.

The Nobel Lecture on Literature, Alexander Solzhenitsyn, Harper & Row Publishers, N.Y., 1973.

One Day in the Life of Ivan Denisovich, Alexander Solzhenitsyn, A Bantam book, 1963.

The Origin of Russian Communism, Nicolas Berdyaev, The University of Michigan Press, 1969.

Political Leadership in Eastern Europe and the Soviet Union, edited by R. Barry Farrell, Aldine Publishing Co., Chicago, 1970.

Preschool Education in the USSR, Alexei Kalinin, Novosti Press Publishing House, Moscow.

Progress, Coexistence & Intellectual Freedom, Andrei D. Sakharov, W.W. Norton & Co., N.Y., 1970.

The Red Executive, A Study of the Organization Man in Russian Industry, David Granick, Doubleday & Company, Inc. 1961.

Religious Minorities in the Soviet Union, published by the Minority Rights Group, London, 1970.

Report of the Central Committee of the Communist Party of the Soviet Union, 24th Congress of the CPSU, Delivered by Leonid Brezhnev, Moscow, 1971.

Russia: Hopes and Fears, Alexander Werth, Penguin Books, Baltimore, Md., 1969.

Russia in Flux, Sir John Maynard, The Macmillan Company, N.Y., 1948.

The Russian Revolution, Alan Moorehead, Harper and Row Publishers, 1958.

Russian Themes, Mihajlo Mihajlov, Farrar, Straus and Girous, N.Y., 1968

Russian Writers — their lives and literature, Janko Lavrin, D. Van Nostrand Inc., N.Y., 1964.

Scientific Communism, V. Afanasyev, Progress Publishers, Moscow, 1967.

Selected Poems of Andrei Voznesensky, Grove Press, Inc., N.Y., 1964.

Solzhenitsyn, A Documentary Record, edited by Leopold Labedz, Harper & Row Publishers, N.Y., 1970.

Soviet Sociology, Alex Simirenko, editor, Quadrangle Books, Chicago, 1966.

The Soviet Union Today, Kenneth R. Whiting, Frederick A. Praeger Publishers, N.Y., 1966.

Three Who Made a Revolution, Bertram D. Wolfe, The Dial Press, N.Y., 1964.

The Trial Begins and On Socialist Realism, Abram Tertz, Vintage Books, N.Y., 1960.

Two Worlds of Childhood, U.S. and U.S.S.R., Urie Bronfenbrenner, Russell Sage Foundation, N.Y., 1970.

USSR, Questions and Answers, Novosti Publishing House, Moscow.

The Unperfect Society Beyond the New Class, Milovan Djilas, Harcourt, Brace & World, Inc., N.Y., 1969.

The View from Lenin Hills, An American Student's Report on Soviet Youth in Ferment, By William Taubman, Coward-McCann, N.Y., 1967.

A Walk in Rural Russia, by Vladimir Soloukhin, E.P. Dutton & Col, N.Y., 1967.

We the Russians, Voices from Russia, edited by Colette Shulman, Praeger Publishers, 1971.

Will the Soviet Union Survive Until 1984? by Andrei Amalrik, Harper & Row Publishers, N.Y., 1970.

Women in the Soviet Union, edited by Donald R. Brown, Teachers College Press, Teachers College, Columbia University, N.Y., 1968.

✿ Index

tolerance within sociology, 262; versus the social sciences, 262-263; myths for a 20th century secular society, 270; mass goals, U.S. and Soviet Union, 277
Ikonnikova, Svetlana, 256-258
Individualism, new ideas about among youth, 73-81; within Marxism, 80; in the theatre, 100; ideas about personal conscience, 103; as reflected in art, 108; within new educational programs, 246; 260; importance of individual initiative among youth, 261
Inner man, 21
Insane asylums, use for dissenters, 177
Intellectuals, idea of one culture for them and one for the people, 92-95; as a class, 92-95; fear of the masses, 94-95
Internationalism, new style among young Soviets, 250
Irkutsk, 43
Islam in Russia, 57
Ivanov, Vladimir, 33

Jacoby, Susan, 200
Janowitz, Dr. Morris, 266
Jazz, 244-245
Jews, emigration and new self-awareness, 78; 163, 285
Juvenile delinquency, 238

Kapitsa, Pyotr, 180
katushev, Konstantin, 139
Kebin, I.G. 11
Keenan, Dr. Edward, 32, 162, 280-281
Kempe, Mirdze, 189, 192
KGB, 156-157, 168-169; blackmail with women, 216
Khamstvo, reaction to it on part of youth, 25
Kharchev, A.G., 221, 262
Kiev, 253-254
Kiev State University, 24
Kochetov, Vsevolod, on anti-war sentiment, 249-250
Kollontai, Madame Alexandra, 205-207
Kolobkov, Vladimir, 24, 49, 80, 194; on importance of sociology, 253-254, 258
Komov, Ivan Tikhonovich, 237-239
Komsomol, new concern over spiritual life of members, 22; historic changes within, 22; call for "humanized" leaders, 22-23; changes in factory operatives, 23; at University of Irkutsk, 44, Young Leninst magazine, Volgograd, 75; resignation from, 143; at Volgograd city headquarters, 243-244; attitudes toward jazz, 244-245; ideological department, 245; in Volgograd 253.
Komsomol Truth, 90
Khrushchev, Nikita, denunciations of Stalin, 52; on Stalinism, 113; criticism of by youth, 145; persons rehabilitated by, 156; educational reforms and elitism, 235-236; 258
Krasin, Victor, trial of, 158
Kronika, 158-163, 284
Krushki, 50, 143, 147
Kurancheva, Zoya, 202-203
Kvasha, Igor, 99

Lanz, Anita, 273
Law, attitudes toward, 73; Stephen Weiner on, 182; history of in U.S.S.R., 184-185
Leadership, the type Russian youth likes, 55; new style leaders, 139; Robert Conquest on new leaders, 140; expertise now more important for leaders than politics, 141; leadership qualities among youth, 259
Leningrad, 144
Limber-Boatkina, Valee, on problems of women, 191-192
Lisovsky, Vladimir, 7, 13, 49, 51, 137, 148; on social sciences and humanism, 177; on Sigmund Freud and youth, 255-258; 259-264; his surveys comparing Soviet youth and American youth, 275
Literary Gazette, 59, 205
Literature, interest in 19th century writers, 109; reading of old Russian writers and philosophers, 288
Litvinov, Pavel, fear of youth on part of older Russians, 11; 155, 186-187
Local government, efforts to make it operate more effectively, 282
London School of Economics, 166, 171-172
Louis, Victor, 88
Love, free love among early Bolsheviks, 218; Madame Alexandra Kollontai on free love, 205-207

Makarenko, Anton, 220, 225-226, 265
Mandelsham, Osip, 101
Manners, concern for, 27
Manual labor, attitudes toward, 148-150, 270
Marriage, problems of women in work and the community, 190; ceremony of, 244
Martinova, Ann, 206
Marx, Karl, new reading of by this generation, 101
Maxla, State Union of Artists in Riga, 103
Mazurov, Kiril T. 139
Medvendev, Zhores and Roy, 181
Melko, Valerie, 20, 46, 76, 258, 273
Merton, Robert, 261
Middle East, attitudes toward, 64-68
Mihajlov, Mihajlo, on merging Christian-Marxist dialogue, 281
Military service, 249
Modern Theatre, 97-100
Molodaya Gvardia, Soviet press debate on interest in the spiritual past, 36
Monastery of the Savior, Movgorod, 34
Moscow Art Theatre, 97
Moscow University, as characterized by American academician, 134; de-Stalinization years, 129-135
Music, renaissance of early Russian church music, 35

Narodniks, 14
Nauka i Religii, 37
Nekrasov, Victor, 9
New Man, concept of in Marxist thought, 81 136; in education, 229-234; 253-254; historical evolution of concept, 259-260; comparisons to American New Man, 284
New World magazine, 37
Nihilists, 15